COMPREHENSIVE GUIDE TO NOVEL DRUG DELIVERY SYSTEMS (NDDS)

MURALIDHAR RAO AKKALADEVI,
VEERAREDDY PRABHAKAR REDDY

Made with ♥ on the Notion Press Platform
www.notionpress.com

Contents

Preface

The field of **Novel Drug Delivery Systems (NDDS)** represents a transformative frontier in pharmaceutical science, offering innovative solutions to address the limitations of traditional drug delivery methods. These advanced systems enhance therapeutic outcomes by improving drug targeting, reducing side effects, and promoting patient compliance. As the demand for precision and efficiency in drug delivery continues to grow, the need for a comprehensive and accessible reference on this subject becomes more critical than ever.

This book, **"Comprehensive Guide to Novel Drug Delivery Systems (NDDS),"** is authored with the primary goal of serving as a definitive resource for students, educators, researchers, and healthcare professionals. It is designed to provide in-depth knowledge of NDDS technologies, from fundamental principles to advanced applications, while maintaining a balance between theoretical insights and practical relevance.

The motivation for writing this book stems from the challenges faced by students and professionals in accessing consolidated and reliable information on NDDS. The rapidly evolving nature of this field often necessitates consulting multiple sources, which can be both time-consuming and overwhelming. This book aims to bridge that gap by presenting all essential concepts, methodologies, and advancements in a single, coherent volume.

Structured to align with academic syllabi and professional requirements, the book begins with an introduction to the evolution of drug delivery systems and progresses to detailed discussions on various NDDS approaches, such as controlled release, transdermal systems, microencapsulation, and nanotechnology. Each chapter is meticulously crafted to ensure clarity, with step-by-step explanations, real-world examples, and detailed illustrations to aid understanding.

The collaborative effort behind this book is a testament to our shared commitment to advancing pharmaceutical education and practice. Drawing from our academic and research expertise, we have endeavored to make the content accessible without compromising on depth or rigor. Whether you are a pharmacy student seeking foundational knowledge or a researcher exploring innovative solutions, we believe this book will be a valuable companion.

We extend our heartfelt gratitude to the many individuals who supported the development of this work. Special thanks are due to our students and colleagues, whose insightful questions and discussions have continually inspired us to explore and clarify complex concepts. We are also deeply appreciative of our families for their unwavering support and encouragement throughout this endeavor.

It is our sincere hope that this book will not only serve as a comprehensive reference but also spark curiosity and inspire innovation in the field of NDDS. As you embark on this journey through the fascinating world of novel drug delivery systems, we welcome your feedback and suggestions to make future editions even more enriching.

With warm regards,

Dr. Muralidhar Rao Akkaladevi

Dr. Veerareddy Prabhakar Reddy

Comprehensive Guide To Novel Drug Delivery Systems

Authors

Dr. Muralidhar Rao Akkaladevi

Principal,

St. Mary's College of Pharmacy,

Secunderabad, Telangana, India

Dr. Prabhakar Reddy Veerareddy

Head,

University College of Pharmaceutical Sciences,

Palamuru University,

Mahabubnagar, Telangana, India

Published by Notion Press

Notion Press, Inc.

800, West El Camino Real #180,

California, USA 94040

Notion Press Media Pvt Ltd

#7, Red Cross Road,

Egmore, Chennai, Tamil Nadu 600008

Email ID: publish@notionpress.com

Phone Number: +91 44 46315631

CHAPTER I

Introduction to Novel Drug Delivery Systems

1.1 Importance of Drug Delivery Systems in Modern Pharmacy

1.1.1 Definition and Scope of Drug Delivery Systems

Drug delivery systems (DDS) are innovative technologies that have transformed the way drugs are administered to patients. These systems are designed to optimize drug therapy by improving the **pharmacokinetics** and **pharmacodynamics** of the drugs. Pharmacokinetics refers to the movement of drugs within the body, including their absorption, distribution, metabolism, and excretion. Pharmacodynamics, on the other hand, is the study of the effects of drugs on the body, including their mechanism of action and the resulting therapeutic effects. The goal of DDS is to deliver drugs more effectively and efficiently, ensuring that they reach the desired target site in the right amount, at the right time, and for the right duration.

One of the primary roles of DDS is to achieve **precise targeting**. Traditional drug delivery methods often result in drugs circulating throughout the body, which can lead to side effects and poor therapeutic outcomes. By targeting the drug delivery to specific sites, DDS help minimize the impact on healthy tissues and organs, thus improving the safety and efficacy of the treatment. For instance, in cancer therapy, DDS can be used to deliver drugs directly to tumor cells, reducing damage to surrounding healthy tissues and improving the overall effectiveness of the drug.

Another important aspect of DDS is **controlled release**. This refers to the ability to release a drug in a controlled manner over an extended period. Controlled-release formulations are designed to release the drug gradually, which helps maintain therapeutic drug levels for a longer duration. This approach not only improves patient compliance but also reduces the frequency of dosing, leading to more consistent and sustained therapeutic effects. For example, sustained-release tablets can be used to treat chronic conditions like diabetes, where the drug needs to be administered over a prolonged period to maintain stable blood sugar levels.

In addition to improving targeting and release, DDS also enhancetherapeutic efficacy. By optimizing the drug's pharmacokinetic profile, DDS can increase the drug's bioavailability, ensuring that the drug is absorbed and utilized by the body more efficiently. This is particularly important for drugs that are poorly absorbed or have a short half-life. Through technologies like liposomes, nanoparticles, and microencapsulation, DDS can enhance drug stability, solubility, and bioavailability, leading to improved therapeutic outcomes.

1.1.2 Evolution of Drug Delivery Systems

The evolution of drug delivery systems has been driven by the need for more efficient, precise, and patient-friendly therapies. Initially, conventional drug delivery methods, such as oral tablets and injections, were the primary means of administering medications. While these traditional dosage forms were effective for certain conditions, they often posed challenges related to **patient compliance, bioavailability**, and **side effects**. For example, oral tablets are subject to the digestive process, which can alter the drug's effectiveness, and injections may cause discomfort and require frequent administration.

The shift toward **advanced delivery methods** emerged as researchers recognized the limitations of conventional systems. One of the first major developments in drug delivery was the introduction of **controlled release systems**. These systems were designed to release drugs gradually over time, reducing the need for frequent dosing. This was a significant advancement, particularly for conditions like **chronic pain** and **hypertension**, where long-term management is required. Controlled release formulations helped maintain therapeutic drug levels in the bloodstream, improving the efficacy and convenience of treatment. They also minimized fluctuations in drug concentrations, which could lead to side effects or inadequate therapeutic responses.

As technology continued to advance, the development of **sustained release** and **targeted delivery systems** took center stage. Sustained-release formulations further improved patient compliance by allowing medications to be administered less frequently, often once a day or even less. This was particularly important for conditions like **diabetes** and **mental health**

disorders, where medications are required over extended periods. The sustained release also helped maintain consistent therapeutic levels, improving the overall effectiveness of the treatment.

The most significant advancement in the evolution of drug delivery systems has been the shift towards **targeted delivery**. This innovation allows drugs to be directed specifically to the site of action, such as a tumor or an infected tissue, reducing the impact on healthy tissues. Targeted delivery methods, such as **liposomes**, **nanoparticles**, and **antibody-drug conjugates**, have revolutionized the treatment of diseases like **cancer** and **autoimmune disorders**. By focusing on specific targets, these systems minimize side effects, increase drug potency, and improve therapeutic outcomes.

1.1.3 Challenges Addressed by Novel Drug Delivery Systems (NDDS)

Novel Drug Delivery Systems (NDDS) have emerged as a solution to the various challenges posed by traditional drug delivery methods. Traditional methods such as oral tablets and injections often struggle with issues like **poor solubility**, **rapid clearance**, and **variable bioavailability**. Many drugs face difficulty in being absorbed into the bloodstream due to their solubility limitations, leading to reduced effectiveness. NDDS aim to solve these issues by enhancing the solubility and stability of drugs, making them more effective in treating a wide range of conditions.

One of the main challenges in conventional drug delivery is **bioavailability**, which refers to the proportion of the drug that enters the systemic circulation and is available for therapeutic effect. Drugs that are poorly soluble in water often have low bioavailability, as they do not dissolve sufficiently in the gastrointestinal tract for absorption. NDDS, such as liposomes, nanoparticles, and cyclodextrin complexes, have been developed to improve the solubility and absorption of such drugs, ensuring that a higher concentration reaches the target site in the body. These systems are specifically designed to enhance the bioavailability of poorly soluble drugs, leading to better therapeutic outcomes.

Another challenge that NDDS address is **drug stability**. Many drugs, especially biologics, are prone to degradation due to environmental factors like temperature, light, and pH changes. Traditional drug formulations often require specific storage conditions to maintain their stability, limiting their use and effectiveness. NDDS such as polymer-based drug systems, microparticles, and hydrogels provide better protection against degradation, maintaining drug stability during storage and while in the body. This increased stability ensures that the drug remains effective throughout its shelf life and treatment period.

Side effects are another concern with conventional drug delivery methods. Many drugs, when administered orally or intravenously, can affect unintended areas of the body, leading to adverse effects. NDDS, through **targeted delivery**, address this issue by ensuring that the drug reaches only the desired site of action. This site-specific targeting reduces the exposure of healthy tissues to the drug, minimizing side effects. For example, **nanoparticles** can be engineered to bind specifically to cancer cells, delivering chemotherapy directly to the tumor site and sparing surrounding healthy tissue from toxic effects.

Patient compliance has long been a challenge with conventional drug delivery methods, particularly in chronic disease management. Frequent dosing schedules and side effects often discourage patients from adhering to their treatment regimens. NDDS, such as sustained-release formulations, can release drugs over an extended period, reducing the need for frequent administration. This improvement in **patient compliance** helps ensure that patients follow their prescribed therapies more effectively, leading to better management of chronic diseases like diabetes, hypertension, and mental health disorders.

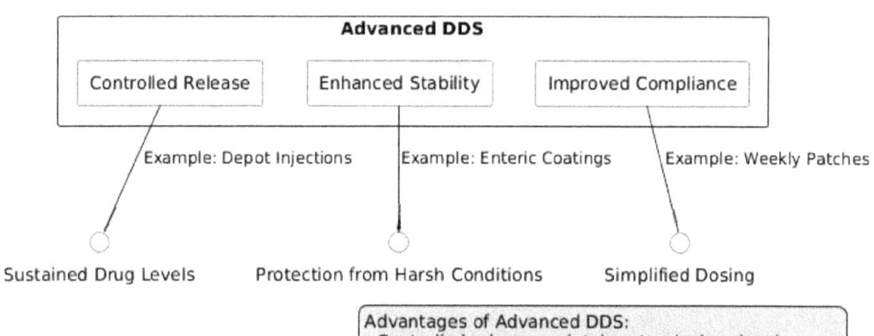

1.2 Principles and Objectives of Novel Drug Delivery Systems

1.2.1 Core Principles of NDDS

The core principles of Novel Drug Delivery Systems (NDDS) revolve around the enhancement of therapeutic efficacy through several key strategies. These strategies include achieving **controlled release, targeted therapy**, and **patient-centric** designs. By implementing these principles, NDDS aim to improve drug delivery by ensuring that drugs are administered in a way that maximizes their effectiveness while minimizing side effects.

One of the fundamental principles of NDDS is **controlled release**. Controlled release systems are designed to release drugs gradually over a prolonged period, instead of a sudden burst or irregular release as seen in conventional dosage forms like tablets or injections. This approach ensures that the drug maintains a steady concentration in the bloodstream, thus maintaining the therapeutic effect for a longer duration. For example, **sustained-release tablets** are designed to release the active ingredient over hours or even days, reducing the need for frequent dosing and improving patient adherence to the prescribed treatment regimen. This principle is particularly important for treating chronic diseases, where long-term drug therapy is needed.

Targeted therapy is another core principle of NDDS. Unlike traditional drug delivery methods, which disperse the drug throughout the body, targeted drug delivery aims to deliver the drug specifically to the site of action. This precise delivery minimizes the exposure of healthy tissues to the drug, thereby reducing side effects and improving the overall therapeutic outcome. For instance, in cancer treatment, **liposomal formulations** and **nanoparticles** can be engineered to target tumor cells specifically, delivering the chemotherapy drugs directly to the cancer site and sparing healthy tissues. This approach enhances the effectiveness of the treatment while minimizing toxicity, a significant concern in conventional cancer therapies.

A crucial aspect of NDDS is their **patient-centric** approach. This principle focuses on designing drug delivery systems that cater to the specific needs of the patient, enhancing both the convenience and comfort of the treatment. By improving patient compliance and reducing the frequency of administration, NDDS make it easier for patients to adhere to their treatment regimens. For example, **transdermal patches** allow for the controlled release of medication over an extended period without the need for injections or frequent oral dosing. This non-invasive method is particularly beneficial for patients who have difficulty swallowing pills or those requiring continuous drug administration.

1.2.2 Key Objectives of NDDS

The key objectives of Novel Drug Delivery Systems (NDDS) are centered around improving the overall effectiveness of drug therapies while minimizing unwanted effects. These objectives include **precision**, **efficiency**, and **safety** in drug delivery, ensuring that medications are delivered in a manner that maximizes their therapeutic benefits while reducing the risks associated with traditional delivery methods.

One of the primary objectives of NDDS is to **minimize side effects**. Traditional drug delivery systems often distribute the drug throughout the body, which can lead to exposure of non-target tissues and cause adverse effects. NDDS aim to precisely deliver the drug to the desired site of action, thereby reducing the interaction with healthy tissues and minimizing systemic toxicity. This is especially beneficial for treatments like chemotherapy, where **targeted delivery** can spare healthy cells and focus the drug's action on cancerous cells, leading to fewer side effects.

Another important objective is to **enhance drug stability**. Many drugs, particularly biologics, are sensitive to environmental factors such as temperature, light, and pH. NDDS help maintain the stability of these drugs by providing protective mechanisms that shield the drug from degradation. For instance, **liposomes** and **nanoparticles** can encapsulate drugs, protecting them from enzymatic breakdown and improving their shelf-life. This is especially crucial for drugs that are prone to degradation and need to be delivered in their active form to be effective.

Efficient delivery to the target site is also a key objective of NDDS. Drugs must not only be delivered in the correct dosage but must reach the right location in the body to be effective. This is especially important for drugs with a **narrow therapeutic window**, where small variations in the drug concentration can result in therapeutic failure or toxicity. NDDS, such as **nanoparticles** and **microspheres**, can be designed to release drugs at specific sites, such as tumors or infected tissues, ensuring that the drug reaches the target site in the optimal concentration for maximum therapeutic effect.

In addition to these objectives, NDDS also aim to improve **patient compliance** by simplifying the administration process. The convenience of controlled release formulations, such as **extended-release tablets** or **transdermal patches**, reduces the frequency of dosing and ensures a more consistent drug level in the bloodstream, making it easier for patients to adhere to their treatment regimens.

1.3 Types of Novel Drug Delivery Systems

1.3.1 Controlled Release Systems

Controlled release systems are a category of drug delivery systems designed to release drugs in a controlled and predictable manner over an extended period. These systems offer several advantages over traditional drug delivery methods, particularly in terms of improving the **efficacy** of treatments and **minimizing side effects**. The primary goal of controlled release systems is to maintain **therapeutic drug levels** in the body for prolonged periods without the need for frequent dosing.

The **sustained release** type of system ensures that the drug is gradually released over an extended period, often from a single dose. This controlled release minimizes the fluctuations in drug levels, which is particularly important for drugs that require a steady concentration in the bloodstream for optimal efficacy. For example, **extended-release formulations** are commonly used for treating chronic conditions such as hypertension, diabetes, and chronic pain. By releasing the drug gradually, these systems help maintain consistent therapeutic levels, reducing the need for frequent dosing.

Pulsatile release systems, on the other hand, are designed to release the drug in a controlled manner at specific intervals, mimicking the natural release of a substance in the body. This type of system is particularly useful for drugs that need to be released in bursts at certain times, such as for drugs used in **hormone replacement therapy** or **disease management**, where the drug is needed at specific times of the day. Pulsatile release systems are designed to respond to physiological signals or external triggers, ensuring that the drug is delivered when needed most.

Another important category within controlled release systems is **diffusion-based systems**. These systems rely on the principles of diffusion to control the rate at which the drug is released. The drug is typically embedded in a matrix or reservoir, and the release is controlled by the diffusion of the drug through the material. Examples of diffusion-based systems include **matrix tablets**, where the drug is dispersed in a polymer matrix, and **reservoir systems**, where the drug is enclosed in a membrane. These systems are widely used in **chronic disease management**, particularly for drugs that require slow, consistent release over an extended period.

The applications of controlled release systems are vast. They play a crucial role in managing **chronic diseases** such as diabetes, cardiovascular diseases, and cancer, where long-term drug therapy is required. By providing controlled release of drugs, these systems help in reducing the side effects associated with high peak concentrations and improve patient compliance by reducing the frequency of drug administration.

1.3.2 Targeted Drug Delivery Systems

Targeted drug delivery systems represent an important advancement in the field of pharmacology, aimed at delivering drugs specifically to the intended site of action, such as diseased tissues or cells, while minimizing exposure to healthy tissues. This precise delivery is designed to enhance the therapeutic effect of the drug and reduce side effects, which are common with traditional drug delivery methods.

There are two main strategies used in targeted drug delivery: **active targeting** and **passive targeting**. **Active targeting** involves the use of specific ligands or antibodies that are designed to bind to receptors present on the surface of target cells. For example, in **cancer therapy**, monoclonal antibodies can be engineered to target tumor-specific antigens on cancer cells. This ensures that the drug is released directly at the tumor site, improving the effectiveness of the treatment while reducing the risk of damage to surrounding healthy tissues.

In contrast, **passive targeting** takes advantage of the natural properties of certain delivery systems, such as the **Enhanced Permeability and Retention (EPR) effect**. This phenomenon occurs because of the leaky blood vessels in tumor tissues, which allow nanoparticles or liposomes to accumulate more readily in the tumor. This form of targeting is commonly used in **liposomal drug delivery systems**, where the drug is encapsulated in liposomes, which then passively accumulate in tumor tissues due to their enhanced permeability.

Targeted drug delivery systems are particularly useful in **cancer therapies**, where conventional chemotherapy drugs can cause severe side effects due to their non-specific distribution in the body. By targeting the drug directly to the tumor, the therapeutic effect is increased while minimizing damage to healthy cells. Similarly, targeted drug delivery has significant applications in **infectious disease treatments**, where drugs can be specifically delivered to infected tissues or cells, improving the drug's efficacy and reducing the risk of systemic side effects.

1.3.3 Specialized Delivery Systems

Specialized drug delivery systems utilize advanced technologies to further enhance the precision and effectiveness of drug delivery. These systems often incorporate **nanotechnology** and **biomolecules** to enable better targeting, stability, and control of drug release. One of the most notable advancements in this area is the use of **liposomes, niosomes, nanoparticles**, and **monoclonal antibodies**.

Liposomes are spherical vesicles composed of lipid bilayers that can encapsulate both hydrophilic and hydrophobic drugs, offering protection against degradation. They are commonly used for **drug delivery in cancer therapy**, as they can encapsulate chemotherapy drugs and target tumors using passive or active targeting strategies. **Niosomes**, similar to liposomes, are composed of non-ionic surfactants and are often used in the delivery of poorly water-soluble drugs.

Nanoparticles, on the other hand, are typically less than 100 nanometers in size and have unique properties that allow for enhanced drug loading and controlled release. Nanoparticles can be functionalized to target specific cells or tissues, making them highly suitable for applications in **biologics** and **gene therapy**. For example, **polymeric nanoparticles** can be used to deliver **DNA, RNA**, or other genetic material to specific cells for gene therapy, which holds great promise for treating genetic disorders and cancers.

Monoclonal antibodies have also gained significant attention in specialized drug delivery systems. These antibodies can be engineered to recognize specific antigens on the surface of diseased cells, particularly cancer cells, allowing for the direct delivery of drugs to the targeted site. This is particularly useful in treating cancers where the immune system's ability to identify and destroy cancer cells is enhanced.

These specialized drug delivery systems offer significant advantages in terms of **precision, efficiency,** and **reduced toxicity.** By using nanotechnology and biomolecules, these systems can deliver drugs more effectively to the site of action, ensuring that the drug remains stable, controlled, and active for a longer period. Furthermore, these technologies allow for the development of **personalized medicine,** where the drug delivery system is tailored to the specific needs of the patient, further improving therapeutic outcomes.

1.4 Advantages and Disadvantages of NDDS

1.4.1 Advantages

Novel drug delivery systems (NDDS) offer numerous benefits that enhance the effectiveness and convenience of drug therapy. One of the primary advantages is the **improved efficacy** of treatments. NDDS, such as **controlled release systems,** allow drugs to be delivered at a consistent rate over time. This ensures that the drug maintains **therapeutic levels** in the bloodstream, improving the **overall effectiveness** of the treatment. For instance, in **chronic disease management,** such as diabetes or hypertension, sustained-release formulations help in maintaining steady blood levels of the drug, leading to better disease control.

Another significant advantage of NDDS is **reduced dosing frequency.** Traditional drug delivery methods often require frequent dosing, which can be challenging for patients, especially those managing chronic conditions. NDDS can **prolong the therapeutic action** of drugs, reducing the need for frequent doses. This leads to **better patient compliance** since patients are more likely to adhere to a treatment regimen if it is less disruptive to their daily life. For example, **transdermal patches** for pain management allow for continuous delivery of medication, improving patient comfort and reducing the burden of multiple daily doses.

Additionally, **NDDS** can help **reduce side effects** associated with conventional drug delivery methods. By controlling the rate and site of drug release, NDDS can minimize fluctuations in drug concentration, which are often responsible for undesirable side effects. Drugs that act on **targeted areas** with minimal systemic exposure lead to a **reduction in systemic side effects**. For instance, **liposomal formulations** for cancer treatment deliver chemotherapy drugs directly to the tumor, sparing healthy cells and reducing adverse effects like hair loss and nausea.

Overall, the key advantages of NDDS include **improved therapeutic outcomes**, **reduced frequency of dosing**, and **enhanced patient adherence**, all of which contribute to better disease management and quality of life.

1.4.2 Disadvantages

While NDDS offer several advantages, they also come with certain **limitations** that can affect their widespread adoption and use. One of the major drawbacks is the **complexity of development**. Designing and producing NDDS involves advanced technologies, such as **nanotechnology**, **polymer science**, and **biomaterials**, which can be intricate and require specialized expertise. The **multifactorial nature** of these systems—such as the need to control drug release rates, ensure stability, and maintain biocompatibility—adds to their complexity.

Moreover, the **high cost** of development is another significant disadvantage. Research and development (R&D) of NDDS often involve substantial investment in specialized equipment, testing, and clinical trials. This can make NDDS significantly more expensive to develop than traditional drug delivery methods. These increased costs may be passed on to the consumer, limiting the accessibility of such advanced treatments, particularly in low-resource settings.

Regulatory hurdles are also a major challenge for NDDS. Since these systems often involve novel technologies and materials, their approval process is more stringent and time-consuming. Regulatory bodies, such as the **FDA**, require extensive data on the **safety**, **efficacy**, and **quality** of NDDS before granting approval. The testing and validation required for NDDS can extend the timeline for product development and delay the availability of these treatments in the market.

Furthermore, the **manufacturing challenges** associated with NDDS, such as ensuring consistency and scalability, can also contribute to higher production costs. Manufacturing processes for NDDS often require specialized facilities, which are not always widely available. This can limit the availability of these systems and increase their cost to both manufacturers and patients.

1.5 Emerging Trends in NDDS

1.5.1 Nanotechnology in NDDS

Nanotechnology is revolutionizing the field of novel drug delivery systems (NDDS) by enabling the development of **nanoscale systems** that can significantly enhance **drug delivery efficacy** and **specificity**. **Nanoparticles** and **dendrimers**, which are materials that operate at the nanometer scale, have emerged as powerful tools for improving drug delivery. These tiny systems possess unique properties, such as an extremely large surface area relative to their volume, which allows for increased interaction with biological systems. As a result, drugs can be **encapsulated** or **conjugated** with nanoparticles to enhance their stability, bioavailability, and targeted delivery to specific tissues or cells.

Precision targeting is one of the key advantages of nanotechnology in NDDS. By manipulating the size, surface charge, and functional groups of nanoparticles, drug formulations can be designed to specifically target areas of the body that require treatment, such as **tumors** or **inflammatory sites**. For example, **liposomal drug formulations** can be used to deliver chemotherapy agents directly to cancer cells, minimizing damage to healthy cells and improving the therapeutic outcome. Additionally, **dendrimers**, which are highly branched molecules, offer a high degree of control over drug release, allowing for precise management of drug dosage over time.

The use of nanotechnology in NDDS also extends to **gene therapy**, where nanoparticles can be used to deliver genetic material directly into target cells, improving the effectiveness of treatments for genetic disorders or cancers. In **vaccine development**, nanoparticles can be employed to create more potent vaccines by enhancing the immune response. Overall, the integration of nanotechnology into NDDS provides substantial improvements in drug delivery, offering **more effective treatments** with fewer side effects.

1.5.2 Smart Drug Delivery Systems

Smart drug delivery systems represent the next step in drug delivery innovation, offering a level of **personalized medicine** that was not possible with traditional drug delivery methods. These systems are designed to be **stimuli-responsive**, meaning they can respond to changes in the **environmental triggers** such as **pH**, **temperature**, or **enzyme presence**. By incorporating these environmental factors, smart systems can release drugs only when needed, ensuring that the drug is delivered at the right time and at the right concentration.

For instance, **pH-sensitive systems** can release drugs specifically in the acidic environment of the stomach or the more neutral pH of the intestines, ensuring that the drug reaches its intended target without premature release. Similarly, **temperature-sensitive systems** can release drugs when they encounter elevated temperatures, such as those found in **inflammatory tissues**. **Thermo-responsive hydrogels** are one such example, where drug release can be triggered by changes in body temperature, making them ideal for localized treatment of conditions like arthritis.

AI integration into smart drug delivery systems is another emerging trend. Artificial intelligence (AI) can be used to optimize the design, production, and administration of smart drug delivery systems, enabling real-time monitoring and adjustment of drug release profiles. This integration allows for a **personalized approach** to medicine, where treatments can be tailored to the individual patient's needs based on their specific genetic profile, lifestyle, and disease progression.

Incorporating **biomarkers** and **diagnostic sensors** into these systems allows for continuous monitoring of therapeutic effects, ensuring that drugs are released only when required and adjusting the release rate according to the patient's needs. This personalized approach to treatment enhances the effectiveness of drug therapy while reducing potential side effects. **Smart drug delivery systems** have the potential to revolutionize the treatment of chronic diseases, cancers, and genetic disorders, offering more precise, safer, and more effective treatments for patients.

1.6 Applications of NDDS

1.6.1 Chronic Disease Management

Novel drug delivery systems (NDDS) play a critical role in the management of chronic diseases, where the need for continuous or prolonged drug therapy is common. **Chronic conditions** such as **diabetes, cardiovascular diseases**, and **pain management** require treatments that provide **steady therapeutic levels** of medication over an extended period. NDDS are designed to release drugs at a controlled, sustained rate, ensuring that patients receive a consistent amount of medication throughout the day. This approach helps to maintain optimal drug concentrations in the bloodstream, improving therapeutic efficacy and patient adherence to treatment regimens.

For diabetes management, **extended-release formulations** of **insulin** or **oral hypoglycemic agents** are examples of NDDS that can provide a **steady supply** of the drug, reducing the need for multiple doses and minimizing fluctuations in blood sugar levels. Similarly, **cardiovascular drugs** like **statins** and **beta-blockers** can be formulated using NDDS to maintain constant drug levels, ensuring the effective management of heart conditions with reduced dosing frequency. In pain management, **transdermal patches** containing analgesics such as **fentanyl** offer **continuous pain relief** without the need for oral administration, which can be especially beneficial for patients suffering from chronic pain conditions such as arthritis or neuropathy. NDDS, by providing a **steady and controlled release** of medication, not only enhance the effectiveness of the drug but also improve **patient compliance**, reducing the risk of missed doses or overmedication.

1.6.2 Oncology

In **oncology**, the use of NDDS is increasingly recognized as an effective strategy to improve treatment outcomes while minimizing side effects associated with **chemotherapy** and **radiotherapy**. **Chemotherapy** drugs are notorious for their toxicity, affecting both cancerous and healthy cells. NDDS, particularly those using **targeted drug delivery systems**, can address this challenge by **delivering chemotherapy agents directly to**

tumor sites, thereby reducing systemic toxicity and enhancing the drug's therapeutic action.

Monoclonal antibodies and **nanoparticle-based delivery systems** are among the most advanced methods used in cancer treatment. These systems can be engineered to specifically recognize and bind to **tumor-specific antigens**, ensuring that the drug is delivered directly to the cancerous cells while sparing normal, healthy tissues. For example, **liposomal formulations** of chemotherapy drugs such as **doxorubicin** are widely used in clinical practice to treat various cancers, as they allow for the drug to accumulate preferentially at the tumor site. In addition, **monoclonal antibodies** like **trastuzumab** are designed to target specific receptors on the surface of cancer cells, enabling precise drug delivery and improving the effectiveness of treatments. By minimizing **side effects** and enhancing the **selectivity** of chemotherapy agents, NDDS significantly improve **patient outcomes** in cancer treatment, offering a more **personalized** and **effective approach** to oncology.

1.6.3 Infectious Diseases

In the treatment of **infectious diseases**, NDDS have the potential to **enhance the effectiveness** of antiviral, antimicrobial, and **vaccine delivery**. Traditional treatments often face challenges such as poor drug solubility, low bioavailability, and the emergence of **drug resistance**. Novel drug delivery systems can address these challenges by providing **site-specific delivery** and improving the **bioavailability** of the drugs, ensuring that they reach the target sites in effective concentrations.

For **antiviral treatments**, NDDS such as **liposomal formulations** can improve the delivery of drugs like **acyclovir** for herpes virus infections or **zidovudine** for HIV, ensuring that the drugs reach the site of infection more efficiently while reducing systemic side effects. In the case of **antimicrobial treatments, nanoparticle-based systems** can help deliver antibiotics directly to the site of infection, improving the drug's ability to overcome bacterial resistance mechanisms and enhance its therapeutic effect. In **vaccine delivery, microneedles, liposomes,** and **nanoparticles** are being used to develop more effective vaccines with improved stability and immune response. These systems can also offer **needle-free vaccination,** which is more comfortable for patients, especially in pediatric and geriatric populations.

1.7 Challenges in NDDS Development

The development of **Novel Drug Delivery Systems (NDDS)** involves overcoming several **technical challenges** to ensure their effectiveness, stability, and successful market acceptance. One of the most prominent challenges in the development of NDDS is **stability**. As these systems often involve complex formulations, maintaining the stability of the drug within the delivery system is crucial. The drug must remain effective over the intended period of delivery, whether it is a few hours or several days. Factors such as **chemical degradation**, **environmental sensitivity**, and **interaction between the drug and the excipients** can impact the stability of the system. To address this, researchers must thoroughly understand the **chemical properties** of the drug and formulation to ensure that it remains stable under various conditions, including temperature, humidity, and pH changes.

Scalability is another major challenge in NDDS development. Many of the advanced **nanoparticles**, **liposomes**, and **microsphere-based systems** that are designed for controlled or targeted drug release are initially developed in small laboratory-scale batches. However, when transitioning to industrial-scale production, the processes must be adapted to handle larger volumes while maintaining the consistency and quality of the drug delivery system. Ensuring that the system's release profile, stability, and effectiveness remain intact during scale-up is a significant challenge. This can require modifications to **formulation processes**, including adjustments to equipment, manufacturing conditions, and even raw materials.

Moreover, **regulatory compliance** presents a considerable hurdle in the development of NDDS. Regulatory authorities such as the **FDA** and **EMA** have stringent guidelines to ensure the safety and efficacy of drug delivery systems before they reach the market. The approval process for NDDS often involves complex and lengthy evaluations, as these systems may need to demonstrate not only their **biological efficacy** but also their **mechanical properties** (e.g., drug release rate, consistency, and stability). This is especially challenging for **novel delivery technologies**, as regulatory frameworks may not be well-defined for new and innovative systems. Ensuring compliance with **Good Manufacturing Practices (GMP)**, **clinical trial protocols**, and **environmental standards** adds layers of complexity to the development process.

Additionally, **safety** and **efficacy** concerns must be thoroughly addressed. Even if a drug delivery system demonstrates effective drug release, the system itself must be biocompatible and non-toxic to ensure patient safety. This includes evaluating **immune reactions, irritation** at the drug delivery site, and any **adverse systemic effects**. As NDDS often involve **novel materials** such as **biodegradable polymers** or **nanoparticles**, long-term safety data is essential to address any potential health risks.

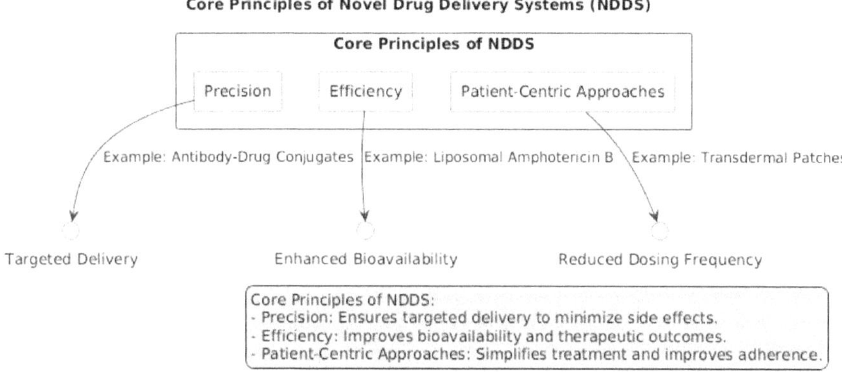

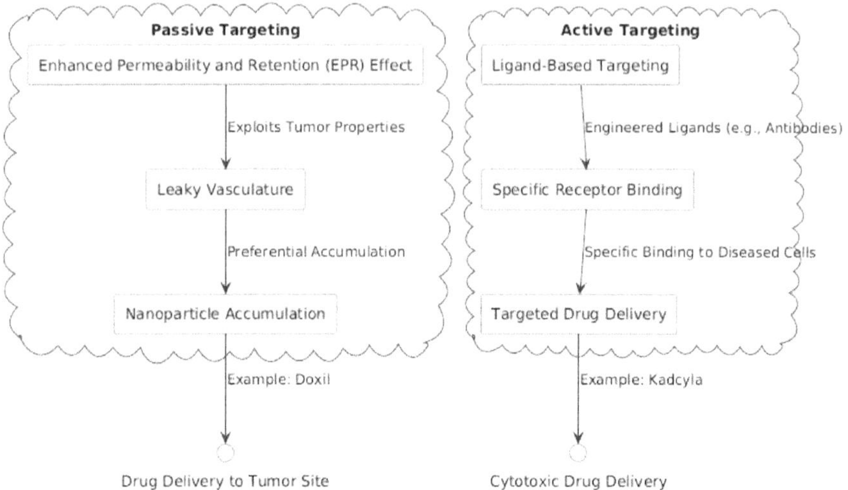

Targeting Approaches in NDDS

CHAPTER II

Controlled Drug Delivery Systems – Basics

2.1 INTRODUCTION TO CONTROLLED DRUG DELIVERY SYSTEMS

Definitions and Key Terminology

Controlled Drug Delivery Systems (CDDS) are advanced pharmaceutical technologies designed to release drugs into the body in a controlled, predictable, and sustainable manner. Unlike traditional drug delivery methods, which often result in fluctuating drug levels in the bloodstream, CDDS aim to maintain consistent therapeutic concentrations over extended periods. This ensures that the drug exerts its intended therapeutic effect without the need for frequent administration.

The primary goal of CDDS is to overcome the limitations of conventional dosage forms, such as tablets or injections, by ensuring that drugs are delivered in a way that aligns with the body's natural processes. These systems are particularly valuable in managing chronic diseases where long-term treatment is required. For instance, controlled-release formulations of medications like metformin or nifedipine are used in diabetes and hypertension to provide sustained therapeutic effects throughout the day.

Core concepts of CDDS include predictable pharmacokinetics, reproducibility, and site-specific action. Predictable pharmacokinetics refers to the ability of the system to release the drug at a consistent rate, ensuring that the concentration of the drug in the bloodstream remains within the therapeutic window. This minimizes the risk of side effects caused by drug peaks or troughs. Reproducibility ensures that the drug release profile remains consistent across different patients and dosing intervals. Site-specific action, on the other hand, refers to the targeted delivery of drugs to a specific tissue or organ, reducing systemic exposure and improving efficacy. For example, drug-eluting stents used in cardiovascular treatments deliver medications directly to the site of arterial blockages, ensuring localized action.

Terminology associated with CDDS includes sustained release, extended release, pulsatile release, and targeted delivery. Sustained release refers to the gradual release of a drug over an extended period, maintaining a steady concentration in the bloodstream. Extended release is similar but often indicates a slightly longer duration of action, as seen in medications like once-daily formulations of antihypertensives. Pulsatile release refers to systems that release drugs in bursts, mimicking natural biological rhythms. Targeted delivery is the precise delivery of drugs to a specific site, such as tumors in cancer therapy, minimizing effects on healthy tissues.

Core Principles of Controlled Drug Delivery Systems (CDDS)

Controlled Drug Delivery Systems (CDDS) are designed to address the limitations of conventional drug delivery methods, focusing on optimizing therapeutic efficacy, safety, and patient convenience. These systems are built upon foundational principles that ensure their reliability and effectiveness in modern therapy.

Maintenance of Stable Therapeutic Levels

One of the primary principles of CDDS is maintaining stable therapeutic levels of a drug within the body over an extended period. Traditional dosage forms often lead to fluctuating drug concentrations, with peaks that may cause side effects and troughs that result in reduced efficacy. CDDS aim to eliminate these fluctuations by releasing the drug at a consistent rate, ensuring that the concentration remains within the therapeutic window.

For example, oral controlled-release formulations of anti-diabetic drugs like metformin provide a steady supply of the medication, avoiding the rapid spikes associated with immediate-release tablets. This stability is particularly beneficial for chronic diseases, where maintaining drug levels is crucial for preventing complications and achieving long-term control. The maintenance of stable drug levels not only enhances the therapeutic effect but also minimizes adverse reactions caused by excessive drug exposure.

Predictable and Reproducible Release Profiles

Another essential principle of CDDS is ensuring predictable and reproducible drug release profiles. Predictability refers to the ability of the system to deliver the drug at a predetermined rate, while reproducibility ensures that this release pattern remains consistent across different doses and patients.

Predictable release profiles are achieved through advanced drug delivery technologies, such as polymeric matrices or osmotic pump systems. For instance, osmotic-controlled oral delivery systems (OROS) release the drug at a constant rate, driven by osmotic pressure. This ensures a uniform release, regardless of variations in gastrointestinal pH or motility.

Reproducibility is critical in ensuring patient safety and confidence in the treatment. Patients can rely on the fact that each dose will perform as expected, reducing variability in therapeutic outcomes. This consistency is achieved through precise manufacturing techniques and rigorous quality control measures that ensure uniformity in drug composition and delivery mechanisms.

Patient-Centric Designs for Improved Adherence

CDDS emphasize patient-centric designs to improve adherence to prescribed treatment regimens. Poor compliance is a common challenge in conventional therapy, often caused by the need for frequent dosing or complex administration schedules. CDDS address this issue by reducing dosing frequency and simplifying drug administration.

For example, transdermal patches that deliver medications like fentanyl for pain management provide a convenient once-daily or weekly option, eliminating the need for multiple daily doses. Similarly, controlled-release formulations of antihypertensive drugs allow patients to take their medication once a day instead of multiple times, enhancing convenience and compliance.

Patient-centric designs also consider individual needs, such as ease of use and reduced discomfort. Subcutaneous implants, which release contraceptives or other medications over months or years, offer a hands-free alternative for individuals who may struggle with daily or monthly regimens. These designs not only improve adherence but also enhance the overall patient experience by reducing the burden of managing chronic conditions.

Historical Evolution and Need

The journey of Controlled Drug Delivery Systems (CDDS) from simple formulations to sophisticated modern technologies reflects the evolving needs of healthcare and the continuous quest for optimizing drug therapy. This evolution has been driven by a deeper understanding of pharmacokinetics, patient behavior, and the limitations of traditional drug delivery methods.

From Early Sustained-Release Tablets to Modern Polymeric Systems

The concept of controlled drug delivery began with the development of sustained-release tablets in the mid-20th century. These formulations aimed to extend the duration of drug action by modifying the release rate of the active ingredient. Early sustained-release systems used basic excipients like waxes and gums to slow drug dissolution, providing a modest improvement over immediate-release formulations.

As pharmaceutical science advanced, researchers began exploring polymer-based systems to achieve more precise control over drug release. Innovations such as hydrophilic matrices, reservoir systems, and membrane-coated tablets emerged, allowing for predictable and reproducible release profiles. The introduction of biodegradable polymers, like polylactic acid (PLA) and polyglycolic acid (PGA), marked a significant milestone, enabling the development of implantable and injectable CDDS. These polymeric systems not only provided sustained drug delivery but also eliminated the need for device removal, enhancing patient convenience.

Modern CDDS have further evolved with the integration of nanotechnology and smart materials. Nanoparticles, liposomes, and dendrimers have enabled site-specific delivery and protection of unstable drugs. Smart drug delivery systems, capable of responding to stimuli like pH or temperature, represent the cutting edge of CDDS innovation. These advancements have expanded the applicability of CDDS to areas like oncology, immunotherapy, and gene delivery, revolutionizing treatment outcomes.

Challenges with Traditional Dosage Forms

Traditional dosage forms, while effective for many conditions, have inherent limitations that necessitated the development of CDDS. One major challenge is the need for frequent dosing. Immediate-release formulations often require multiple doses per day to maintain therapeutic drug levels, which can lead to poor patient compliance. This is especially problematic in chronic diseases like hypertension or diabetes, where long-term adherence is critical for treatment success.

Plasma drug level fluctuations are another significant drawback of conventional drug delivery. Rapid absorption following drug administration often leads to high plasma concentrations, increasing the risk of side effects. As drug levels decline, they may fall below the therapeutic threshold, reducing efficacy. These peaks and troughs in drug concentration not only compromise therapeutic outcomes but also increase the risk of dose-related toxicity.

Traditional dosage forms also face challenges in targeting drugs to specific sites. Systemic drug delivery often exposes non-target tissues to the active ingredient, leading to undesirable side effects. For example, systemic chemotherapy drugs can harm healthy cells alongside cancerous ones, resulting in significant toxicity.

Drivers for CDDS Development

The development of CDDS has been propelled by the need to overcome these challenges and improve the overall quality of drug therapy. One key driver is the goal of achieving improved pharmacokinetics. CDDS are designed to release drugs in a controlled manner, maintaining plasma concentrations within the therapeutic window. This eliminates peaks and troughs, enhancing efficacy and reducing the risk of side effects.

Patient convenience has also been a major focus. By reducing dosing frequency, CDDS simplify treatment regimens, leading to better compliance. For instance, once-daily controlled-release formulations of antihypertensive drugs provide the same therapeutic benefits as multiple daily doses, making them more user-friendly.

Another critical driver is the reduction of systemic toxicity. CDDS enable localized drug delivery, minimizing exposure to non-target tissues.

Drug-eluting stents, for example, release anti-proliferative agents directly at the site of arterial blockages, reducing restenosis without affecting other parts of the body.

Rationale Behind Controlled Release Formulations

Controlled release formulations are designed to address the limitations of conventional drug delivery systems by optimizing drug pharmacokinetics and enhancing therapeutic outcomes. These formulations are developed with a scientific understanding of drug absorption, distribution, metabolism, and excretion (ADME), alongside various factors that influence the design of the delivery system. Controlled release systems aim to provide precise, predictable, and prolonged drug delivery, improving efficacy, safety, and patient adherence.

Role of ADME in CDDS Design

The ADME processes—absorption, distribution, metabolism, and excretion—are foundational to the design of controlled drug delivery systems (CDDS). Absorption determines how quickly and efficiently a drug enters the systemic circulation. Conventional dosage forms often result in rapid absorption, leading to high plasma concentrations that can cause side effects. CDDS, on the other hand, are engineered to release the drug at a controlled rate, ensuring steady absorption and reducing plasma level fluctuations.

Distribution refers to the spread of the drug throughout the body. Conventional systems distribute drugs systemically, often affecting both target and non-target tissues. Controlled release systems, such as targeted delivery mechanisms, aim to concentrate the drug at the desired site of action. For example, liposomal formulations in cancer therapy deliver drugs preferentially to tumor cells, minimizing effects on healthy tissues.

Metabolism plays a critical role in determining the duration of a drug's therapeutic action. Many drugs undergo rapid first-pass metabolism in the liver, reducing their bioavailability. Controlled release formulations NDDS bypass this issue by maintaining steady plasma concentrations, reducing the need for repeated dosing. For instance, transdermal patches for hormones like estradiol avoid hepatic first-pass metabolism, providing consistent therapeutic effects.

Excretion determines how long a drug remains in the body. Drugs with short half-lives require frequent dosing to maintain therapeutic levels. Controlled release formulations extend the duration of action by slowing the rate at which the drug is released and metabolized, ensuring prolonged therapeutic effects.

Factors Influencing Design

Several factors influence the design of controlled release formulations, including drug properties and the mechanisms of release.

Drug Properties

The physical and chemical properties of a drug are pivotal in determining the design of its controlled release system. Solubility is a critical factor, as poorly soluble drugs may have limited absorption and bioavailability. Techniques like nanoparticle encapsulation or polymeric matrices are used to improve the solubility of these drugs. For instance, poorly soluble drugs like paclitaxel are formulated into nanoparticle-based systems for enhanced delivery.

Stability is another important consideration. Many drugs degrade in the presence of light, moisture, or enzymes, reducing their therapeutic efficacy. Controlled release systems protect these drugs from degradation. For example, enteric-coated tablets shield acid-labile drugs from the acidic environment of the stomach, ensuring their release in the intestine.

The half-life of a drug also influences its suitability for controlled release formulations. Drugs with short half-lives are ideal candidates for these systems, as they require prolonged release to maintain therapeutic levels. Conversely, drugs with very long half-lives may not benefit significantly from controlled release formulations.

Mechanisms of Release

Controlled release formulations utilize various mechanisms to regulate drug release, including diffusion, dissolution, and osmotic pressure systems.

Diffusion-based systems control drug release through a polymer matrix or membrane. In these systems, the drug diffuses through the polymer at a controlled rate, ensuring steady release. Examples include matrix tablets and transdermal patches.

Dissolution-based systems rely on the gradual dissolution of the drug or its surrounding polymeric coating. These systems provide sustained release by controlling the rate at which the drug dissolves in bodily fluids. Enteric-coated tablets, designed to release the drug in the intestine, exemplify this mechanism.

Osmotic pressure systems use osmotic gradients to drive drug release. These systems consist of a drug reservoir enclosed in a semi-permeable membrane. Water enters the reservoir through the membrane, creating pressure that pushes the drug out through a small orifice. Osmotic pumps, such as those used for the delivery of nifedipine in hypertension, provide highly predictable release profiles.

2.2 ADVANTAGES AND DISADVANTAGES OF CONTROLLED DRUG DELIVERY SYSTEMS

Advantages

Controlled Drug Delivery Systems (CDDS) have revolutionized modern therapeutics by addressing several limitations associated with conventional drug delivery methods. These systems offer numerous benefits that enhance patient compliance, therapeutic efficacy, and overall healthcare outcomes.

Improved Patient Compliance

One of the most significant advantages of CDDS is their ability to improve patient compliance, particularly in managing chronic conditions. Conventional drug formulations often require frequent administration, which can lead to missed doses and suboptimal treatment outcomes. Controlled release systems reduce dosing frequency by providing a sustained and predictable release of the drug. For instance, transdermal patches delivering medications like fentanyl or estradiol allow once-daily or even weekly administration, eliminating the need for multiple daily doses.

This convenience is especially beneficial for chronic diseases such as hypertension or diabetes, where long-term adherence is critical. Controlled-release formulations of antihypertensive medications like nifedipine ensure steady drug levels, reducing the burden of frequent dosing. Similarly, extended-release formulations of metformin help diabetic patients maintain consistent blood glucose control without the inconvenience of multiple daily doses. By simplifying treatment regimens, CDDS significantly enhance patient adherence and improve overall therapeutic success.

Enhanced Therapeutic Efficacy

CDDS also contribute to enhanced therapeutic efficacy by maintaining stable plasma drug concentrations. Traditional dosage forms often result in peaks and troughs in drug levels, where high peaks may cause toxicity and low troughs reduce effectiveness. Controlled drug delivery systems ensure that drug levels remain within the therapeutic window, minimizing these fluctuations.

For example, sustained-release tablets used in pain management, such as morphine extended-release formulations, provide consistent analgesic effects while reducing the risk of side effects like sedation or respiratory depression. This stability not only improves treatment outcomes but also enhances patient comfort and safety.

Prolonged drug action is another key benefit of CDDS. By extending the duration of therapeutic effects, these systems reduce the frequency of dosing and associated side effects. Depot injections of antipsychotic medications, administered once a month, maintain steady drug levels, offering significant advantages over daily oral medications.

Targeted Drug Delivery

CDDS enable targeted drug delivery, which minimizes systemic toxicity and improves therapeutic outcomes. Targeted delivery ensures that the drug reaches the specific site of action, reducing exposure to non-target tissues. This is particularly beneficial in cancer therapy, where conventional chemotherapy often affects healthy cells alongside cancerous ones, leading to significant side effects.

Drug-eluting stents used in cardiovascular treatments exemplify targeted delivery. These stents release anti-proliferative agents directly at the site of arterial blockages, preventing restenosis while avoiding systemic side effects. Similarly, liposomal formulations of doxorubicin deliver the drug preferentially to tumor cells, enhancing its efficacy and reducing cardiotoxicity.

In localized infections, CDDS improve outcomes by concentrating antibiotics at the site of infection, reducing the risk of resistance and systemic adverse effects. For example, antibiotic-loaded bone cements used in orthopedic surgeries provide localized drug release, ensuring effective treatment of infections without systemic exposure.

Economic and Social Benefits

CDDS offer significant economic and social benefits by improving treatment efficiency and reducing healthcare costs. By minimizing dosing frequency and enhancing adherence, these systems reduce the likelihood of treatment failure and associated complications. This translates into fewer hospital visits, reduced need for follow-up interventions, and overall cost savings for both patients and healthcare systems.

For instance, the use of controlled-release formulations in chronic disease management decreases the economic burden on healthcare systems by reducing the incidence of hospitalizations related to poor medication adherence. Socially, CDDS empower patients by simplifying their treatment regimens, improving their quality of life, and enabling them to manage their conditions more effectively.

Disadvantages of Controlled Drug Delivery Systems

While Controlled Drug Delivery Systems (CDDS) offer numerous advantages, they are not without their challenges. The complexity and costs associated with their development, as well as patient-specific and regulatory hurdles, present significant disadvantages that must be carefully considered.

Complexity in Formulation Development

The development of CDDS involves advanced technologies and sophisticated manufacturing processes. Formulations often require techniques like microencapsulation, where the drug is encased in a polymeric shell to control its release. Similarly, nanotechnology-based systems, such as nanoparticles or liposomes, are utilized for targeted and sustained delivery. These technologies demand specialized knowledge, state-of-the-art facilities, and precise quality control measures, significantly increasing the complexity of production.

High research and development (R&D) costs are another major challenge. Developing a novel controlled-release system requires extensive preclinical and clinical testing to establish its safety, efficacy, and reliability. These costs, coupled with the need for specialized manufacturing equipment, make CDDS significantly more expensive than conventional dosage forms. For example, the production of a transdermal patch involves multiple steps, including drug loading, adhesive application, and quality assurance, all of which contribute to its higher cost.

Risks of Dose Dumping

Dose dumping is a serious concern associated with CDDS, where a sudden and unintended release of the drug occurs due to formulation failure. This can lead to dangerously high drug concentrations in the bloodstream, posing significant toxicity risks.

Polymeric systems, often used in CDDS, are susceptible to degradation or mechanical failure under certain conditions. For instance, exposure to heat, moisture, or physical stress during storage or use can compromise the integrity of the formulation. In osmotic systems, malfunction of the delivery mechanism can result in uncontrolled drug release.

The consequences of dose dumping are particularly severe in drugs with a narrow therapeutic index, where the margin between therapeutic and toxic doses is small. For example, in sustained-release formulations of opioids like morphine, dose dumping can lead to life-threatening respiratory depression. These risks necessitate stringent quality control measures and careful patient monitoring.

Patient-Specific Challenges

Physiological variability among patients can impact the performance of CDDS. Factors such as gastrointestinal (GI) motility, enzyme activity, and pH levels vary significantly between individuals, affecting the rate and extent of drug release and absorption. For example, in patients with gastrointestinal disorders like Crohn's disease, the altered GI environment can compromise the effectiveness of oral controlled-release formulations.

Resistance to novel delivery systems is another challenge. Many patients and healthcare providers may be unfamiliar with advanced CDDS, leading to hesitation or reluctance to adopt these technologies. This resistance can stem from concerns about safety, cost, or the perceived complexity of using such systems. Patient education and provider training are essential to overcome these barriers and ensure the successful implementation of CDDS in clinical practice.

Regulatory and Market Barriers

The stringent regulatory requirements for CDDS present significant challenges for their development and commercialization. These systems must undergo rigorous testing to ensure their safety, efficacy, and reliability, often resulting in prolonged approval timelines. Regulatory agencies such as the US Food and Drug Administration (FDA) and the European Medicines Agency (EMA) require extensive data from preclinical and clinical trials, as well as detailed manufacturing process validation.

High initial costs and limited accessibility further hinder the widespread adoption of CDDS. The complex manufacturing processes and lengthy approval timelines contribute to the high cost of these systems, making them less accessible to patients in low-resource settings. For instance, while advanced drug-eluting stents have revolutionized cardiovascular treatment, their cost limits their availability in developing countries.

2.3 MECHANISMS AND APPLICATIONS OF CONTROLLED DRUG DELIVERY SYSTEMS

Mechanisms of Controlled Drug Delivery Systems

Controlled drug delivery systems (CDDS) rely on sophisticated mechanisms to regulate the release of drugs over a prolonged period or in response to specific physiological triggers. These mechanisms are carefully designed to ensure consistent therapeutic effects while minimizing side effects. Among the most widely used mechanisms are diffusion-controlled systems, dissolution-controlled systems, and osmotic systems.

Diffusion-Controlled Systems

In diffusion-controlled systems, the drug is released through a polymer matrix or membrane at a controlled rate. The release mechanism depends on the diffusion of drug molecules through the polymeric material, which acts as a barrier.

There are two primary types of diffusion-controlled systems: matrix systems and reservoir systems. In matrix systems, the drug is uniformly dispersed within a polymeric matrix. The release occurs as the drug molecules near the surface diffuse out first, followed by those from deeper layers. These systems are commonly used in sustained-release tablets, where the polymer matrix ensures a steady release of the active ingredient over time.

In reservoir systems, the drug is encased in a polymeric shell or membrane. The release is regulated by the thickness and permeability of the membrane. Implantable devices, such as hormone-releasing implants, often use this mechanism to deliver drugs over months or even years. An example is Norplant, a subdermal implant for contraceptive hormone delivery, which provides effective contraception for up to five years.

Dissolution-Controlled Systems

Dissolution-controlled systems regulate drug release by relying on the dissolution of a polymer or coating surrounding the drug. These systems are particularly effective for controlling the timing and site of drug release.

There are two main types of dissolution-controlled systems: erosion-controlled and encapsulated systems. In erosion-controlled systems, the drug is embedded in a polymer matrix that gradually erodes in the presence of biological fluids, releasing the drug. In encapsulated systems, the drug core is coated with a polymeric material that dissolves at a predetermined rate.

Enteric-coated tablets are a common example of dissolution-controlled systems. These tablets are coated with materials that resist gastric acid but dissolve in the alkaline environment of the intestine. This ensures that the drug is released only in the intestine, protecting acid-sensitive drugs like omeprazole from degradation in the stomach.

Osmotic Systems

Osmotic systems use osmotic pressure gradients to drive the controlled release of drugs. These systems consist of a drug reservoir surrounded by a semi-permeable membrane with a small orifice for drug release.

When the system is exposed to aqueous fluids, water enters through the semi-permeable membrane due to osmotic pressure differences. This creates pressure within the reservoir, pushing the drug out through the orifice at a controlled rate. Osmotic systems are highly reliable and independent of physiological factors like pH or motility, making them ideal for maintaining steady drug levels.

One widely recognized application of osmotic systems is the osmotic pump tablet, such as the OROS (Osmotic Release Oral System) used for drugs like nifedipine in hypertension management. These systems provide a consistent release rate, ensuring effective blood pressure control over a 24-hour period.

Applications of Controlled Drug Delivery Systems (CDDS)

Controlled Drug Delivery Systems (CDDS) have transformed the landscape of therapeutic interventions by offering precise, sustained, and targeted delivery of drugs across various medical fields. Their applications span chronic disease management, oncology, pain management, and infectious diseases, providing innovative solutions that enhance efficacy and patient outcomes.

Chronic Disease Management

CDDS are particularly valuable in managing chronic diseases, where long-term treatment adherence and consistent therapeutic levels are crucial. One prominent example is the use of extended-release formulations of metformin for diabetes management. These formulations ensure a steady release of the drug over 24 hours, improving glycemic control while minimizing the gastrointestinal side effects often associated with immediate-release tablets. By reducing dosing frequency to once daily, extended-release metformin enhances patient adherence, a critical factor in managing a chronic condition like diabetes.

In hypertension, transdermal patches delivering medications such as clonidine or nitroglycerin provide sustained blood pressure control. These patches release the drug through the skin into systemic circulation at a consistent rate, bypassing gastrointestinal metabolism and reducing the risk of first-pass degradation. The convenience of once-daily application further improves patient compliance, especially for elderly individuals managing multiple medications.

Oncology

Cancer treatment has greatly benefited from the advent of CDDS, particularly in the form of localized chemotherapy. Traditional systemic chemotherapy often affects healthy tissues, leading to severe side effects. CDDS, such as drug-eluting implants, address this limitation by delivering chemotherapeutic agents directly to the tumor site.

For instance, gliadel wafers are implantable devices used in the treatment of brain tumors. These wafers are loaded with carmustine, a chemotherapeutic drug, and placed in the surgical cavity after tumor resection. The wafers release the drug locally over several weeks, targeting residual cancer cells while minimizing systemic toxicity. Such localized delivery improves therapeutic efficacy and reduces adverse effects, offering a significant advancement in oncology.

Pain Management

Pain management, particularly for chronic conditions, has been revolutionized by CDDS like transdermal patches. Fentanyl transdermal patches are a widely used example, providing sustained analgesia for patients with severe chronic pain, such as those with cancer or advanced arthritis.

These patches deliver fentanyl, a potent opioid, through the skin at a controlled rate, maintaining consistent plasma levels over 72 hours. This prolonged action eliminates the need for frequent dosing and reduces the risk of breakthrough pain, a common challenge with conventional oral or injectable formulations. Additionally, transdermal patches bypass the gastrointestinal tract, reducing the risk of gastrointestinal side effects and first-pass metabolism, which is particularly important for patients with compromised digestive systems.

Infectious Diseases

In the field of infectious diseases, CDDS enable site-specific delivery of antibiotics, addressing challenges like resistance and systemic toxicity. Conventional systemic antibiotic administration often exposes healthy tissues to the drug, increasing the likelihood of adverse effects and promoting the development of antibiotic resistance.

Drug delivery systems such as antibiotic-loaded bone cements or beads are used in the treatment of osteomyelitis, a severe bone infection. These systems release antibiotics like vancomycin or gentamicin directly at the infection site over an extended period, achieving high local concentrations while minimizing systemic exposure. Similarly, CDDS are employed in the treatment of tuberculosis, where sustained-release formulations of rifampicin or isoniazid improve adherence and therapeutic outcomes in patients undergoing prolonged therapy.

2.4 EMERGING TRENDS AND INNOVATIONS IN CONTROLLED DRUG DELIVERY

Controlled Drug Delivery Systems (CDDS) have seen remarkable advancements in recent years, driven by the integration of smart technologies, nanotechnology, and personalized medicine. These innovations aim to enhance the precision, efficiency, and adaptability of drug delivery systems to meet evolving therapeutic needs.

Smart and Responsive Systems

Smart drug delivery systems are designed to respond to specific physiological stimuli, ensuring precise and timely drug release. These systems can be programmed to release drugs in response to changes in pH, temperature, or the presence of specific enzymes.

pH-sensitive systems exploit the variations in pH levels within the human body to deliver drugs selectively to certain regions. For instance, cancerous tissues often exhibit a slightly acidic environment compared to healthy tissues. pH-sensitive nanoparticles can release their drug payload specifically in these acidic regions, enhancing therapeutic efficacy while reducing systemic toxicity. These systems are particularly beneficial in oncology, where targeted delivery is crucial for minimizing harm to healthy tissues.

Temperature-responsive systems leverage the differences in temperature between diseased and healthy tissues. For example, certain thermosensitive hydrogels remain in a liquid state at room temperature but gel at body temperature, providing localized and sustained drug release. These systems are useful in applications like localized cancer therapy and tissue regeneration.

Wearable devices represent another innovation in smart drug delivery. These devices combine real-time monitoring with controlled drug release, allowing for precise, on-demand administration. For instance, insulin pumps equipped with continuous glucose monitors can adjust insulin delivery based on real-time blood sugar levels, offering superior glycemic control for diabetic patients. This integration of monitoring and delivery not only improves therapeutic outcomes but also enhances patient convenience.

Nanotechnology Integration

Nanotechnology has revolutionized CDDS by enabling precision targeting and sustained drug release at a microscopic scale. Nanoparticles, which are particles measuring less than 100 nanometers, are increasingly used to enhance the solubility, stability, and bioavailability of drugs.

Liposomal formulations are among the most well-established applications of nanotechnology in drug delivery. These lipid-based vesicles encapsulate drugs, protecting them from degradation and directing them to specific tissues. For example, liposomal doxorubicin, marketed as Doxil, is used in cancer therapy to deliver the chemotherapeutic agent directly to tumor cells while sparing healthy tissues. This targeted delivery reduces the cardiotoxicity associated with conventional doxorubicin therapy.

Dendrimers, another nanotechnology-based innovation, are highly branched, tree-like structures with a high degree of surface functionality. These characteristics make them ideal for site-specific delivery, as they can be engineered to carry multiple drug molecules and targeting ligands. Dendrimers have shown promise in delivering anticancer drugs, imaging agents, and gene therapies with exceptional precision.

Personalized Medicine

The emergence of personalized medicine has introduced a paradigm shift in the design and application of CDDS. Tailored drug delivery systems are developed based on an individual's genetic profile, physiological conditions, and disease characteristics, ensuring optimal therapeutic outcomes.

Pharmacogenomics, the study of how genes affect an individual's response to drugs, plays a pivotal role in personalized CDDS. By analyzing genetic variations that influence drug metabolism, transport, and targets, personalized drug delivery systems can be optimized to enhance efficacy and minimize side effects. For instance, patients with genetic polymorphisms affecting the cytochrome P450 enzymes may benefit from CDDS designed to bypass extensive first-pass metabolism.

Personalized CDDS are also being developed for advanced therapeutics such as immunotherapy and gene therapy. These systems incorporate nanotechnology and bioinformatics to deliver drugs or genetic material specifically to diseased tissues. For example, mRNA vaccines for COVID-19, which utilize lipid nanoparticles for delivery, represent a milestone in personalized and targeted therapy.

Emerging trends such as smart systems, nanotechnology integration, and personalized medicine signify the ongoing transformation of controlled drug delivery systems. These innovations not only address existing limitations but also open new possibilities for treating complex and chronic diseases, paving the way for a future of more precise and patient-centered therapies.

CHAPTER III

Controlled Drug Delivery Systems – Design Approaches

3.1 SELECTION CRITERIA FOR DRUG CANDIDATES

Physicochemical Properties
  Solubility and Dissolution Rate

The solubility and dissolution rate of a drug are critical factors in designing controlled-release formulations. Solubility refers to the ability of a drug to dissolve in a given solvent, while the dissolution rate is the speed at which the drug dissolves in bodily fluids. These properties directly impact the drug's absorption and bioavailability. Drugs with low solubility pose a significant challenge in controlled drug delivery systems (CDDS) because they may not dissolve sufficiently in gastrointestinal fluids to maintain consistent plasma levels. For example, poorly soluble drugs like carbamazepine require formulation strategies such as the use of solubilizing agents or nanoparticle technologies to enhance their release and absorption.

Hydrophilic and hydrophobic properties also influence the release behavior of a drug. Hydrophilic drugs, which readily dissolve in water, are more suitable for immediate or sustained-release formulations due to their ability to achieve predictable release rates. On the other hand, hydrophobic drugs require specialized techniques such as encapsulation in lipophilic matrices to ensure controlled release. For instance, hydrophobic drugs like paclitaxel are often formulated into nanoparticles or liposomes to improve their solubility and achieve sustained delivery.

Molecular Weight and Size

The molecular weight and size of a drug determine its ability to diffuse through polymers, membranes, or biological barriers, which is a key consideration in diffusion-controlled systems. Drugs with smaller molecular weights can diffuse more easily through polymeric matrices, leading to a steady release profile. For instance, small molecule drugs like propranolol are often used in matrix-based controlled-release formulations because their small size allows for consistent diffusion.

In contrast, large molecule drugs such as peptides and proteins present unique challenges due to their size and complexity. These molecules require advanced delivery systems like hydrogels, nanoparticles, or conjugation with carrier molecules to facilitate controlled release and improve stability. An example is insulin, which is a large protein that cannot diffuse through conventional matrices and is instead delivered through specialized systems like biodegradable implants or microneedles.

Stability

Stability is a fundamental property that influences the design and efficacy of controlled drug delivery systems. Drugs must maintain their chemical and physical stability during formulation, storage, and administration to ensure therapeutic effectiveness. Chemical stability refers to the drug's resistance to degradation processes such as oxidation, hydrolysis, or photodegradation. For example, drugs like ascorbic acid are highly sensitive to light and require protective packaging and stabilizing agents to preserve their efficacy.

Physical stability involves maintaining the drug's structural integrity under varying environmental conditions, including temperature and humidity. Drugs that exhibit polymorphic changes, such as ritonavir, can experience significant reductions in solubility and bioavailability due to instability in different crystalline forms.

The stability of a drug in biological fluids is also critical for controlled-release formulations. Many drugs degrade rapidly in the acidic environment of the stomach or under enzymatic activity in the intestines. To address this, formulation strategies such as enteric coatings or encapsulation in pH-sensitive polymers are employed. For instance, omeprazole, a proton pump inhibitor, is formulated with an enteric coating to protect it from degradation in gastric acid and ensure its release in the alkaline environment of the intestine.

Partition Coefficient (Log P)

The partition coefficient, often expressed as Log P, is a measure of a drug's lipophilicity, indicating its ability to dissolve in lipids relative to water. It is a critical parameter in the selection of drug candidates for controlled drug delivery systems (CDDS). Lipophilicity significantly affects a drug's membrane permeability, a key factor in determining its absorption and distribution within the body.

For efficient membrane permeation, a drug requires an optimal Log P value. Highly lipophilic drugs (with a high Log P) readily pass through lipid membranes but may face challenges in dissolving in aqueous biological fluids, leading to poor bioavailability. Conversely, highly hydrophilic drugs (with a low Log P) dissolve easily in water but struggle to cross lipid bilayers, limiting their absorption.

An optimal Log P, generally ranging between 1 and 3, strikes a balance between these properties, enabling adequate solubility in biological fluids and efficient transport across lipid membranes. For example, propranolol, a beta-blocker with a Log P of approximately 3.4, demonstrates good membrane permeability and effective systemic absorption.

In formulation design, achieving the ideal balance between hydrophilicity and lipophilicity is crucial. This balance ensures that the drug is both bioavailable and capable of sustained or controlled release. Strategies such as the use of co-solvents, surfactants, or encapsulation within hydrophilic or lipophilic matrices can be employed to optimize a drug's partition coefficient for specific delivery systems. For instance, hydrophobic drugs like paclitaxel are often encapsulated in liposomal formulations to enhance their aqueous solubility and improve delivery to target tissues.

Ionization and pKa

Ionization, governed by a drug's pKa value, is another vital parameter influencing solubility, permeability, and overall performance in controlled-release formulations. The pKa of a drug represents the pH at which 50% of the drug exists in its ionized form, while the remainder remains unionized.

The ionization state of a drug affects its solubility and permeability. Ionized drugs are more soluble in aqueous environments due to their charged nature, but their ability to cross lipid membranes is significantly reduced. On the other hand, unionized drugs are more lipophilic, making them better suited for membrane permeation but less soluble in water. This interplay necessitates careful consideration in the formulation of CDDS to achieve effective drug delivery.

For example, weakly acidic drugs such as aspirin (pKa ~3.5) remain predominantly unionized in the acidic environment of the stomach, facilitating their absorption. However, in the more alkaline environment of the small intestine, these drugs become ionized, which can limit their absorption. In contrast, weakly basic drugs like propranolol (pKa ~9.5) are better absorbed in the small intestine due to their ionization state in that environment.

pH-sensitive release systems take advantage of this behavior by designing formulations that release the drug in environments where its ionization state optimizes therapeutic effect. For instance, enteric-coated tablets protect acid-labile drugs like omeprazole in the stomach and allow their release in the intestine, where they are less prone to degradation.

Biological Factors

Absorption Window

The absorption window of a drug refers to the specific regions within the gastrointestinal tract (GIT) where optimal drug absorption occurs. This concept is critical in designing controlled drug delivery systems (CDDS) to ensure maximum therapeutic efficacy.

Different drugs exhibit varying absorption profiles depending on their physicochemical properties and interactions with the GIT environment. The stomach, with its acidic pH and limited surface area, is ideal for absorbing weakly acidic drugs such as aspirin. These drugs remain unionized in the stomach's acidic environment, facilitating membrane permeation. However, the short residence time of drugs in the stomach limits the duration of absorption.

The small intestine is the most significant site for drug absorption due to its large surface area, extensive blood supply, and neutral to slightly alkaline pH. Many drugs, including weakly basic drugs like propranolol, are efficiently absorbed here. Controlled-release formulations often aim to extend the drug's release in the small intestine to maximize absorption.

The colon, while less permeable than the small intestine, is a valuable target for certain drugs, especially in cases where delayed or site-specific release is desired. Drugs for treating colonic diseases, such as ulcerative colitis, are formulated to release their active ingredients in the colon. For example, mesalamine is delivered through pH-sensitive coatings that dissolve only in the alkaline environment of the colon.

Understanding the absorption window allows for designing CDDS tailored to the drug's absorption site, ensuring prolonged release and enhanced therapeutic outcomes. For instance, gastro-retentive systems like floating tablets are used to extend the gastric residence time of drugs absorbed primarily in the stomach, while enteric-coated tablets ensure drug release in the intestine.

Metabolism and First-Pass Effect

The metabolism of drugs, particularly the first-pass effect, plays a crucial role in determining their bioavailability and suitability for controlled-release formulations. The first-pass effect occurs when drugs are extensively metabolized in the liver before reaching systemic circulation, leading to reduced bioavailability.

Strategies to bypass liver metabolism are essential for drugs with high first-pass metabolism. One common approach is the development of prodrugs, which are pharmacologically inactive derivatives that convert to the active drug after absorption. For instance, enalapril, a prodrug of enalaprilat, is designed to enhance oral bioavailability by evading extensive hepatic metabolism.

Transdermal delivery systems offer another effective strategy to bypass the first-pass effect. Drugs like nitroglycerin, used in managing angina, are delivered through the skin directly into systemic circulation. Transdermal patches provide controlled and sustained release while avoiding gastrointestinal degradation and hepatic metabolism, making them an ideal choice for drugs with poor oral bioavailability.

Several drugs are significantly impacted by the first-pass effect, necessitating innovative delivery systems. For example, propranolol undergoes extensive hepatic metabolism, reducing its bioavailability when administered orally. Controlled-release formulations, such as osmotic systems, help maintain steady plasma levels, minimizing the impact of metabolism. Similarly, morphine, which has a high first-pass metabolism, benefits from alternative delivery methods like sublingual or transdermal systems to improve its therapeutic efficacy.

Incorporating biological factors like absorption windows and metabolism into the design of CDDS ensures that the drug reaches its intended site of action at optimal concentrations. This understanding enables the development of formulations that overcome physiological barriers, improve bioavailability, and provide sustained therapeutic effects.

Half-Life of the Drug

The half-life of a drug, which represents the time required for its concentration in the bloodstream to reduce by half, is a critical factor in determining its suitability for controlled-release formulations. Drugs with a half-life in the range of 2–6 hours are considered ideal candidates for controlled drug delivery systems (CDDS).

Drugs with very short half-lives (<2 hours) are rapidly cleared from the body, necessitating frequent dosing to maintain therapeutic levels. For example, dopamine has a short half-life and requires continuous infusion to achieve consistent plasma concentrations. Formulating such drugs into controlled-release systems poses challenges, as achieving sustained release often requires the use of advanced technologies like polymeric matrices or reservoir systems. Additionally, the rapid clearance of the drug may demand large doses, increasing the risk of dose dumping or toxicity in the event of formulation failure.

On the other hand, drugs with very long half-lives (>6 hours) naturally maintain prolonged therapeutic effects without the need for controlled-release systems. These drugs are less suited for CDDS because their inherent pharmacokinetics already provide extended duration of action. For example, amiodarone, with a half-life of several days, does not benefit significantly from controlled-release formulations. However, for long-half-life drugs with significant side effects, controlled-release systems may still be valuable in minimizing peak plasma concentrations and reducing adverse effects.

Designing CDDS for drugs with intermediate half-lives enables the extension of dosing intervals and maintenance of steady-state plasma concentrations. This not only improves patient compliance but also enhances therapeutic outcomes by reducing fluctuations in drug levels. Extended-release formulations of metformin, for instance, leverage its moderate half-life to provide sustained glycemic control with once-daily dosing, significantly improving adherence in diabetic patients.

Target Site Considerations

The choice between localized and systemic delivery is an essential consideration in the design of controlled-release formulations. Localized delivery focuses on directing the drug to a specific site within the body, minimizing systemic exposure and reducing the risk of side effects. Systemic delivery, on the other hand, involves distributing the drug throughout the bloodstream to reach multiple sites of action.

Topical formulations are prime examples of localized delivery systems. These are widely used in dermatological conditions, where the drug is applied directly to the skin. For instance, corticosteroid creams for eczema provide high local concentrations of the drug at the site of inflammation, avoiding systemic side effects like immunosuppression. Similarly, topical antifungal creams for conditions like athlete's foot target the affected area with minimal systemic absorption.

Implantable drug delivery systems represent another approach to localized delivery, especially in oncology. Implants such as gliadel wafers are placed directly at the tumor site during surgery to deliver chemotherapeutic agents like carmustine. This localized delivery ensures high drug concentrations at the tumor while sparing healthy tissues, reducing systemic toxicity and improving therapeutic efficacy.

Systemic delivery remains essential for conditions requiring widespread distribution of the drug, such as hypertension or diabetes. Controlled-release tablets and transdermal patches are commonly used to provide consistent drug levels in systemic circulation, ensuring prolonged therapeutic effects.

The decision to pursue localized or systemic delivery depends on the nature of the condition being treated, the drug's properties, and the desired therapeutic outcomes. By aligning the delivery method with the target site, controlled drug delivery systems can optimize efficacy, safety, and patient convenience.

Case Studies of Successful Controlled-Release Drugs

Metformin Extended-Release (XR)

Metformin Extended-Release (XR) formulations are widely recognized for their role in managing Type 2 diabetes mellitus. These formulations use a **matrix-based controlled-release mechanism**, ensuring a gradual and predictable release of the drug over an extended period. The matrix system is typically composed of hydrophilic polymers like hydroxypropyl methylcellulose (HPMC), which swell upon contact with gastrointestinal fluids, forming a gel barrier. This barrier regulates the diffusion of metformin, maintaining steady plasma concentrations.

The extended-release formulation offers significant advantages over immediate-release tablets. It minimizes gastrointestinal side effects, such as nausea and diarrhea, which are commonly associated with high peak concentrations of metformin in the bloodstream. Additionally, it enhances patient compliance by reducing dosing frequency to once daily, making it more convenient for long-term diabetes management. The consistent release profile of Metformin XR helps maintain optimal glycemic control throughout the day, providing therapeutic benefits without significant fluctuations in blood glucose levels.

Nifedipine Extended-Release Tablets

Nifedipine, a calcium channel blocker used in the treatment of hypertension and angina, has been successfully developed into an extended-release tablet using an **osmotic pump-based design**. This system consists of a core containing the drug, surrounded by a semi-permeable membrane with a laser-drilled orifice.

When ingested, water enters the tablet through the semi-permeable membrane, creating osmotic pressure within the core. This pressure forces the drug solution out through the orifice at a controlled rate, independent of gastrointestinal pH or motility. This design overcomes the challenges associated with immediate-release nifedipine, such as rapid onset of action leading to reflex tachycardia and short duration of effect requiring multiple daily doses.

The extended-release formulation ensures steady-state plasma concentrations, providing consistent blood pressure control over 24 hours. This improves patient adherence by reducing dosing frequency and minimizes adverse effects like excessive vasodilation or hypotension. Nifedipine extended-release tablets exemplify the application of advanced delivery systems to enhance therapeutic outcomes for chronic conditions.

Fentanyl Transdermal Patch

The Fentanyl Transdermal Patch is a landmark innovation in pain management, offering **sustained diffusion-based release** of the drug for patients with severe chronic pain, such as those with cancer or advanced arthritis. The patch is composed of multiple layers, including a drug reservoir, an adhesive layer, and a rate-controlling membrane.

Once applied to the skin, the patch releases fentanyl at a controlled rate, ensuring steady plasma concentrations over 72 hours. This prolonged action eliminates the need for frequent dosing, a significant benefit for patients requiring continuous pain relief. The transdermal route also bypasses gastrointestinal metabolism and hepatic first-pass effects, making it particularly advantageous for patients with compromised digestive systems or those at risk of opioid-induced gastrointestinal side effects.

The Fentanyl Transdermal Patch has transformed chronic pain management by providing consistent and effective analgesia while reducing the risk of overdose associated with rapid-release formulations. Its ease of use and reliability make it a preferred option for both patients and healthcare providers.

These case studies highlight the success of controlled-release formulations in addressing specific therapeutic challenges, improving patient compliance, and optimizing drug efficacy. By leveraging advanced delivery mechanisms like matrix systems, osmotic pumps, and transdermal technologies, these formulations exemplify the potential of controlled-release systems to revolutionize drug therapy.

3.2 APPROACHES TO DESIGN CONTROLLED RELEASE FORMULATIONS

Diffusion-Based Systems

Diffusion-based systems are among the most commonly employed approaches in designing controlled-release drug formulations. These systems rely on the movement of drug molecules from a region of higher concentration (within the formulation) to a region of lower concentration (the surrounding biological environment). This process is governed by Fick's laws of diffusion, which describe the rate of drug release in relation to the properties of the diffusion medium and the concentration gradient.

Mechanism

The mechanism of diffusion-based drug release involves the passage of drug molecules through a polymer matrix or membrane. In such systems, the polymer acts as a physical barrier that controls the rate of drug diffusion. Depending on the system's design, the polymer may remain intact or erode gradually, influencing the drug release kinetics. The drug's solubility, molecular weight, and the polymer's permeability are critical factors that determine the overall release profile.

Types of Diffusion-Based Systems

Matrix Systems

Matrix systems are characterized by the dispersion of the drug within a polymer matrix. As the drug diffuses through the matrix, the release rate decreases over time due to a diminishing concentration gradient. In some cases, matrix erosion also contributes to drug release, providing a combined mechanism of diffusion and erosion.

Hydrophilic polymers such as hydroxypropyl methylcellulose (HPMC) are widely used in matrix systems. When exposed to aqueous environments, HPMC matrices swell and form a gel layer, which acts as a diffusion barrier. This swelling not only controls the rate of drug release but also protects the drug from premature degradation. HPMC-based formulations are extensively used in sustained-release tablets, such as extended-release metformin for diabetes management.

Reservoir Systems

In reservoir systems, the drug core is enclosed within a polymeric membrane that regulates its release. Unlike matrix systems, reservoir systems can achieve zero-order release kinetics, where the drug is released at a constant rate over time. This makes them particularly suitable for applications requiring prolonged and predictable drug delivery.

The rate-controlling membrane in reservoir systems is often composed of semi-permeable polymers that allow the drug to diffuse out while preventing the influx of external fluids. For example, osmotic pump tablets utilize a reservoir design with a laser-drilled orifice, ensuring precise and sustained drug release over 24 hours.

Advantages and Limitations

Diffusion-based systems offer several advantages, including predictable release profiles and flexibility in designing formulations with varying release durations. Reservoir systems, in particular, provide consistent drug delivery, enhancing therapeutic outcomes for conditions requiring long-term management.

However, these systems also present limitations. Matrix systems often exhibit non-linear release profiles due to changes in the concentration gradient over time. Reservoir systems, while capable of zero-order release, carry risks of dose dumping if the rate-controlling membrane fails. Such failures can result in a sudden release of the entire drug dose, leading to potential toxicity.

Applications

Diffusion-based systems are widely used in developing sustained-release tablets and implantable devices. Sustained-release tablets designed with matrix or reservoir systems ensure prolonged drug action, reducing dosing frequency and improving patient compliance. For example, nifedipine extended-release tablets leverage reservoir systems to provide consistent blood pressure control in hypertensive patients.

Implantable devices, such as hormone-releasing implants or drug-eluting stents, also utilize diffusion-based mechanisms. These devices release therapeutic agents locally over months or years, offering significant advantages in conditions requiring site-specific delivery. Examples include Norplant, a contraceptive implant, and drug-eluting stents for preventing restenosis in cardiovascular treatments.

Diffusion-based systems exemplify the sophistication of modern controlled-release formulations, addressing critical therapeutic challenges and improving patient outcomes. By tailoring the design to the drug's properties and therapeutic goals, these systems continue to play a vital role in advancing pharmaceutical science.

Dissolution-Based Systems

Dissolution-based systems are a foundational approach in the design of controlled-release drug formulations. These systems regulate the release of a drug through the dissolution of a polymer or coating material. The dissolution rate of the polymer governs the timing and extent of drug release, making this method highly effective for creating formulations with predictable release profiles.

Mechanism

The mechanism of dissolution-based systems revolves around the gradual breakdown or solubilization of a polymeric material that encapsulates or embeds the drug. As the polymer dissolves in the surrounding biological fluid, the drug is released at a controlled rate. The polymer dissolution rate can be tailored through the selection of materials and their properties, allowing for precise control over drug release. This method ensures that the release is not immediate but occurs over a prolonged period, enhancing therapeutic efficacy and reducing the need for frequent dosing.

Types of Dissolution-Based Systems

Encapsulation Systems

Encapsulation systems involve coating individual drug particles or the entire dosage form with a polymer layer. The thickness and composition of this coating determine the rate at which the drug is released. For example, sustained-release capsules are designed with polymer coatings that dissolve slowly, ensuring a steady release of the drug over several hours.

An application of encapsulation systems is in the development of enteric-coated tablets. These formulations are coated with pH-sensitive polymers that resist dissolution in the acidic environment of the stomach but dissolve readily in the alkaline environment of the intestine. This approach protects acid-labile drugs like omeprazole from degradation in gastric acid and ensures their release in the intestine, where absorption occurs.

Matrix-Based Dissolution Systems

Matrix-based dissolution systems embed the drug within a polymeric matrix that dissolves gradually in biological fluids. As the matrix dissolves, the drug is released in a controlled manner. Unlike encapsulation systems, which rely on a surrounding coating, matrix-based systems distribute the drug throughout the polymer.

These systems are particularly effective for drugs requiring a prolonged release profile. For instance, hydrophilic polymers like hydroxypropyl methylcellulose (HPMC) are commonly used in matrix formulations. When exposed to aqueous environments, the matrix swells and dissolves, releasing the drug over time. This approach is frequently employed in the design of sustained-release tablets, such as those used for metformin or diclofenac.

Considerations

The use of pH-sensitive polymers is a critical consideration in dissolution-based systems. These polymers enable site-specific drug release by responding to the pH variations in the gastrointestinal tract. For example, poly(methacrylic acid-co-methyl methacrylate) polymers are often used in enteric coatings to achieve delayed release in the intestine. This ensures that the drug is released in the target region, improving its bioavailability and minimizing potential side effects.

Other factors, such as the drug's solubility, stability, and intended therapeutic application, must also be carefully evaluated during formulation. The polymer's solubility and erosion properties, along with the desired release kinetics, play a significant role in determining the overall efficacy of the system.

Applications

Dissolution-based systems find applications across various therapeutic areas. Enteric-coated tablets, for example, are widely used for drugs requiring protection from gastric acid or for targeting the intestine. Examples include delayed-release formulations of mesalamine for inflammatory bowel disease and omeprazole for acid reflux management.

Pulsatile release formulations represent another innovative application of dissolution-based systems. These formulations are designed to release the drug in bursts at specific intervals, mimicking the body's natural rhythms or addressing the timing of disease symptoms. Such systems are beneficial in conditions like asthma, where drug release can be timed to coincide with nocturnal symptoms.

Dissolution-based systems offer a versatile and effective approach to controlled drug delivery. By tailoring the dissolution characteristics of the polymer or matrix, these systems provide precise control over drug release, enhancing therapeutic outcomes and improving patient compliance.

Ion Exchange Systems

Ion exchange systems represent a unique and effective approach in the design of controlled drug delivery systems (CDDS). These systems leverage the interaction between charged drug molecules and ion exchange resins to achieve controlled and sustained release. Their application is particularly valuable for drugs that require prolonged therapeutic effects and consistent plasma levels.

Mechanism

The mechanism of ion exchange systems is based on the exchange of ions between the drug-resin complex and the surrounding gastrointestinal tract (GIT) fluids. Ion exchange resins are insoluble, cross-linked polymers with charged functional groups that bind to oppositely charged drug molecules, forming a stable drug-resin complex.

When the drug-resin complex encounters the GIT fluids, the ions present in the fluid (e.g., sodium, chloride) displace the drug molecules from the resin. This ionic interaction causes the drug to be released in a controlled manner. The rate of release depends on factors such as the strength of the ionic bond, the pH of the surrounding environment, and the concentration of competing ions in the fluid.

For example, in acidic stomach conditions, the release of a basic drug bound to a cationic resin is influenced by the availability of hydrogen ions. As the complex moves to the intestine, where the environment is more alkaline, the release profile changes due to variations in ion concentrations and pH. This pH-dependent release allows for sustained drug delivery throughout the GIT.

Components

Ion exchange systems primarily rely on drug-resin complexes for controlled ionic interaction. These complexes are formed by binding the drug molecules to ion exchange resins, which act as carriers. The resins are typically classified into two types based on their charge:

1. **Cationic Resins**: These resins possess negatively charged functional groups, such as sulfonate or carboxylate groups, which attract and bind positively charged drug molecules.
2. **Anionic Resins**: These resins carry positively charged functional groups, such as quaternary ammonium groups, which bind negatively charged drug molecules.

The selection of the resin depends on the drug's ionic nature and the desired release profile. Resins are carefully chosen to ensure stability in the GIT and compatibility with the drug's chemical properties.

Applications

Ion exchange systems have been successfully employed in various therapeutic applications. One common use is in the formulation of **antihistamines**, such as chlorpheniramine. By binding chlorpheniramine to an ion exchange resin, a controlled-release formulation is achieved, which prolongs its action and reduces the frequency of dosing. This approach enhances patient compliance and provides consistent symptom relief in conditions like allergies.

Similarly, **bronchodilators** used for respiratory conditions like asthma benefit from ion exchange systems. For instance, the extended-release formulation of theophylline employs ion exchange resins to maintain therapeutic drug levels over an extended period. This ensures effective symptom control without the need for frequent dosing.

Ion exchange systems are also applied in pediatric and geriatric formulations, where taste masking is a concern. The drug-resin complex not only controls the release but also reduces the bitterness of certain drugs, improving palatability for these patient populations.

3.3 COMPARATIVE ANALYSIS OF DESIGN APPROACHES

Diffusion vs. Dissolution Systems

The comparison between diffusion-based and dissolution-based controlled drug delivery systems highlights their distinct mechanisms and applications.

Diffusion systems rely on the movement of drug molecules through a polymer matrix or membrane. The release rate depends on the drug's concentration gradient and the permeability of the polymer. These systems are best suited for drugs that require a steady and prolonged release over time, as seen in reservoir and matrix diffusion designs. For instance, hydroxypropyl methylcellulose (HPMC) matrices in extended-release formulations of metformin achieve sustained glucose control, reducing the frequency of dosing.

In contrast, dissolution systems regulate drug release through the gradual breakdown or solubilization of the polymer or coating material. The release rate is determined by the dissolution rate of the polymer and can be tailored for site-specific delivery using pH-sensitive materials. Enteric-coated tablets, such as those used for mesalamine in inflammatory bowel disease, exemplify the effectiveness of dissolution systems in targeting specific regions of the gastrointestinal tract.

While diffusion systems are ideal for achieving consistent plasma levels, dissolution systems offer the advantage of flexibility in timing and site-specific release, making them suitable for drugs with unique absorption characteristics.

Case Studies

Matrix-diffusion systems, such as those in sustained-release nifedipine tablets, provide a controlled and predictable release, addressing the need for prolonged blood pressure management in hypertensive patients. On the other hand, dissolution-based systems, like enteric-coated omeprazole tablets, ensure drug stability in the acidic stomach environment and effective release in the intestine, enhancing therapeutic efficacy in acid-related disorders.

Ion Exchange vs. Diffusion Systems

Ion exchange systems differ significantly from diffusion systems in their reliance on ionic interactions for controlled release. In ion exchange systems, the drug is bound to a resin and released via exchange with ions in gastrointestinal fluids. These systems are particularly effective for drugs that are ionizable and require controlled release over extended periods.

Diffusion systems, by contrast, depend on the movement of drug molecules through a polymer barrier and are less influenced by ionic interactions. They are better suited for non-ionizable drugs or those requiring a consistent release rate regardless of the ionic environment.

Selection criteria for these systems depend on the drug's chemical properties and therapeutic goals. For instance, ion exchange systems are used in taste-masked pediatric formulations of antihistamines like chlorpheniramine, while diffusion systems are preferred for maintaining steady-state plasma levels in drugs like propranolol.

Combination Strategies

Combination strategies represent a hybrid approach, integrating multiple mechanisms to optimize drug delivery. These systems leverage the benefits of diffusion, dissolution, and ion exchange to achieve improved control and flexibility in drug release.

Matrix-diffusion-dissolution hybrids are a notable example. In these systems, the drug is embedded in a polymer matrix that both dissolves and allows diffusion, providing dual control over the release kinetics. For instance, certain multi-layered tablets use an outer dissolution layer for immediate release and an inner diffusion-controlled layer for sustained release, addressing both rapid onset and prolonged therapeutic action.

Such combination strategies are particularly valuable in complex therapeutic scenarios, such as in managing conditions requiring both immediate symptom relief and long-term control. For example, a hybrid system might deliver an anti-inflammatory drug with an initial burst release for acute relief, followed by sustained delivery for ongoing management.

3.4 CHALLENGES IN DESIGNING CONTROLLED RELEASE SYSTEMS

Controlled drug delivery systems (CDDS) offer significant advantages in improving therapeutic outcomes, but their design and implementation come with substantial challenges. These challenges span across formulation, manufacturing, and patient-specific factors, requiring careful consideration to ensure efficacy, safety, and consistency.

Formulation Challenges

One of the primary challenges in designing controlled release systems lies in ensuring compatibility between drugs, polymers, and excipients. Polymers, which serve as the backbone for most controlled-release formulations, must interact harmoniously with the drug and other excipients. Incompatibilities can lead to instability, reduced drug efficacy, or altered release profiles. For instance, drugs sensitive to moisture or light may require protective coatings, which need to be chemically and physically stable in the formulation environment.

Additionally, reproducible release profiles are critical in CDDS to maintain consistent therapeutic outcomes. Variability in the properties of raw materials, such as differences in polymer grade or drug particle size, can lead to fluctuations in drug release rates. This issue is particularly significant in systems like matrix or reservoir designs, where precise control over material properties is essential. Advanced analytical techniques and stringent quality control measures are required to ensure uniformity across batches.

Manufacturing and Scale-Up

Manufacturing controlled-release formulations on a large scale introduces technical complexities. Processes such as coating, encapsulation, and matrix formation require precise control over parameters like temperature, humidity, and particle size distribution. For example, creating consistent polymer coatings in reservoir systems demands highly specialized equipment and expertise, as even minor variations can affect the release rate.

Scale-up from laboratory to industrial production often presents additional challenges. Techniques that are effective at a small scale may not translate directly to large-scale operations due to differences in mixing efficiency, heat transfer, or drying rates. These discrepancies can lead to issues such as uneven drug distribution or incomplete coating, compromising the product's performance.

Quality control is another critical area in manufacturing controlled-release systems. Advanced formulations like reservoir and diffusion systems require rigorous testing to ensure that the release profile matches the intended design. Tests such as dissolution studies, particle size analysis, and polymer integrity assessments must be performed consistently to detect and address deviations.

Patient-Related Variability

Patient-specific factors can significantly influence the performance of controlled-release systems, posing a challenge in achieving consistent therapeutic outcomes. Variability in gastrointestinal (GI) conditions, such as pH, motility, and enzyme activity, affects the release and absorption of drugs. For instance, a patient with a higher gastric pH may experience delayed drug release from enteric-coated formulations designed to dissolve in acidic environments.

Differences in GI transit time also impact the effectiveness of controlled-release systems. For example, drugs targeting the colon may fail to reach the desired site if the transit time through the small intestine is too rapid.

Conversely, prolonged gastric retention in patients with delayed gastric emptying can lead to unpredictable release kinetics and reduced efficacy.

Enzyme activity levels, which vary among individuals due to genetic and environmental factors, further complicate the design of enzyme-sensitive formulations. A formulation designed for average enzyme levels may underperform or overperform in patients with atypical enzyme activity, leading to suboptimal drug release and therapeutic effects.

3.5 FUTURE TRENDS IN CONTROLLED RELEASE DESIGN APPROACHES

The field of controlled drug delivery systems (CDDS) is evolving rapidly, driven by advancements in material science, nanotechnology, and personalized medicine. These innovations aim to enhance therapeutic outcomes, minimize side effects, and cater to individual patient needs through smarter, more efficient delivery systems.

Smart and Responsive Systems

Smart and responsive drug delivery systems represent the next generation of CDDS, offering precise control over drug release in response to physiological or external stimuli. These systems utilize advanced polymers that change their properties under specific conditions, enabling targeted and on-demand drug release.

Stimuli-responsive polymers are engineered to respond to internal cues such as pH, temperature, or enzymes. For example, pH-sensitive polymers release drugs in specific regions of the gastrointestinal tract, such as the colon, where the pH differs significantly from other segments. This property is particularly useful for treating conditions like inflammatory bowel disease, where site-specific drug delivery is crucial.

External triggers such as light, ultrasound, or magnetic fields also offer promising avenues for on-demand drug release. Light-activated systems, for instance, use photosensitive materials that release drugs upon exposure to specific wavelengths of light. Similarly, ultrasound-responsive formulations employ acoustic waves to trigger drug release, making them ideal for localized treatments, such as in cancer therapy. These innovations reduce systemic exposure, enhancing safety and efficacy.

Nanotechnology in CDDS

Nanotechnology has revolutionized controlled drug delivery, enabling the development of nanoparticles that provide sustained and precise targeting. These nanoscale carriers offer high surface area-to-volume ratios, allowing for efficient drug encapsulation and controlled release.

Nanoparticles can be designed to release drugs over extended periods or in response to specific stimuli. For example, liposomal drug delivery systems use lipid bilayers to encapsulate drugs, protecting them from degradation and enabling gradual release. Liposomal formulations, such as doxorubicin-loaded liposomes, have shown significant success in reducing toxicity and improving outcomes in cancer therapy.

Nanocapsules, another innovation in nanotechnology, consist of a polymer shell surrounding a liquid or solid core. These structures provide enhanced stability and controlled drug release, making them ideal for delivering biologics like proteins or peptides. For instance, insulin-loaded nanocapsules are being explored for oral delivery, overcoming the challenges of enzymatic degradation in the gastrointestinal tract.

Personalized Medicine

The integration of pharmacogenomics into CDDS design is paving the way for personalized medicine, where drug delivery systems are tailored to an individual's genetic and physiological profile. Personalized CDDS account for variations in metabolism, enzyme activity, and drug response, ensuring optimal therapeutic outcomes.

Tailored formulations can adjust drug release rates based on a patient's unique pharmacokinetic profile. For example, patients with rapid drug metabolism may benefit from systems that deliver higher doses over shorter durations, while slow metabolizers may require extended-release formulations.

Wearable devices integrated with controlled-release systems are also emerging as tools for personalized medicine. These devices monitor real-time physiological parameters, such as glucose levels in diabetic patients, and adjust drug release accordingly. By combining advanced CDDS with wearable technology, personalized approaches offer unprecedented control over treatment regimens.

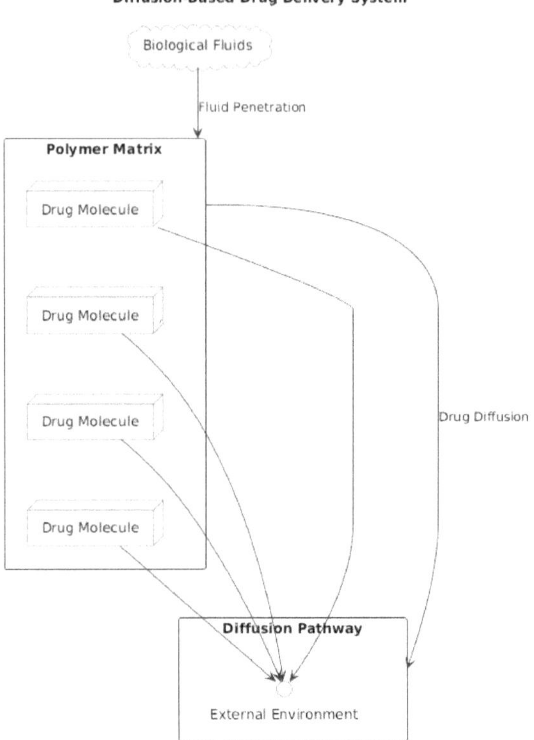

Mechanism of Diffusion-Based Drug Delivery System: This diagram demonstrates a system where drug molecules are embedded within a polymer matrix or enclosed in a reservoir surrounded by a rate-controlling membrane. Biological fluids penetrate the system, initiating the diffusion of the drug. The drug molecules travel through the polymer matrix or membrane and are released at a controlled rate into the external environment. This ensures a predictable and sustained drug release for consistent therapeutic effects.

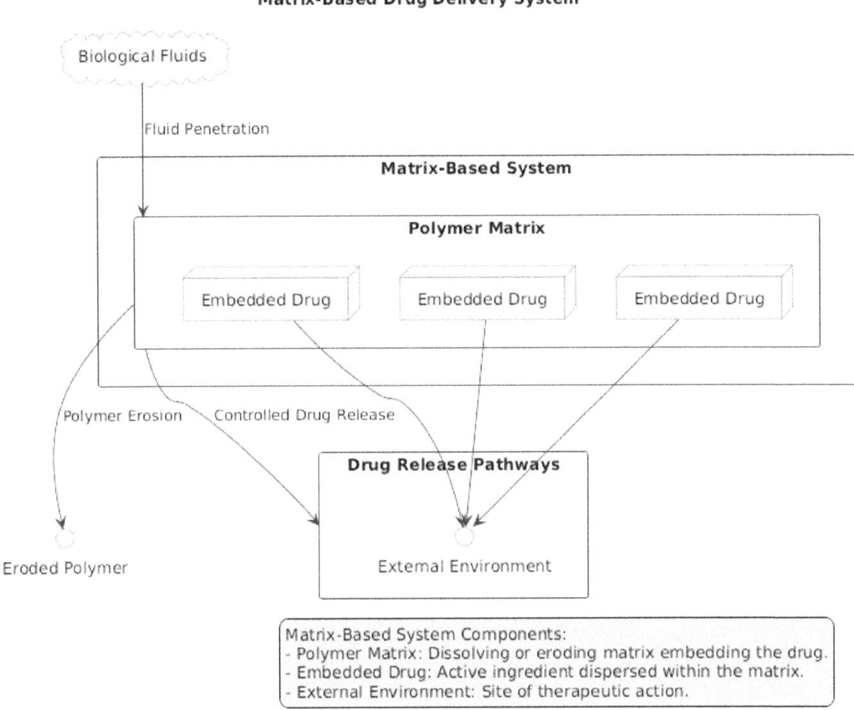

This diagram illustrates a system where drug molecules are embedded in a polymer matrix. When biological fluids interact with the matrix, it gradually dissolves or erodes, releasing the drug in a controlled manner. The process ensures a sustained release of the drug over time, providing consistent therapeutic effects. The polymer matrix acts as both a carrier and a release regulator, while the external environment represents the target site for drug action.

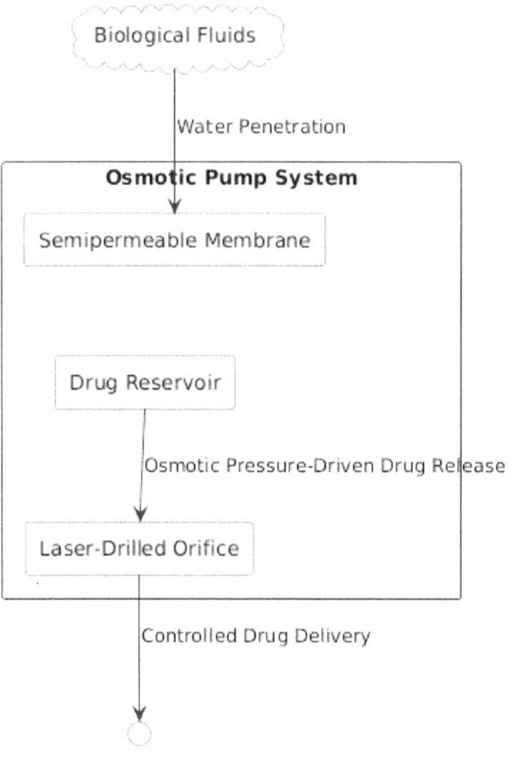

This diagram illustrates an osmotic pump system where water from biological fluids enters through a semipermeable membrane, creating osmotic pressure inside the drug reservoir. This pressure pushes the drug out through a laser-drilled orifice at a controlled rate. The system ensures consistent and predictable drug delivery over an extended period, making it ideal for sustained-release formulations.

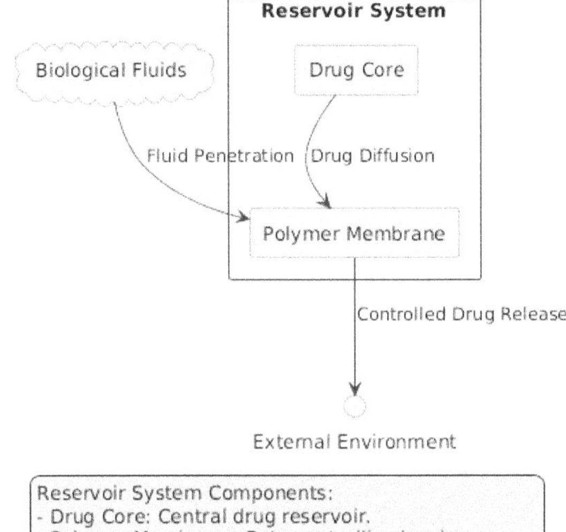

This diagram illustrates a system where the drug is stored in a central reservoir surrounded by a semipermeable polymer membrane. Biological fluids penetrate the membrane, dissolving the drug in the reservoir. The drug then diffuses through the membrane at a controlled rate and is released into the external environment. This system ensures a consistent and predictable drug release, often achieving zero-order kinetics for sustained therapeutic effects.

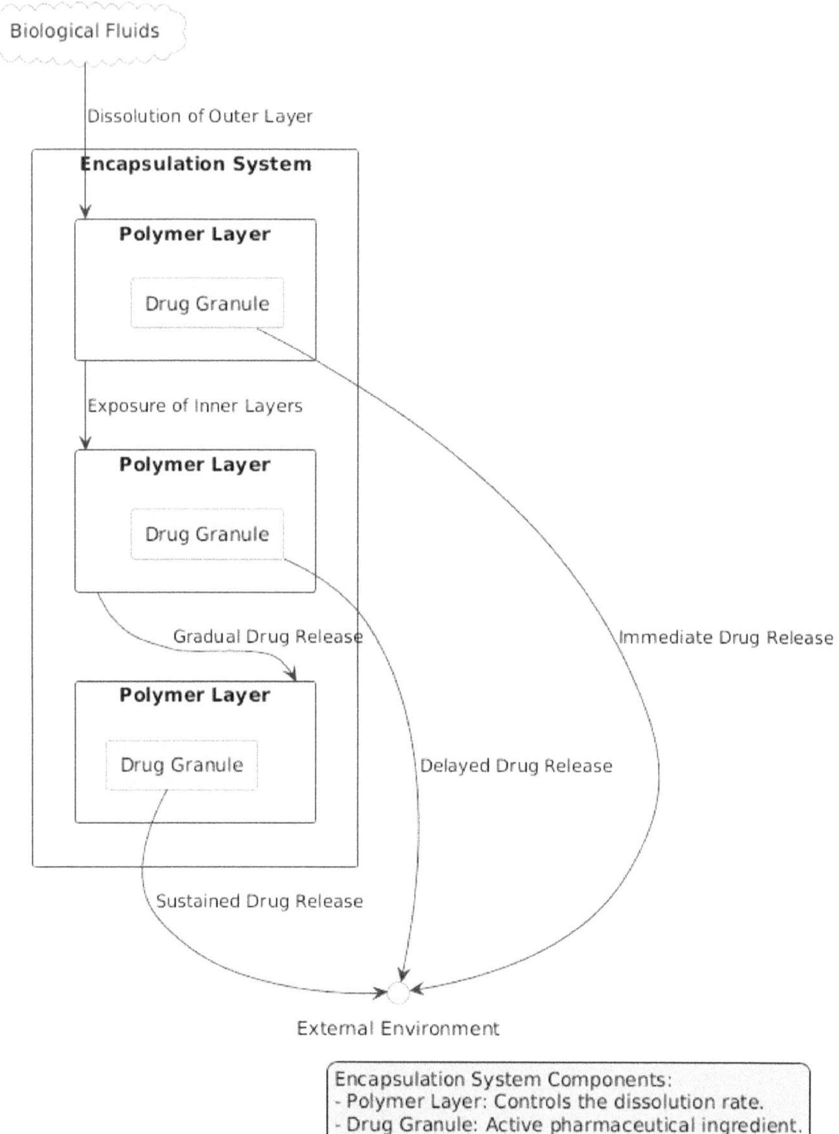

This diagram represents an encapsulation system where drug granules are surrounded by dissolvable polymer layers. Upon contact with biological fluids, the outermost polymer layer dissolves, gradually exposing the drug granules. The drug is then released in a controlled manner, layer by layer, ensuring sustained and sequential drug delivery over time. This mechanism provides steady therapeutic effects and reduces dosing frequency.

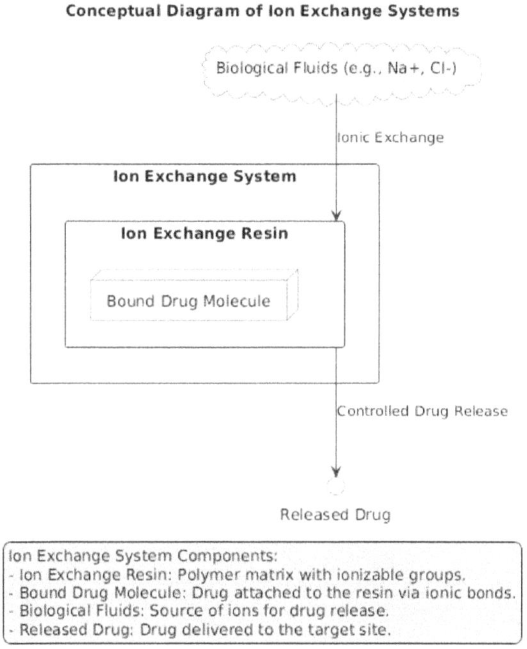

This diagram shows how ion exchange systems work by using a resin that binds drug molecules through ionic interactions. When biological fluids containing ions (e.g., Na+ or Cl-) interact with the resin, the ions exchange places with the drug molecules. This controlled ionic exchange releases the drug gradually into the target environment, ensuring sustained and predictable delivery.

Feature	Diffusion Systems	Dissolution Systems
Predictability	Consistent release, often zero-order kinetics.	Variable release depending on polymer and pH sensitivity.
Formulation Complexity	Requires precise membrane fabrication.	Simpler to manufacture, especially matrix-based systems.
Suitability for Drugs	Suitability for Drugs	Suitability for Drugs
Risk Factors	Mechanical failure can cause dose dumping.	Non-uniform coating may lead to variable release.

Diffusion vs. Dissolution Systems

CHAPTER IV

Role of Polymers in Controlled Drug Delivery Systems

4.1 INTRODUCTION TO POLYMERS IN DRUG DELIVERY

4.1.1 Definition and Role of Polymers

Polymers are large molecules composed of repeating structural units called monomers, linked together by covalent bonds. These materials have become indispensable in the design and development of **Novel Drug Delivery Systems (NDDS)** and controlled drug delivery systems (CDDS). The versatility, biocompatibility, and tunable properties of polymers make them ideal for achieving precise control over drug release, enhancing therapeutic efficacy, and minimizing side effects.

In drug delivery, polymers serve multiple roles. They can act as carriers, encapsulating the drug and providing protection from environmental factors like light, moisture, or enzymatic degradation. This protection is particularly important for sensitive drugs such as proteins and peptides, which are prone to denaturation under harsh conditions. Polymers also facilitate sustained and targeted drug release, ensuring that the therapeutic agent reaches the desired site of action at optimal concentrations over an extended period.

For instance, hydrophilic polymers such as **hydroxypropyl methylcellulose (HPMC)** swell in the presence of water, forming a gel barrier that regulates drug diffusion in matrix systems. Hydrophobic polymers like **polylactic-co-glycolic acid (PLGA)** degrade slowly in biological fluids, enabling sustained drug release in depot formulations and implantable devices. These materials are used extensively in formulations for conditions requiring long-term management, such as diabetes or cancer.

The adaptability of polymers allows for the design of delivery systems tailored to specific therapeutic needs. For example, **pH-sensitive polymers** are used in enteric coatings to protect acid-labile drugs like omeprazole during their transit through the stomach, ensuring their release in the intestine. Similarly, **temperature-sensitive polymers** are employed in smart drug delivery systems, where drug release is triggered by changes in body temperature, as seen in some cancer therapies.

Polymers are not only functional but also play a critical role in improving patient compliance. By enabling controlled release, polymers reduce the frequency of dosing, which is particularly beneficial in chronic diseases. For instance, once-weekly injections of exenatide for diabetes management, formulated with PLGA microspheres, have significantly improved adherence compared to daily injections.

4.1.2 Historical Background

The use of polymers in drug delivery has a rich historical context, evolving alongside advancements in pharmaceutical science. Early applications of polymers in drug formulations were relatively simple, primarily focusing on their role as stabilizing agents or excipients in conventional dosage forms. For instance, natural polymers like gelatin were used in the late 19th century for encapsulating drugs in soft gelatin capsules, providing a convenient means of administration and improving drug stability.

The mid-20th century marked a significant milestone in the evolution of polymer applications with the development of sustained-release formulations. Polymers were increasingly utilized to modulate the release of drugs, addressing challenges such as frequent dosing and fluctuating plasma drug levels. Hydrophilic polymers like methylcellulose and ethylcellulose were among the first to be employed in controlled-release matrix systems, paving the way for more sophisticated delivery mechanisms.

The advent of synthetic polymers in the latter half of the 20th century brought about a paradigm shift in drug delivery. Polymers such as **polyethylene glycol (PEG)** and **polyvinyl alcohol (PVA)** introduced unprecedented versatility, enabling the design of systems tailored to specific therapeutic needs. The introduction of **poly(lactic-co-glycolic acid) (PLGA)** as a biodegradable polymer in the 1970s revolutionized drug delivery by allowing for sustained release over weeks or months. PLGA-based formulations became particularly valuable in oncology and hormone replacement therapies, where consistent drug levels are critical.

In recent decades, the role of polymers has expanded significantly with the rise of **Novel Drug Delivery Systems (NDDS)**. Advances in material science and nanotechnology have enabled the development of smart polymers capable of responding to external stimuli such as pH, temperature, or light. These innovations have led to the creation of intelligent systems that can release drugs on demand, improving therapeutic outcomes and reducing side effects. For example, pH-sensitive polymers in enteric coatings now protect acid-labile drugs and ensure site-specific release, while thermoresponsive polymers are employed in cancer therapies to deliver drugs to hyperthermic tumor sites.

The integration of polymers into nanotechnology-based systems has further transformed drug delivery. Polymers are now used to create nanoparticles, micelles, and hydrogels, offering targeted and controlled delivery for a wide range of therapeutic agents, including biologics and gene therapies. **Liposomal formulations**, where polymers enhance the stability and functionality of lipid carriers, exemplify the advanced use of polymers in modern drug delivery systems.

4.1.3 Key Characteristics

Polymers play an indispensable role in drug delivery systems, primarily due to their unique and versatile characteristics. These properties enable polymers to meet the complex requirements of controlled and targeted drug delivery, improving therapeutic outcomes and patient compliance.

Biocompatibility

Biocompatibility is one of the most critical characteristics of polymers used in drug delivery. A biocompatible polymer does not provoke adverse reactions when introduced into the body, such as inflammation or immune responses. This ensures that the drug delivery system is safe for prolonged use, especially in applications requiring implants or injectable formulations. For example, **polyethylene glycol (PEG)** is widely used due to its excellent biocompatibility, reducing immunogenicity in protein-based drugs and prolonging their half-life in circulation

. Similarly, natural polymers like **chitosan** and **hyaluronic acid** are biocompatible and often used in ophthalmic and dermal applications, ensuring patient safety.

Biodegradability

Biodegradability is another essential trait, particularly for polymers used in sustained-release systems and implants. Biodegradable polymers break down into non-toxic byproducts that are naturally eliminated from the body, eliminating the need for surgical removal. **Poly(lactic-co-glycolic acid) (PLGA)** is a prominent example of a biodegradable polymer used in depot injections and implants for chronic conditions. Its degradation rate can be tailored by adjusting the ratio of lactic acid to glycolic acid, providing flexibility in drug release duration.

Controlled Release

Polymers are instrumental in achieving controlled and sustained drug release, a cornerstone of modern drug delivery systems. Their ability to regulate drug diffusion, degradation, or dissolution enables precise control over the release kinetics. For instance, **hydroxypropyl methylcellulose (HPMC)** swells to form a gel barrier, controlling drug diffusion in matrix systems. Similarly, polymers like **ethylcellulose** are used in reservoir systems, where a rate-controlling membrane ensures steady drug release over time.

Flexibility in Formulation Design

Polymers offer unmatched flexibility in designing drug delivery systems, accommodating a wide range of drugs and therapeutic requirements. They can be processed into various forms, such as nanoparticles, hydrogels, films, or microspheres, to suit specific applications. For example, **pH-sensitive polymers**, such as **methacrylic acid copolymers**, enable site-specific release by dissolving at a particular pH, protecting drugs from degradation in the acidic environment of the stomach. Thermoresponsive polymers, like **poly(N-isopropylacrylamide)**, undergo phase changes in response to temperature, making them ideal for localized drug delivery in hyperthermic conditions.

4.1.4 Overview of Polymer-Based Drug Delivery Systems

Polymer-based drug delivery systems have revolutionized the field of pharmaceuticals, offering advanced solutions for sustained release, targeted delivery, and improved therapeutic efficacy. These systems utilize the versatile properties of polymers to address the limitations of conventional drug delivery methods, such as poor bioavailability, frequent dosing, and non-specific drug distribution.

One of the most significant applications of polymer-based systems is **sustained release formulations.** By incorporating drugs into polymeric matrices, it is possible to achieve prolonged and predictable drug release over hours, days, or even months. For instance, **poly(lactic-co-glycolic acid) (PLGA)** is widely used in injectable depots and implantable devices for conditions requiring long-term management, such as diabetes and hormone replacement therapy. The slow degradation of PLGA ensures a consistent release of the drug, maintaining therapeutic levels and enhancing patient compliance.

Another transformative use of polymer-based systems is in **targeted drug delivery**. Polymers can be engineered to release drugs at specific sites in the body, minimizing systemic exposure and reducing side effects. **pH-sensitive polymers**, such as methacrylic acid derivatives, are used in enteric coatings to deliver drugs to the intestine, protecting acid-sensitive compounds like omeprazole from degradation in the stomach. Similarly, polymers functionalized with ligands enable **active targeting**, directing drugs to diseased tissues, such as tumors, through receptor-mediated mechanisms.

Nanocarriers, such as polymeric nanoparticles, micelles, and hydrogels, represent another cutting-edge application of polymer-based systems. These nanoscale carriers offer precise control over drug release and enhanced stability, making them ideal for delivering biologics and poorly soluble drugs. For example, **dendrimers**, a class of highly branched polymers, are used for targeted delivery of anticancer drugs, ensuring that the therapeutic agent is concentrated at the tumor site while sparing healthy tissues. Similarly, **polymeric micelles** are employed to solubilize hydrophobic drugs like paclitaxel, improving their bioavailability and therapeutic efficacy.

4.2 CLASSIFICATION OF POLYMERS

4.2.1 Biodegradable and Non-Biodegradable Polymers
Polymers used in drug delivery systems are broadly classified into biodegradable and non-biodegradable types based on their degradation behavior in biological environments. This classification significantly influences their mechanisms of drug release, applications, and overall suitability for specific therapeutic requirements.

Biodegradable Polymers
Biodegradable polymers are materials that break down into non-toxic byproducts, such as water, carbon dioxide, and biomass, within the body. These byproducts are subsequently eliminated through natural metabolic pathways. Polymers like **polylactic acid (PLA), polyglycolic acid (PGA)**, and their copolymer **polylactic-co-glycolic acid (PLGA)** are among the most widely used biodegradable materials in controlled drug delivery

systems.

The degradation rate of these polymers can be precisely tailored by modifying their chemical composition. For example, increasing the glycolic acid content in PLGA accelerates degradation due to its higher hydrophilicity compared to lactic acid. This feature makes PLGA particularly suitable for long-acting injectables and implants, such as those used in cancer therapy and contraceptives.

Biodegradable polymers are especially advantageous for applications requiring **temporary therapeutic effects**, such as post-surgical implants that release anti-inflammatory drugs or antibiotics. Since these systems degrade over time, they eliminate the need for surgical removal, reducing patient discomfort and healthcare costs.

Non-Biodegradable Polymers

Non-biodegradable polymers, on the other hand, maintain their structural integrity in biological environments. These polymers are often used in systems where **long-term stability** is essential. Examples include **polyethylene glycol (PEG), polydimethylsiloxane (silicone rubber)**, and **polyvinyl alcohol (PVA)**.

Non-biodegradable systems are commonly employed in reservoir-type devices, such as drug-eluting stents, which provide sustained drug release for extended periods. However, these systems require eventual removal or replacement, as their permanence may lead to complications, such as biofouling or inflammation, if left in the body indefinitely.

The choice between biodegradable and non-biodegradable polymers depends on the therapeutic context. Biodegradable systems are preferred for transient therapies, while non-biodegradable systems are ideal for applications demanding prolonged stability and robustness.

4.2.2 Hydrophilic and Hydrophobic Polymers

Polymers can also be classified based on their affinity for water, into hydrophilic and hydrophobic types. This distinction significantly impacts their drug release behavior and applications in controlled drug delivery systems.

Hydrophilic Polymers

Hydrophilic polymers have a strong affinity for water and tend to absorb it, forming gels or swelling upon contact with aqueous environments. This property is crucial for controlled drug release, as the swelling behavior creates a diffusion barrier that regulates the release rate.

Hydroxypropyl methylcellulose (HPMC) is a commonly used hydrophilic polymer in matrix systems. In aqueous environments, HPMC swells to form a gel layer that controls the diffusion of the drug, providing sustained release over hours. Such systems are widely used in extended-release tablets for chronic conditions like diabetes or hypertension.

Hydrophilic polymers are also used in **mucoadhesive systems**, where their ability to adhere to mucosal surfaces prolongs drug residence time. For example, chitosan-based hydrophilic formulations are employed in ocular and nasal drug delivery systems.

Hydrophobic Polymers

Hydrophobic polymers repel water and do not swell significantly, making them ideal for applications requiring minimal interaction with biological fluids. These polymers, such as **ethylcellulose**, are often used as coatings in reservoir systems or in matrix systems where water-insolubility is critical for drug stability.

Ethylcellulose, for instance, is used to coat drug particles in sustained-release capsules, where the coating acts as a barrier to water, controlling drug release over time. Hydrophobic polymers are also essential in developing **implantable devices**, such as contraceptive implants, where prolonged and consistent drug release is required.

The balance between hydrophilic and hydrophobic properties in a polymer system can be fine-tuned to achieve specific release kinetics. For instance, combining hydrophilic and hydrophobic polymers in a matrix can provide dual control, with the hydrophilic component facilitating initial swelling and drug release, while the hydrophobic component ensures sustained action.

4.2.3 Natural vs. Synthetic Polymers

Polymers used in drug delivery systems can be classified into **natural** and **synthetic** categories based on their origin. Both types of polymers offer unique advantages and limitations, making them suitable for different applications in controlled drug delivery systems.

Natural Polymers

Natural polymers are derived from biological sources such as plants, animals, or microorganisms. These materials are inherently biocompatible, biodegradable, and renewable, making them highly attractive for pharmaceutical applications.

Chitosan, derived from chitin found in crustacean shells, is a widely used natural polymer in drug delivery. Its biocompatibility and ability to form hydrogels make it suitable for mucoadhesive systems, such as ocular and nasal drug delivery. Chitosan also exhibits antimicrobial properties, enhancing its utility in wound healing and infection management.

Alginate, extracted from seaweed, is another commonly used natural polymer. It forms hydrogels in the presence of divalent cations like calcium, making it ideal for encapsulating drugs or cells. Alginate-based systems are employed in tissue engineering and sustained-release formulations for conditions like diabetes.

However, natural polymers have limitations, including variability in quality and properties due to their biological origin. Additionally, their mechanical strength and processability may be inferior to synthetic counterparts, restricting their use in applications requiring high precision or robustness.

Synthetic Polymers

Synthetic polymers are man-made materials, offering consistent quality, tunable properties, and greater mechanical strength. These polymers are extensively used in modern drug delivery systems for their versatility and precision in design.

Poly(lactic-co-glycolic acid) (PLGA) is one of the most commonly used synthetic polymers in pharmaceutical formulations. Its biodegradability and biocompatibility, combined with its ability to provide controlled drug release over weeks or months, make it suitable for applications like depot injections and implantable devices.

Polyethylene and **polyethylene glycol (PEG)** are other examples of synthetic polymers widely used in drug delivery. PEG, in particular, is valued for its ability to improve the solubility and stability of biologics. It is also employed to modify drug pharmacokinetics, as seen in PEGylated proteins that exhibit prolonged circulation times.

Despite their advantages, synthetic polymers may pose challenges such as higher production costs and potential toxicity associated with their degradation products. These factors must be carefully evaluated during formulation development.

Applications and Selection

Natural polymers are often preferred for applications requiring high biocompatibility and biodegradability, such as wound dressings and cell encapsulation. Synthetic polymers, on the other hand, are chosen for applications demanding precision and structural integrity, such as implantable devices and nanoparticle formulations.

4.2.4 Comparison of Polymer Types

The classification of polymers into biodegradable, hydrophilic, hydrophobic, natural, and synthetic types allows for tailored applications in drug delivery systems. Each type offers distinct characteristics that make it suitable for specific therapeutic needs.

Biodegradable Polymers are ideal for temporary applications, such as depot injections or post-surgical implants. Their ability to degrade into non-toxic byproducts eliminates the need for removal, enhancing patient compliance. However, their degradation rates must be carefully controlled to match the therapeutic requirements.

Hydrophilic Polymers, such as hydroxypropyl methylcellulose (HPMC), are excellent for matrix systems that require sustained drug release. Their swelling and gel-forming properties regulate drug diffusion, making them effective in extended-release formulations.

Hydrophobic Polymers, like ethylcellulose, are better suited for applications requiring minimal water interaction. They are commonly used in reservoir systems and implantable devices, providing consistent release over extended durations.

Natural Polymers offer biocompatibility and biodegradability, making them suitable for mucoadhesive and hydrogel-based systems. However, their variability and lower mechanical strength may limit their use in high-precision applications.

Synthetic Polymers provide unmatched versatility and consistency, allowing for the design of sophisticated delivery systems like nanoparticles and implantable reservoirs. Their higher cost and potential toxicity must be managed during formulation.

4.3 PROPERTIES OF POLYMERS RELEVANT TO NDDS

Polymers used in **Novel Drug Delivery Systems (NDDS)** must possess specific properties that influence their performance in drug formulation and delivery. These properties determine the polymer's suitability for encapsulating drugs, controlling their release, and ensuring stability and efficacy throughout the delivery process.

4.3.1 Physicochemical Properties

The **physicochemical properties** of polymers, such as molecular weight, solubility, and miscibility, significantly impact their functionality in NDDS.

Molecular Weight plays a crucial role in defining the mechanical strength, degradation rate, and drug release behavior of polymers. High molecular weight polymers, such as **poly(lactic-co-glycolic acid) (PLGA)**, exhibit slower degradation and prolonged drug release, making them ideal for applications like depot injections or implants. Conversely, low molecular weight polymers degrade more rapidly, facilitating faster drug release in systems requiring short-term therapy.

Solubility determines the polymer's ability to interact with solvents during formulation. Hydrophilic polymers, such as **polyvinyl alcohol (PVA)** and **chitosan**, are soluble in aqueous environments, making them suitable for hydrophilic drug encapsulation and gel formation. Hydrophobic polymers like **ethylcellulose**, on the other hand, are used for encapsulating lipophilic drugs and ensuring controlled release in non-aqueous environments.

Miscibility with drugs and excipients ensures homogeneity in formulations, preventing phase separation and ensuring consistent drug release profiles. Polymers that exhibit good miscibility with active pharmaceutical ingredients (APIs) are preferred for matrix systems and film coatings. For instance, the miscibility of **hydroxypropyl methylcellulose (HPMC)** with water and various drugs makes it a popular choice in extended-release formulations.

The balance of these physicochemical properties is essential for optimizing drug loading capacity, release kinetics, and formulation stability, ensuring effective and predictable therapeutic outcomes.

4.3.2 Thermal Properties

Thermal properties are critical in the design and manufacturing of polymer-based NDDS. These properties influence the polymer's stability during processing and its performance during drug delivery.

The **glass transition temperature (Tg)** is a key thermal property that defines the transition of a polymer from a rigid, glassy state to a flexible, rubbery state. Polymers with a high Tg, such as **polycarbonate**, remain rigid at body temperature, making them suitable for structural applications like implants. Polymers with a low Tg, such as **polyethylene glycol (PEG)**, are more flexible and can be used in formulations requiring elasticity or flow, such as transdermal patches.

Thermal stability is another essential factor, ensuring that the polymer can withstand the high temperatures involved in manufacturing processes like extrusion, molding, or coating without degrading. Polymers like **PLGA** and **polycaprolactone (PCL)** are known for their excellent thermal stability, making them suitable for advanced drug delivery systems like nanoparticles and microspheres.

Understanding and leveraging the thermal properties of polymers also aids in designing systems that respond to temperature changes. For example, **thermoresponsive polymers**, such as **poly(N-isopropylacrylamide)**, exhibit phase transitions near body temperature, enabling targeted drug release in hyperthermic conditions.

The **physicochemical** and **thermal properties** of polymers are integral to the success of NDDS. By tailoring these properties, researchers can design delivery systems that are efficient, stable, and aligned with therapeutic requirements, advancing the possibilities of personalized medicine and patient-centered care.

4.3.3 Biodegradability and Biocompatibility

Biodegradability and biocompatibility are crucial properties for polymers used in **Novel Drug Delivery Systems (NDDS)**, ensuring the development of sustainable and patient-safe formulations. These properties not only influence the polymer's performance in drug delivery but also play a significant role in regulatory approval and patient acceptance.

Biodegradability refers to the ability of a polymer to break down into non-toxic byproducts that are naturally eliminated from the body. This property is particularly important in drug delivery systems like implants, injectable depots, and microspheres. Biodegradable polymers such as **polylactic-co-glycolic acid (PLGA)** degrade into lactic and glycolic acids, which are metabolized and excreted via the Krebs cycle. This eliminates the need for surgical removal of the delivery system, reducing patient discomfort and healthcare costs.

Biodegradable polymers are extensively used in formulations requiring prolonged drug release, such as contraceptive implants and cancer therapies. For instance, **Lupron Depot**, a PLGA-based formulation, provides controlled release of leuprolide acetate over several months, improving patient compliance and therapeutic outcomes.

Biocompatibility ensures that the polymer does not elicit adverse biological responses, such as inflammation or immunogenicity, when introduced into the body. Biocompatible polymers like **polyethylene glycol (PEG)** are widely used to coat nanoparticles and biologics, enhancing their stability and reducing immune recognition. For example, PEGylation of proteins like interferon has significantly improved their half-life and therapeutic efficacy.

Case studies further highlight the importance of these properties. For example, **dexamethasone-eluting stents** made from biodegradable polymers have been successful in reducing restenosis rates in cardiovascular applications. Similarly, chitosan-based wound dressings leverage both biodegradability and biocompatibility to enhance healing and minimize complications.

By integrating biodegradable and biocompatible polymers, NDDS can achieve a balance between efficacy, safety, and sustainability, making them an essential component of advanced drug delivery technologies.

4.3.4 Mechanical Properties

The mechanical properties of polymers, such as strength, elasticity, and durability, are critical in determining their suitability for specific drug delivery systems like transdermal patches and implants. These properties ensure that the polymeric material can withstand the stresses encountered during manufacturing, storage, and application, while maintaining its functionality.

Strength refers to the polymer's ability to resist deformation or failure under stress. This property is especially important in implantable devices, where the material must retain its structural integrity within the body. For instance, polymers like **polysulfone** and **polycarbonate** are used in orthopedic implants due to their high tensile strength and durability.

Elasticity defines the polymer's capacity to return to its original shape after deformation. Elastic materials are essential for applications like **transdermal patches**, which need to adhere to the skin's contours without cracking or peeling. Polymers like **silicone rubber** and **ethylene vinyl acetate** provide the required flexibility and resilience for such systems.

Durability ensures that the polymer can perform reliably over the intended duration of drug release. This is crucial for long-term implants and depot systems, where premature degradation or mechanical failure could compromise therapeutic outcomes. Polymers like **polyurethane** are commonly used in long-acting delivery systems due to their excellent wear resistance and stability.

In transdermal patches, a combination of mechanical properties is essential to ensure proper adhesion, flexibility, and patient comfort. For example, nicotine patches rely on **polyisobutylene-based adhesives**, which provide both strength and elasticity, ensuring consistent drug release while adhering securely to the skin.

In implantable systems, the mechanical properties must also account for biocompatibility and biodegradability. For instance, **PLGA-based implants** offer the right balance of strength and controlled degradation, making them ideal for applications like contraceptives and chemotherapy.

The mechanical properties of polymers directly influence their application in NDDS. By tailoring these properties, researchers can create robust, reliable, and patient-friendly delivery systems, meeting the diverse demands of modern therapeutics.

4.3.5 Swelling Behavior

Swelling behavior is a fundamental property of certain polymers, particularly hydrogels, that plays a vital role in the design of **controlled release systems**. This property refers to the ability of a polymer to absorb water or biological fluids, resulting in an increase in its volume and a change in its structure. Swelling behavior is crucial in regulating drug release rates, enhancing bioavailability, and ensuring site-specific delivery.

Hydrogels, a class of highly absorbent polymers, exhibit pronounced swelling behavior. These polymers are composed of a network of hydrophilic chains that absorb water, forming a gel-like structure. This swelling can create a diffusion barrier that controls the rate at which a drug is released. For example, **polyacrylic acid (PAA)** and **hydroxypropyl methylcellulose (HPMC)** are used in matrix systems for sustained drug release.

pH sensitivity is another critical aspect of swelling behavior. Polymers such as **poly(methacrylic acid-co-ethyl acrylate)** swell in response to changes in pH, making them ideal for **enteric coatings**. These coatings protect acid-labile drugs during transit through the stomach and release them in the intestine, where the pH is higher. This approach is commonly used for drugs like **omeprazole** and **insulin**.

Swelling behavior is also influenced by **ionic strength** in the surrounding environment. Polymers such as **alginate** and **chitosan** swell in response to the ionic composition of the medium, enabling tailored drug release in specific biological conditions. For example, alginate-based hydrogels are used for localized drug delivery in wound healing applications, where the ionic environment can vary significantly.

By leveraging swelling behavior, controlled release systems can achieve prolonged and predictable drug release profiles, improving therapeutic efficacy and patient compliance.

4.3.6 Surface Properties

The surface properties of polymers, including mucoadhesion and tissue interaction, are critical determinants of their performance in **transdermal** and **mucosal drug delivery systems**. These properties influence how well a polymer-based system adheres to biological surfaces, interacts with tissues, and facilitates drug absorption.

Mucoadhesion

is the ability of a polymer to adhere to mucosal surfaces, such as those found in the oral, nasal, or gastrointestinal tracts. This property is particularly advantageous for drug delivery systems that require prolonged contact with the mucosa to enhance drug absorption and therapeutic efficacy. Polymers like **chitosan** and **carbopol** exhibit strong mucoadhesive properties due to their ability to form hydrogen bonds and ionic interactions with mucosal glycoproteins. For example, chitosan-based formulations are widely used in nasal sprays and buccal patches, where prolonged adhesion enhances drug residence time and bioavailability.

Tissue interaction refers to how polymers interact with biological tissues, influencing their ability to deliver drugs effectively. In transdermal systems, for instance, the surface properties of the polymer must ensure proper adhesion to the skin while allowing for controlled drug permeation. **Polyisobutylene** and **silicone adhesives** are commonly used in transdermal patches because they provide the necessary balance between adhesion and drug release.

In mucosal delivery, surface properties also determine the polymer's ability to penetrate mucus layers and deliver drugs directly to the underlying tissues. Polymers like **hyaluronic acid** and **poloxamers** are employed in ophthalmic and vaginal drug delivery systems because they interact effectively with the mucosa, ensuring sustained and localized drug action.

By tailoring surface properties, researchers can enhance the performance of polymer-based drug delivery systems. Improved mucoadhesion and tissue interaction not only increase drug absorption but also reduce the dosing frequency, making these systems more patient-friendly and effective in achieving therapeutic goals.

4.3.7 Cross-Linking in Polymers

Cross-linking is a critical property in polymers that significantly impacts their structural integrity and functionality, especially in **hydrogels** and advanced drug delivery systems. Cross-linking refers to the formation of bonds—either physical or chemical—between polymer chains, resulting in a three-dimensional network structure. This network enhances the mechanical strength, stability, and drug release modulation capabilities of the polymer.

Physical cross-linking involves non-covalent interactions such as hydrogen bonding, ionic interactions, or van der Waals forces. This type of cross-linking is reversible and often responsive to environmental conditions like pH, temperature, or ionic strength. For example, **alginate hydrogels** cross-linked with calcium ions are widely used in wound dressings and drug encapsulation, where the ionic cross-links can be modulated to control drug release.

Chemical cross-linking, on the other hand, involves covalent bonds between polymer chains, creating a more stable and permanent network. Polymers such as **polyvinyl alcohol (PVA)** and **polyethylene glycol (PEG)** are chemically cross-linked using agents like glutaraldehyde to form robust hydrogels. These systems are particularly useful in sustained-release formulations, where long-term stability and controlled release are critical.

Cross-linking also plays a vital role in advanced drug delivery systems. For instance, **stimuli-responsive hydrogels** rely on cross-linked networks that swell or contract in response to external triggers, such as pH or temperature. This property enables precise control over drug release, making them suitable for applications in oncology or localized drug delivery.

The degree of cross-linking directly influences drug release profiles. High cross-linking density reduces the swelling of hydrogels and slows down drug diffusion, while low-density cross-linking allows faster drug release. This tunability makes cross-linked polymers an indispensable component in designing sophisticated drug delivery systems tailored to specific therapeutic needs.

4.3.8 Environmental Impact

The environmental impact of polymers used in drug delivery is an increasingly important consideration, given the global emphasis on **sustainability** and eco-friendly practices. Traditional synthetic polymers, while highly effective in drug delivery, often pose challenges related to environmental degradation and waste management. Addressing these concerns involves lifecycle assessments and the development of green alternatives.

Lifecycle assessment (LCA) evaluates the environmental footprint of a polymer, from its production and use to disposal or degradation. Non-biodegradable polymers like **polyethylene (PE)** and **polypropylene (PP)**, commonly used in packaging and medical applications, can persist in the environment for decades, contributing to plastic pollution. In contrast, **biodegradable polymers** such as **polylactic acid (PLA)** and **polycaprolactone (PCL)** break down into natural byproducts, significantly reducing their environmental impact.

The development of **green polymers** is a key step toward sustainable drug delivery. Green polymers are derived from renewable sources, such as **chitosan**, extracted from crustacean shells, or **alginate**, obtained from seaweed. These materials not only minimize environmental harm but also align with the principles of green chemistry by reducing the use of toxic chemicals in their synthesis.

Polymers like **starch-based plastics** and **cellulose derivatives** are being explored for single-use drug delivery systems, such as biodegradable implants or capsules. These materials degrade naturally, leaving no harmful residues, thus offering a sustainable alternative to traditional synthetic polymers.

Incorporating sustainability into polymer design also involves improving manufacturing processes. For instance, advances in **solvent-free production techniques** and energy-efficient polymerization methods reduce the carbon footprint of polymer-based drug delivery systems.

By focusing on the environmental impact, the pharmaceutical industry can strike a balance between innovation and sustainability. The adoption of green polymers and eco-friendly practices not only addresses environmental concerns but also enhances the societal acceptance and long-term viability of advanced drug delivery systems.

4.4 Applications of Polymers in Controlled Release Systems

Polymers serve as the backbone of controlled release systems, enabling precise and sustained drug delivery across various routes of administration. Their versatility in design and functionality allows for the development of advanced delivery systems that cater to diverse therapeutic needs.

4.4.1 Oral Controlled Release Systems

Oral controlled release systems represent one of the most common applications of polymers in drug delivery. These systems rely on polymers to modulate drug release, ensuring sustained therapeutic effects and minimizing dosing frequency.

Matrix tablets are a popular oral delivery system where drugs are embedded within a polymeric matrix. Polymers such as **hydroxypropyl methylcellulose (HPMC)** and **carbopol** are frequently used to control drug diffusion and dissolution. These systems release the drug gradually as the matrix swells or erodes, providing sustained action. For instance, extended-release formulations of metformin rely on matrix systems to maintain consistent plasma levels in diabetes management.

Enteric coatings protect drugs from the acidic environment of the stomach, ensuring their release in the intestine where the pH is higher. Polymers like **Eudragit** (a family of methacrylate copolymers) are widely used for enteric coatings, as they dissolve at specific pH levels. This technology is critical for drugs like **omeprazole**, which are unstable in gastric acid.

By leveraging the properties of polymers, oral controlled release systems enhance bioavailability, reduce side effects, and improve patient compliance.

4.4.2 Transdermal Drug Delivery Systems

Polymers are integral to the development of **transdermal drug delivery systems (TDDS)**, which deliver drugs through the skin into systemic circulation. These systems offer the advantage of bypassing the gastrointestinal tract and first-pass metabolism, making them ideal for certain therapeutic applications.

Polymers such as **polyisobutylene** and **acrylates** are used as adhesives in transdermal patches. These materials ensure proper adhesion to the skin while allowing controlled drug permeation. For example, nicotine patches use polyisobutylene adhesives to provide a steady release of nicotine, helping patients quit smoking.

In **reservoir systems**, polymers act as rate-controlling membranes that regulate drug release. Polymers like **ethylene-vinyl acetate (EVA)** and **silicone rubber** are used in these systems to maintain consistent drug delivery over several days or weeks.

The durability, flexibility, and biocompatibility of polymers ensure that transdermal systems are comfortable to wear and effective in achieving therapeutic goals.

4.4.3 Injectable and Implantable Systems

Injectable and implantable systems represent advanced applications of polymers in drug delivery, offering long-term therapeutic effects and localized drug action.

Microspheres and **nanoparticles** are commonly used injectable systems where drugs are encapsulated within biodegradable polymers like **polylactic-co-glycolic acid (PLGA)**. These systems provide controlled release over weeks or months, making them suitable for conditions like cancer and chronic pain. For instance, **Lupron Depot**, a PLGA-based formulation, releases leuprolide acetate over several months for the treatment of prostate cancer.

Implantable systems utilize both biodegradable and non-biodegradable polymers. Biodegradable implants, such as those made from **polycaprolactone (PCL)**, gradually degrade while releasing the drug, eliminating the need for surgical removal. Non-biodegradable implants, such as **silicone-based devices**, offer long-term drug release and are commonly used in contraceptive systems like Norplant.

Drug-eluting stents, another application of implantable systems, use polymers to deliver anti-proliferative drugs locally, preventing restenosis in cardiovascular treatments. Polymers like **polyethylene glycol (PEG)** are used to coat the stent and regulate drug release.

By integrating polymers into injectable and implantable systems, these delivery methods provide precise, localized, and sustained drug release, reducing systemic toxicity and improving therapeutic outcomes.

4.4.4 Targeted Drug Delivery Systems

Targeted drug delivery systems represent a significant advancement in therapeutic interventions by directing drugs to specific cells or tissues while minimizing exposure to healthy areas. Polymers play an essential role in these systems by providing functionalization capabilities for active targeting. Nanoparticles, created using polymers like **polyethylene glycol (PEG)**, are widely employed for this purpose. PEGylation involves attaching PEG chains to nanoparticles or drug molecules to enhance their stability and circulation time in the bloodstream. This modification reduces immune recognition and prolongs systemic circulation, enabling drugs to reach their target efficiently.

Active targeting is often achieved through surface functionalization of nanoparticles with ligands, such as antibodies or peptides, that bind specifically to receptors on target cells. For instance, in cancer therapy, nanoparticles functionalized with anti-HER2 antibodies are used to target HER2-positive tumors, delivering drugs like doxorubicin directly to the cancer cells. Such systems improve the therapeutic efficacy while reducing systemic toxicity. Polymers provide the structural and functional foundation for these targeted delivery systems, making them indispensable in modern precision medicine.

4.4.5 Mucoadhesive Drug Delivery Systems

Mucoadhesive drug delivery systems leverage the adhesive properties of polymers to enhance drug retention at mucosal sites, such as the buccal, nasal, and vaginal regions. This prolonged retention ensures better drug absorption and therapeutic outcomes. Polymers like **chitosan** and **carbopol** exhibit excellent mucoadhesive properties due to their ability to interact with mucosal glycoproteins through hydrogen bonding and electrostatic interactions.

Buccal delivery systems, such as mucoadhesive films or patches, are used for drugs like fentanyl, providing sustained release and bypassing first-pass metabolism. Similarly, nasal formulations employing mucoadhesive polymers enhance drug delivery for conditions like migraines, where rapid onset of action is critical. Vaginal delivery systems using bioadhesive polymers offer targeted treatment for infections and hormone replacement therapies, ensuring localized action with minimal systemic exposure.

Mucoadhesive systems exemplify how polymers can improve the performance of drug delivery systems by optimizing drug retention and absorption in specific anatomical locations.

4.4.6 Smart Polymers in Drug Delivery

Smart polymers represent an innovative class of materials capable of responding to external stimuli, such as pH, temperature, or enzymes, to regulate drug release. These systems enable on-demand drug release tailored to specific physiological conditions, enhancing therapeutic precision.

pH-sensitive polymers, like **poly(methacrylic acid-co-ethyl acrylate)**, are designed to release drugs in response to pH changes along the gastrointestinal tract. For example, these polymers prevent drug release in the acidic stomach environment, ensuring delivery in the more neutral or alkaline pH of the intestine. This approach is commonly used for acid-sensitive drugs like proteins and peptides.

Thermo-responsive polymers, such as **poly(N-isopropylacrylamide)**, undergo a phase transition at specific temperatures, enabling controlled drug release. These polymers are particularly useful in localized cancer therapy, where hyperthermia-induced drug release can enhance the treatment's efficacy.

Smart polymers represent the future of drug delivery, offering unprecedented control over drug release profiles and therapeutic effects.

4.4.7 Combination Therapy

Combination therapy involves the co-delivery of multiple drugs in a single formulation, aiming to achieve synergistic effects in treating complex diseases like cancer and infectious conditions. Polymers facilitate this approach by enabling the encapsulation and controlled release of multiple drugs simultaneously.

Nanoparticles made from polymers like **PLGA** and **PEG** can encapsulate both hydrophilic and hydrophobic drugs, ensuring their stability and bioavailability. For example, in cancer therapy, nanoparticles co-delivering doxorubicin and paclitaxel provide a dual mechanism of action, enhancing cytotoxicity against tumor cells while reducing drug resistance.

Polymeric systems also allow for the sequential release of drugs, ensuring that the therapeutic agents act in a specific order for optimal efficacy. This approach is particularly beneficial in treating infections, where a combination of antibiotics with different mechanisms can prevent resistance and improve patient outcomes.

Combination therapy systems highlight the versatility of polymers in addressing the complexities of modern therapeutic strategies.

4.4.8 Polymer-Drug Compatibility and Stability

Ensuring polymer-drug compatibility and stability is critical for the safety and efficacy of drug delivery systems. Compatibility refers to the ability of the polymer to interact with the drug without causing degradation or adverse reactions. Stability involves maintaining the structural and functional integrity of the formulation throughout its shelf life.

Analytical techniques like **Fourier-transform infrared spectroscopy (FTIR)** and **X-ray diffraction (XRD)** are commonly used to assess compatibility. FTIR identifies potential chemical interactions between the polymer and drug, while XRD evaluates the crystalline or amorphous nature of the formulation, which can influence drug release profiles.

Biodegradable polymers like PLGA must be carefully evaluated for stability, as their degradation products can affect the drug's efficacy and safety. For instance, in microsphere formulations, polymer degradation could lead to premature drug release or dose dumping if not adequately controlled.

By ensuring polymer-drug compatibility and stability, researchers can develop safe, effective, and reliable drug delivery systems that meet stringent regulatory standards and patient needs.

CHAPTER V

Microencapsulation Technology

5.1 Introduction to Microencapsulation

Microencapsulation technology is a widely utilized method in pharmaceutical sciences that involves the coating or encapsulation of drugs and other active substances into micron-sized particles. This technique plays a crucial role in improving drug delivery by providing controlled release, enhancing stability, and masking unpleasant tastes or odors.

5.1.1 Definition and Overview

Microencapsulation refers to the process of enclosing drugs or active ingredients within a microscopic coating material, forming particles that range in size from a few microns to several hundred microns. The coating materials are typically polymers, lipids, or natural gums, chosen based on their compatibility with the drug and the desired release profile.

This technology serves as a bridge between macro- and nano-encapsulation, combining the advantages of both scales. Compared to macro-encapsulation, such as tablets or capsules, microencapsulation offers improved control over drug release and better patient compliance due to its ability to deliver drugs in small, uniform doses. On the other hand, while nano-encapsulation achieves more precise targeting and enhanced cellular uptake, microencapsulation is more cost-effective and easier to scale up for industrial production.

Microencapsulation is used in diverse pharmaceutical applications, including oral, parenteral, and topical drug delivery systems. For instance, it is commonly employed to protect sensitive drugs like vitamins or probiotics from degradation during storage and transit through the gastrointestinal tract. Moreover, this technology is extensively applied in controlled-release formulations, where drugs are released over an extended period to maintain therapeutic efficacy.

5.1.2 Key Features

Microencapsulation technology offers several distinctive features that make it a valuable tool in pharmaceutical and biomedical applications. One of the primary features is **controlled release**, where the encapsulated drug is released gradually over a predetermined time. This property helps maintain consistent therapeutic levels of the drug in the bloodstream, minimizing the need for frequent dosing and enhancing patient compliance. Controlled release can be achieved by tailoring the composition and thickness of the encapsulation material, enabling precise modulation of the drug release profile.

Another critical feature of microencapsulation is **environmental protection**. Sensitive drugs, such as those prone to oxidation, hydrolysis, or photodegradation, can be safeguarded within the microcapsules. The encapsulation layer acts as a protective barrier, shielding the active ingredient from adverse environmental conditions like moisture, light, and oxygen. This ensures the drug remains stable and effective during storage and throughout its intended shelf life.

Additionally, microencapsulation provides flexibility in drug delivery, allowing for the encapsulation of both hydrophilic and hydrophobic drugs. This versatility makes the technology applicable to a wide range of therapeutic agents and formulations, further solidifying its importance in modern pharmaceutical sciences.

5.1.3 Purpose and Importance

The purpose of microencapsulation extends beyond simple drug containment, addressing various challenges in drug formulation and delivery. One of the most significant benefits is **stability enhancement**, especially for drugs that are chemically or physically unstable. For example, probiotics encapsulated in polymeric coatings are protected from the acidic conditions of the stomach, ensuring their viability upon reaching the intestines.

Another critical purpose is **taste masking**, which is essential for improving the palatability of bitter or unpleasant-tasting drugs. Encapsulation creates a barrier between the drug and the taste receptors, making it easier for patients to take medications such as pediatric formulations.

Targeted delivery is another vital application of microencapsulation. By functionalizing the outer layer of the microcapsules, drugs can be directed to specific tissues or cells, enhancing therapeutic efficacy and reducing systemic side effects. For instance, microencapsulated chemotherapeutic agents can be engineered to release the drug only in the tumor microenvironment, sparing healthy tissues from toxic exposure.

Through its multifaceted purposes, microencapsulation addresses critical issues in drug delivery, enabling the development of advanced formulations that meet patient and clinical needs.

5.1.4 Materials Used

The choice of material for microencapsulation is crucial as it directly affects the drug's release profile, stability, and compatibility. A wide range of materials, including polymers, lipids, and inorganic substances, are employed in microencapsulation based on the desired application and drug properties.

Polymers are the most commonly used materials in microencapsulation due to their versatility and tunable properties. Natural polymers like **gelatin** are frequently used for encapsulating water-soluble drugs, while synthetic polymers such as **polylactic-co-glycolic acid (PLGA)** and **ethylcellulose** are preferred for their biodegradability and controlled release capabilities. For example, PLGA microspheres are extensively used in depot injections to release drugs like leuprolide acetate over several months.

Lipids, including **paraffin** and **waxes**, are often used for their ability to create hydrophobic barriers. These materials are particularly effective for encapsulating lipophilic drugs or protecting moisture-sensitive drugs. Lipid-based microcapsules are widely used in oral formulations and nutraceuticals.

Inorganic substances, such as **silica** and **calcium phosphate**, provide unique advantages in specific applications. Silica is used for its high thermal stability and ability to adsorb hydrophilic drugs, while calcium phosphate is biocompatible and ideal for applications like bone-targeted drug delivery.

The selection of encapsulation material is guided by the drug's physicochemical properties, the route of administration, and the intended therapeutic outcome. The versatility of these materials makes microencapsulation a highly adaptable and effective technology in drug delivery.

5.2 Methods of Microencapsulation

Microencapsulation can be achieved through a variety of methods, each tailored to meet specific formulation requirements and drug delivery goals. These methods differ in their processes and applications, offering flexibility in designing encapsulated systems for diverse therapeutic needs.

5.2.1 Spray Drying and Coating

5.2.1.1 Spray Drying

Spray drying is one of the most widely used methods in microencapsulation, known for its efficiency and scalability. This process involves atomizing a liquid feed containing the drug and encapsulation material into fine droplets using a high-pressure nozzle or rotary atomizer.

The droplets are then introduced into a chamber containing hot air, causing rapid evaporation of the solvent. This results in the formation of solid microcapsules or microspheres containing the drug within the encapsulation matrix.

This method is particularly suitable for heat-sensitive drugs, as the rapid drying minimizes thermal exposure. Spray drying is extensively used in the encapsulation of vitamins, probiotics, and other bioactive compounds that require protection from environmental factors. For instance, ascorbic acid, a highly unstable vitamin, is commonly encapsulated using spray drying to enhance its shelf life and stability in nutritional supplements.

The particle size, morphology, and release profile of the microcapsules can be controlled by adjusting the feed composition, atomization pressure, and drying temperature. This versatility makes spray drying a preferred choice for developing formulations with specific therapeutic and industrial needs.

5.2.1.2 Spray Coating

Spray coating is a highly effective method for microencapsulation, particularly suitable for modifying the surface properties of solid particles or tablets. In this process, the drug or core material is coated with a thin layer of polymeric or lipid-based material to achieve the desired functionality, such as controlled release or taste masking.

Pan coating involves placing the drug particles or cores in a rotating pan and applying the coating material in the form of a fine spray. This technique is commonly used for coating tablets and pellets. The rotation ensures uniform coating while facilitating the drying of the applied material. Pan coating is widely employed for enteric-coated tablets, which are designed to resist dissolution in the stomach and release the drug in the intestine.

Fluidized bed coating is another popular spray coating method, particularly suited for encapsulating small particles or granules. In this technique, the drug particles are suspended in a stream of air within a fluidized bed chamber, where the coating material is sprayed onto their surface. The continuous circulation of particles ensures uniform coating and efficient drying. Fluidized bed systems are frequently used for developing controlled-release granules and multiparticulate dosage forms, offering precise control over the coating thickness and release profile.

Spray coating techniques are versatile and scalable, making them a preferred choice for various pharmaceutical and nutraceutical applications.

5.2.1.3 Applications

Spray coating finds extensive applications in pharmaceutical formulations, particularly for **taste masking** and **controlled release**. For taste masking, bitter or unpleasant-tasting drugs are coated with a polymeric layer that prevents the drug from interacting with taste receptors during administration. This application is especially beneficial in pediatric and geriatric formulations, improving patient compliance.

Controlled-release formulations utilize spray coating to regulate the release of drugs over an extended period. For example, fluidized bed coating is employed to develop sustained-release granules of drugs like theophylline, which ensures consistent plasma levels and reduces dosing frequency.

5.2.2 Coacervation Phase Separation

Coacervation phase separation is a sophisticated method of microencapsulation that relies on the principle of phase separation within a polymer solution to form microcapsules. This technique is widely used to encapsulate sensitive drugs, offering precise control over encapsulation efficiency and release profiles.

5.2.2.1 Principle

The core principle of coacervation phase separation involves the separation of a polymer-rich phase (coacervate droplets) from a homogeneous polymer solution under specific conditions. These droplets surround the drug or active ingredient, forming a protective coating. The process is typically induced by altering factors such as temperature, pH, or the addition of a third component (e.g., a nonsolvent or electrolyte) to the polymer solution.

The encapsulation occurs as the polymer coacervates deposit onto the drug particles. This deposition creates a uniform coating that solidifies upon further processing, resulting in stable microcapsules.

5.2.2.2 Types

Coacervation can be classified into two main types: simple coacervation and complex coacervation.

In **simple coacervation**, phase separation is induced by a single polymer in solution, typically by altering temperature or the addition of a nonsolvent. This method is commonly used for hydrophilic drugs and proteins.

Complex coacervation involves two or more polymers with opposite charges interacting in solution to form coacervates. For example, gelatin and gum arabic are often used in complex coacervation to encapsulate hydrophobic drugs or sensitive compounds like vitamins. The electrostatic interactions between the polymers facilitate coacervate formation, creating robust and uniform microcapsules.

5.2.2.3 Steps

The process of coacervation phase separation typically involves three key steps:

1. **Polymer Solution Preparation**: The polymer is dissolved in a suitable solvent to form a homogeneous solution. The drug or active ingredient to be encapsulated is dispersed or dissolved in the solution.
2. **Encapsulation**: Phase separation is induced by altering the solution's conditions, such as by changing the temperature, pH, or adding a nonsolvent. This causes the polymer to separate into coacervate droplets, which surround the drug particles.
3. **Solidification**: The coacervate layer solidifies to form stable microcapsules. This step can be achieved by cooling, cross-linking, or solvent removal, depending on the polymer and drug properties.

Coacervation phase separation is widely used in applications requiring high encapsulation efficiency and tailored release profiles. For instance, this method is employed to encapsulate vitamins, essential oils, and peptides in food and pharmaceutical products, ensuring their stability and prolonged activity. The precision and adaptability of this technique make it invaluable in developing advanced drug delivery systems.

5.2.3 Solvent Evaporation Technique

The solvent evaporation technique is a widely used method for the microencapsulation of drugs, especially in the preparation of microspheres and nanospheres. This technique relies on the evaporation of a volatile solvent to form solid particles containing the encapsulated drug. It is particularly suitable for hydrophobic drugs and is commonly used with biodegradable polymers like polylactic-co-glycolic acid (PLGA).

5.2.3.1 Process

The solvent evaporation process typically involves an **oil-water emulsion system**, where the drug is dissolved or dispersed in an organic solvent containing the polymer. This organic phase is emulsified into an aqueous phase, usually containing a stabilizer like polyvinyl alcohol, to form droplets.

Once the emulsion is stable, the solvent is removed by evaporation under reduced pressure or by stirring at an elevated temperature. As the solvent evaporates, the polymer solidifies, encapsulating the drug within microspheres or nanospheres. The solid particles are then collected by filtration or centrifugation, followed by washing and drying to obtain the final product.

This method offers precise control over particle size and drug loading by adjusting the solvent, emulsifier concentration, and processing conditions. It is particularly effective for producing uniform particles with high encapsulation efficiency.

5.2.3.2 Factors

Several factors influence the success and efficiency of the solvent evaporation technique:

- **Solvent Properties**: The choice of solvent affects the emulsion stability and the rate of solvent evaporation. Solvents like dichloromethane and ethyl acetate are commonly used due to their volatility and compatibility with polymers like PLGA.
- **Stirring Speed**: The speed of stirring during the emulsification step plays a crucial role in determining the particle size. Higher stirring speeds result in smaller droplets and, consequently, smaller microspheres.
- **Emulsifier Concentration**: The amount and type of emulsifier impact the stability of the emulsion and the uniformity of the particles. Stabilizers like polyvinyl alcohol ensure that the droplets remain discrete during the process.

By optimizing these factors, it is possible to produce microcapsules or microspheres with desired properties for specific applications.

5.2.3.3 Applications

The solvent evaporation technique is extensively used in the pharmaceutical industry for the preparation of **PLGA microspheres**, which are biodegradable and biocompatible. These microspheres are ideal for controlled drug delivery, as they degrade slowly in the body, releasing the drug over weeks or months.

For example, depot formulations like **Lupron Depot**, which delivers leuprolide acetate for prostate cancer and endometriosis treatment, are manufactured using this method. Similarly, the technique is applied in encapsulating proteins, peptides, and vaccines to protect them from degradation and ensure sustained release.

5.2.4 Interfacial Polymerization

Interfacial polymerization is a highly specialized technique used for microencapsulation, where polymers are formed at the interface of two immiscible phases. This method is particularly effective for encapsulating volatile drugs and sensitive compounds, providing a robust and protective polymer shell around the active ingredient.

5.2.4.1 Mechanism

The core mechanism of interfacial polymerization involves the formation of a polymer layer at the boundary between two immiscible phases. Typically, one phase contains the monomer or pre-polymer dissolved in an organic solvent, while the other is an aqueous phase containing a co-reactant or catalyst. When these phases are brought into contact, polymerization occurs at the interface, forming a solid shell around the dispersed droplets of the drug or active substance.

This technique allows precise control over the thickness and composition of the polymer shell by varying the concentration of reactants and the duration of the polymerization reaction. The resulting microcapsules offer excellent protection against environmental factors and controlled release properties.

5.2.4.2 Steps

The process of interfacial polymerization typically involves three main steps:

1. **Immiscible Phases**: The core material (drug or active ingredient) is dissolved or suspended in one phase, such as an organic solvent. This phase is then emulsified into a second immiscible phase, typically aqueous, creating a stable emulsion.

2. **Polymerization**: Reactants are introduced into their respective phases, initiating a polymerization reaction at the interface. For instance, a diacid chloride dissolved in the organic phase reacts with a diamine present in the aqueous phase, forming a polyamide shell around the droplets.

3. **Solidification**: The polymer shell solidifies, encapsulating the core material. The formed microcapsules are then separated from the reaction medium, washed to remove residual reactants, and dried to obtain the final product.

5.2.4.3 Applications

Interfacial polymerization is widely used for the encapsulation of **volatile drugs** and other sensitive compounds. For example, volatile anesthetics like halothane can be encapsulated using this method to prevent evaporation and enhance stability. Similarly, the technique is employed in encapsulating fragrances, essential oils, and pesticides to protect them from environmental degradation and ensure controlled release.

In the pharmaceutical industry, this method is particularly useful for developing formulations that require high stability and precise release profiles. For instance, interfacial polymerization is used to encapsulate hydrophobic drugs in polymer shells for targeted and sustained delivery, ensuring optimal therapeutic outcomes.

5.3 Applications of Microencapsulation in Pharmacy

Microencapsulation technology is a cornerstone of modern pharmaceutical sciences, offering a wide range of applications that address key challenges in drug delivery, stability, and patient compliance. Its versatility has made it an essential tool for enhancing therapeutic efficacy and expanding the scope of pharmaceutical and healthcare products.

5.3.1 Controlled and Sustained Release

One of the most significant applications of microencapsulation in pharmacy is achieving controlled and sustained drug release. By encapsulating drugs in polymers that dissolve or degrade slowly, it is possible to maintain therapeutic levels of the drug in the bloodstream over an extended period. This is particularly beneficial in chronic disease management, where frequent dosing can be burdensome for patients.

For example, microencapsulated formulations of drugs like metformin provide sustained glucose control in diabetes, reducing the need for multiple daily doses. Similarly, depot injections of leuprolide acetate, prepared using biodegradable polymers like PLGA, release the drug over several months, improving adherence and therapeutic outcomes.

5.3.2 Protection from Environmental Degradation

Microencapsulation provides an effective barrier against environmental factors that can degrade sensitive drugs. Active ingredients prone to **hydrolysis, oxidation**, or **photodegradation** are encapsulated in protective coatings that shield them from adverse conditions.

For instance, vitamins like ascorbic acid are encapsulated to prevent oxidation during storage and administration. Probiotics, which are highly sensitive to stomach acid and moisture, are microencapsulated to ensure they remain viable until they reach the intestines. Such formulations enhance the stability and shelf life of pharmaceutical and nutraceutical products, ensuring efficacy.

5.3.3 Taste Masking

Taste masking is a crucial application of microencapsulation, particularly in pediatric and geriatric formulations. Encapsulating bitter or unpleasant-tasting drugs prevents the active ingredient from interacting with taste receptors, making medications more palatable.

For example, bitter drugs like ibuprofen are coated with polymers that dissolve only in the stomach, masking their taste during administration. This application significantly improves patient compliance, especially in children who are sensitive to the taste of medicines.

5.3.4 Targeted Delivery

Microencapsulation enables precise targeting of drugs to specific tissues or organs, reducing systemic side effects and improving therapeutic efficacy. This is particularly valuable in cancer therapy, where site-specific delivery minimizes damage to healthy tissues.

For instance, microencapsulated chemotherapeutic agents can be engineered to release the drug only within the acidic microenvironment of a tumor. Similarly, microcapsules functionalized with ligands for specific receptors enable targeted delivery to diseased tissues. This approach is used in advanced formulations of drugs like doxorubicin for cancer treatment.

5.3.5 Beyond Drug Delivery

The applications of microencapsulation extend beyond traditional drug delivery. In **diagnostics**, imaging agents like contrast media are encapsulated to improve their stability and controlled release, enhancing imaging accuracy in procedures like MRI or CT scans.

In the field of **nutraceuticals**, microencapsulation is employed to encapsulate bioactive compounds such as omega-3 fatty acids, ensuring their stability and controlled release in dietary supplements. This technology also allows for the co-encapsulation of multiple nutrients, enhancing the nutritional value of functional foods.

The versatility of microencapsulation continues to expand its role in pharmacy, providing innovative solutions for drug delivery, diagnostics, and beyond. Its ability to address diverse challenges while enhancing product performance ensures its relevance in advancing healthcare and improving patient outcomes.

CHAPTER VI

Mucosal and Implantable Drug Delivery Systems

6.1 Mucosal Drug Delivery Systems

Mucosal drug delivery systems represent an advanced approach to drug administration, utilizing the mucous membranes that line various parts of the body, such as the oral cavity, nasal passages, gastrointestinal tract, and reproductive organs. These systems offer the advantage of enhanced absorption, reduced systemic side effects, and site-specific drug delivery, making them highly effective for therapeutic applications.

6.1.1 Principles of Bioadhesion and Mucoadhesion

The concepts of **bioadhesion** and **mucoadhesion** are central to mucosal drug delivery systems, as they enable the prolonged retention of drug formulations at mucosal surfaces. Bioadhesion refers to the general adhesion of a material, often a polymer, to a biological surface. Mucoadhesion, a subset of bioadhesion, specifically involves the adhesion of a material to mucus or mucosal tissues. This property is crucial for ensuring that the drug remains localized at the site of action or absorption, thereby enhancing its therapeutic efficacy.

The mechanisms underlying mucoadhesion are complex and involve multiple stages. Initially, **wetting** occurs when the formulation comes into contact with the mucus layer. This step is facilitated by the hydrophilic nature of the polymers used, which allows them to absorb moisture and adhere to the mucosal surface. Once the polymer is sufficiently hydrated, **swelling** occurs, which increases the surface area available for interaction. This stage is critical for the next mechanism, known as **polymer-mucus chain interpenetration**.

During interpenetration, the polymer chains diffuse into the mucus network, forming strong physical and sometimes chemical bonds. These interactions are reinforced by secondary forces such as hydrogen bonding, Van der Waals forces, and ionic interactions. The strength of these bonds determines the degree of adhesion and the retention time of the formulation.

The importance of bioadhesion and mucoadhesion in drug delivery systems cannot be overstated. By ensuring prolonged retention of the drug at the site of administration, these mechanisms allow for increased contact time between the drug and the absorptive mucosal surface. This prolonged retention enhances drug absorption and bioavailability, especially for drugs with short half-lives or those that require localized action. Additionally, site-specific delivery enabled by mucoadhesion reduces systemic exposure, thereby minimizing potential side effects.

For example, buccal mucoadhesive films containing drugs like fentanyl are designed to adhere to the inner lining of the cheek, providing rapid pain relief while avoiding gastrointestinal metabolism and hepatic first-pass effects. Similarly, vaginal mucoadhesive gels containing antifungal agents ensure localized treatment of infections without systemic drug exposure.

Mucosal drug delivery systems, driven by the principles of bioadhesion and mucoadhesion, are increasingly being recognized as innovative solutions for a wide range of therapeutic needs. Their ability to improve drug retention, absorption, and site-specific delivery makes them an indispensable tool in modern pharmaceutical development.

6.1.2 Factors Affecting Mucoadhesion

Mucoadhesion is a complex phenomenon influenced by a combination of physicochemical, physiological, and environmental factors. Understanding these factors is critical for the effective design of mucosal drug delivery systems, as they directly impact the adhesion strength, drug retention time, and overall therapeutic efficacy.

Physicochemical Factors

The properties of the polymer used in mucoadhesive formulations play a pivotal role in determining the strength and duration of adhesion. **Polymer molecular weight** is one of the key parameters. Polymers with higher molecular weights generally exhibit stronger mucoadhesive properties due to their increased chain length, which facilitates deeper penetration into the mucus layer and stronger interactions with mucin molecules. For example, polymers like chitosan and carbopol with high molecular weights are widely used in mucoadhesive formulations for their robust adhesion.

Viscosity of the polymer also significantly affects mucoadhesion. Polymers with optimal viscosity can form a stable adhesive layer without compromising their ease of application. High viscosity polymers create a more cohesive network that resists detachment from the mucosal surface, ensuring prolonged retention of the formulation.

Flexibility of the polymer chains determines their ability to interact with the mucus network. Flexible polymers can adapt to the topography of the mucosal surface, enhancing chain interpenetration and adhesion strength. In contrast, rigid polymers may have limited interaction with the mucus layer, resulting in weaker adhesion.

Physiological Factors

The physiological environment of the mucosal surface also influences mucoadhesion. **pH** variations across different mucosal sites affect the ionization of both the polymer and mucin, altering the strength of their interactions. For instance, anionic polymers like polycarbophil show enhanced mucoadhesion in acidic environments, making them suitable for gastric and vaginal formulations.

Mucosal turnover is another critical factor. The natural renewal of the mucosal layer can reduce the residence time of mucoadhesive formulations by detaching the adhered layer. This turnover rate varies across different mucosal surfaces, with higher rates observed in the gastrointestinal tract compared to the buccal cavity.

Enzymatic degradation of the polymer or active ingredient by mucosal enzymes can also impact mucoadhesion. Polymers that are resistant to enzymatic breakdown, such as synthetic or cross-linked polymers, are preferred for applications requiring prolonged adhesion and drug release.

Environmental Factors

Environmental conditions, including **temperature** and **moisture levels**, further influence mucoadhesion. Higher temperatures can enhance polymer hydration and chain flexibility, improving adhesion strength. However, excessive heat may also lead to degradation of temperature-sensitive polymers or active ingredients.

Moisture levels are crucial for polymer swelling and interaction with the mucus layer. Insufficient moisture may hinder polymer hydration and reduce adhesion, while excessive moisture could dilute the adhesive layer, weakening the bond between the polymer and the mucosa.

6.1.3 Mechanisms of Mucoadhesion

The phenomenon of mucoadhesion is governed by intricate mechanisms that involve a series of physical and chemical interactions between the polymer and the mucus layer. These interactions occur in distinct steps and are influenced by the properties of both the polymer and the mucosal surface. A detailed understanding of these mechanisms is essential for designing effective mucoadhesive drug delivery systems.

Step-by-Step Mechanism of Mucoadhesion

The process of mucoadhesion can be divided into two primary stages: the initial **contact stage** and the subsequent **consolidation stage**.

In the **contact stage**, the polymer comes into close proximity with the mucus layer. This initial contact is facilitated by the application of the formulation, often aided by the natural movement of the mucosa or by external forces like rubbing or pressing. The wettability of the polymer and its ability to absorb moisture from the mucus layer play a crucial role in ensuring intimate contact between the two surfaces. Hydrophilic polymers, such as hydroxypropyl methylcellulose (HPMC), readily interact with the moist mucosal surface, initiating the adhesion process.

In the **consolidation stage**, the interactions between the polymer and the mucus layer are stabilized, forming a strong adhesive bond. This stage involves three key mechanisms:

1. **Hydrogen Bonding**: Hydrogen bonds are formed between functional groups in the polymer (such as hydroxyl, carboxyl, and amine groups) and the glycoproteins in the mucus layer. Polymers like chitosan, which contain abundant amino groups, establish strong hydrogen bonding, enhancing adhesion strength.

2. **Van der Waals Forces**: These weak, nonspecific forces contribute to the overall adhesion by creating an attractive interaction between the polymer and the mucus layer. Although individually weak, van der Waals forces collectively provide substantial adhesion in systems with large surface areas.

3. **Ionic Interactions**: In some cases, ionic interactions occur between charged groups in the polymer and the mucus glycoproteins. For example, anionic polymers like polycarbophil form ionic bonds with positively charged mucin molecules, creating a stable adhesive interface.

Examples of Polymer-Mucus Interactions

Polymers such as **HPMC** and **chitosan** are widely used in mucoadhesive formulations due to their ability to form strong interactions with the mucus layer. HPMC, a hydrophilic polymer, absorbs moisture and swells upon contact with mucus, enhancing hydrogen bonding and surface contact. This property makes it an ideal choice for buccal films and ocular formulations.

Chitosan, a naturally occurring cationic polymer, exhibits excellent mucoadhesion due to its ability to interact with negatively charged mucins through ionic interactions and hydrogen bonding. Its biocompatibility and biodegradability further make it suitable for nasal and vaginal delivery systems.

Significance of Understanding Mechanisms

By elucidating the mechanisms of mucoadhesion, researchers can tailor drug delivery systems to achieve optimal adhesion, retention, and drug release. For instance, in buccal patches for chronic pain relief, polymers with strong mucoadhesive properties ensure prolonged contact with the oral mucosa, enhancing drug absorption and reducing dosing frequency. Similarly, in nasal sprays for allergy relief, optimized mucoadhesion improves drug efficacy by maintaining the formulation at the site of action for extended periods.

This mechanistic understanding underscores the importance of selecting appropriate polymers and designing formulations that leverage these interactions to achieve superior therapeutic outcomes.

6.1.4 Transmucosal Drug Delivery Systems

Transmucosal drug delivery systems utilize the mucosal membranes for administering drugs, offering advantages such as bypassing first-pass metabolism, rapid onset of action, and improved bioavailability. These systems are especially beneficial for drugs that are poorly absorbed through the gastrointestinal tract or are extensively metabolized by the liver. The primary routes for transmucosal delivery include buccal and sublingual administration, each with distinct mechanisms and applications.

Buccal Drug Delivery

Buccal drug delivery involves administering drugs through the inner lining of the cheek. This route provides a direct pathway for drug absorption into the systemic circulation, avoiding the first-pass metabolism in the liver. The buccal mucosa has a relatively permeable structure and a rich vascular supply, facilitating effective drug absorption.

One of the primary benefits of buccal drug delivery is the ability to deliver drugs with low oral bioavailability due to hepatic metabolism. For example, buprenorphine, an opioid analgesic, is commonly administered via buccal films to manage severe pain and opioid dependence. The buccal route also supports the delivery of peptides and hormones, which are typically degraded in the gastrointestinal tract.

Buccal drug delivery systems, such as films, tablets, and patches, are designed to adhere to the mucosa, ensuring prolonged drug contact and consistent absorption. These systems are particularly useful for delivering drugs that require controlled or sustained release, such as hormones for hormone replacement therapy.

Sublingual Drug Delivery

Sublingual drug delivery involves placing the drug under the tongue, where it rapidly dissolves and is absorbed through the highly vascular sublingual mucosa. This route is favored for drugs requiring a rapid onset of action, as the drug bypasses both the gastrointestinal tract and hepatic metabolism, entering the systemic circulation almost immediately.

The high vascularity of the sublingual mucosa ensures quick and efficient drug absorption. For example, nitroglycerin, used for treating acute episodes of angina pectoris, is administered sublingually to provide prompt relief by dilating blood vessels. The sublingual route is also suitable for other drugs requiring rapid systemic effects, such as certain anxiolytics and cardiovascular agents.

Sublingual tablets and films are common formulations, designed to dissolve quickly without requiring water. These systems improve patient compliance, especially in emergencies where rapid drug action is critical.

Transmucosal drug delivery systems represent a significant advancement in pharmaceutical sciences, offering targeted and efficient solutions for various therapeutic needs. By leveraging the unique properties of mucosal membranes, these systems enhance drug efficacy and patient outcomes, particularly for drugs with specific pharmacokinetic challenges.

6.1.5 Buccal Patches

Buccal patches are innovative drug delivery systems designed to adhere to the buccal mucosa, providing prolonged drug retention and site-specific delivery. These thin adhesive films are gaining prominence for their ability to bypass the gastrointestinal tract and first-pass metabolism, offering improved drug bioavailability and controlled release.

Buccal patches are typically made from biocompatible and mucoadhesive polymers, ensuring they remain securely attached to the mucosa while gradually releasing the drug. They are available in two primary types: **matrix-type** and **reservoir-type** patches. Matrix-type patches distribute the drug uniformly throughout the polymer matrix, allowing for a continuous release profile. In contrast, reservoir-type patches contain the drug within a separate compartment or reservoir, which is surrounded by a rate-controlling membrane to achieve a more predictable release pattern.

One of the key applications of buccal patches is in **pain management**, particularly for the delivery of buprenorphine, an opioid analgesic. These patches offer a controlled and sustained release of the drug, ensuring consistent pain relief over extended periods. Another notable application is in **hormone replacement therapy**, where buccal patches containing estradiol provide effective and targeted hormone delivery, bypassing hepatic metabolism and improving bioavailability.

The advantages of buccal patches are manifold. Their ability to enhance drug bioavailability and provide site-specific delivery makes them suitable for drugs with poor oral bioavailability or those prone to extensive first-pass metabolism. Additionally, the ease of use and non-invasive nature of buccal patches improve patient compliance, particularly for individuals who have difficulty swallowing traditional oral dosage forms.

Despite their advantages, buccal patches face certain challenges. **Mucosal irritation** is a common concern, especially with drugs or excipients that may be harsh on the sensitive buccal lining. **Adhesion issues** can also arise, where the patch may fail to remain securely attached to the mucosa, compromising drug delivery. Addressing these challenges requires careful selection of polymers and optimization of formulation properties to ensure comfort and effectiveness.

Buccal patches represent a promising advancement in drug delivery, combining the benefits of controlled release, improved bioavailability, and ease of administration. Their versatility and efficacy continue to drive their adoption in diverse therapeutic areas, making them a valuable addition to modern pharmaceutical technology.

6.1.6 Formulation and Evaluation of Buccal Drug Delivery Systems

The formulation and evaluation of buccal drug delivery systems are critical for ensuring their effectiveness in delivering drugs through the buccal mucosa. These systems are designed to enhance drug absorption, provide controlled release, and ensure patient comfort and compliance. Various components and techniques are used to achieve these objectives, along with rigorous evaluation to ensure quality and efficacy.

Components

The formulation of buccal drug delivery systems involves the careful selection of **mucoadhesive polymers**, **permeation enhancers**, and **plasticizers**. Mucoadhesive polymers, such as hydroxypropyl methylcellulose (HPMC) and chitosan, are the cornerstone of these systems. These polymers ensure the formulation adheres to the buccal mucosa and facilitates prolonged drug retention. HPMC is particularly favored for its hydrophilic nature and swelling properties, while chitosan, a cationic polymer, enhances mucoadhesion through ionic interactions with negatively charged mucin.

Permeation enhancers are included to improve the permeability of the buccal mucosa, allowing drugs with low absorption rates to penetrate effectively. Common permeation enhancers include surfactants, bile salts, and fatty acids. These agents temporarily disrupt the integrity of the mucosal barrier or modify the drug's solubility, enhancing its diffusion across the mucosa.

Plasticizers, such as polyethylene glycol and glycerol, are used to improve the flexibility and mechanical properties of buccal films and patches. They ensure the formulation remains pliable and comfortable for the patient, reducing the risk of irritation or detachment.

Types of Buccal Drug Delivery Systems

Buccal drug delivery systems are available in various forms, including **tablets**, **patches**, **films**, and **gels**, each tailored to specific therapeutic needs.

- **Buccal tablets** are small, flat, and designed to adhere to the mucosa while providing controlled drug release.
- **Buccal patches** and **films** are thin and flexible, offering better comfort and patient compliance. These systems are particularly useful for sustained-release formulations.

- **Buccal gels** are viscous preparations that spread easily over the mucosal surface, making them suitable for localized drug delivery.

Evaluation

The evaluation of buccal drug delivery systems involves a series of tests to ensure their performance, safety, and efficacy.

Mucoadhesion strength is measured using tensile or shear tests to determine the formulation's ability to adhere to the mucosal surface. Strong mucoadhesion is essential for prolonged retention and effective drug delivery.

Drug release kinetics are evaluated using in vitro dissolution studies, where the rate and extent of drug release from the formulation are assessed. This provides insights into the release mechanism and ensures consistent delivery of the drug.

Bioavailability studies assess the amount of drug absorbed into the systemic circulation, comparing the buccal system's performance to other delivery methods. These studies are often complemented by in vitro permeation testing, where drug diffusion across excised mucosal tissues is analyzed.

6.2 Implantable Drug Delivery Systems

Implantable drug delivery systems represent a sophisticated approach to achieving long-term, controlled drug release. These systems are placed subcutaneously or at specific anatomical sites, offering significant advantages in terms of consistent drug delivery, improved patient compliance, and reduced dosing frequency. The advanced design and engineering of these systems make them invaluable in managing chronic diseases, hormone replacement therapy, and localized cancer treatment.

6.2.1 Concept and Mechanism of Implants

Implantable drug delivery systems are long-term devices designed to deliver drugs in a controlled and sustained manner. These systems are made from biocompatible materials that minimize immune responses and tissue irritation. Their ability to maintain therapeutic drug levels over weeks, months, or even years eliminates the need for frequent administration, offering a convenient solution for managing chronic conditions.

The mechanism of drug release from implants depends on the system's design and the materials used. Three primary mechanisms govern drug release in these systems:

1. **Diffusion-Controlled Release**

   In diffusion-based systems, the drug is encapsulated within a polymer matrix or reservoir. The release occurs as the drug molecules diffuse through the polymer, driven by a concentration gradient. For example, implants like **Norplant**, used for long-term contraception, rely on diffusion through a silicone-based matrix to release the hormone levonorgestrel consistently over time.

2. **Erosion-Controlled Release**

   In erosion-based systems, biodegradable polymers like polylactic acid (PLA) and polyglycolic acid (PGA) degrade over time, releasing the encapsulated drug. These systems are particularly useful for applications where the implant does not need to be removed after the drug is depleted. For instance, **Zoladex** implants, used in prostate cancer treatment, release goserelin as the polymer matrix erodes in the body.

3. **Osmotic-Driven Release**

   Osmotic pumps represent an advanced mechanism where drug release is driven by osmotic pressure. These implants consist of a drug reservoir enclosed in a semipermeable membrane. When exposed to bodily fluids, water enters the reservoir through the membrane, creating pressure that pushes the drug out at a controlled rate. An example is the **Duros implant**, used for chronic pain management, which delivers drugs like hydromorphone using osmotic principles.

Implantable drug delivery systems offer precise control over the rate and duration of drug release. Their ability to deliver drugs locally or systemically makes them suitable for a wide range of therapeutic applications. For instance, localized implants used in cancer therapy release chemotherapeutic agents directly at the tumor site, minimizing systemic side effects. Similarly, systemic implants provide consistent drug levels in conditions like hormone deficiencies or chronic pain.

6.2.2 Types of Implantable Systems

Implantable drug delivery systems can be broadly classified into biodegradable and non-biodegradable systems based on the materials used in their construction. These classifications determine the implant's behavior in the body, including its duration of action and the need for removal after the drug is depleted. Both types have specific applications, advantages, and limitations, making them suitable for different therapeutic scenarios.

Biodegradable Implants

Biodegradable implants are designed using polymers that degrade into non-toxic byproducts within the body. These byproducts are eventually metabolized or excreted, eliminating the need for surgical removal of the implant after the drug is exhausted.

Common materials for biodegradable implants include **polylactic acid (PLA)** and **polycaprolactone (PCL)**. PLA is widely used due to its predictable degradation profile and biocompatibility. PCL, known for its slower degradation rate, is suitable for applications requiring prolonged drug release.

An example of a biodegradable implant is the **Gliadel wafer**, used in brain cancer treatment. This implant delivers the chemotherapeutic agent carmustine directly to the tumor site, ensuring localized action while minimizing systemic toxicity. The polymer matrix degrades over time, releasing the drug as it dissolves in the surrounding tissue.

Biodegradable implants are ideal for temporary treatments where long-term retention of the implant is not required. They are commonly used in applications like cancer therapy, localized infections, and hormone delivery.

Non-Biodegradable Implants

Non-biodegradable implants are constructed from durable materials that remain intact within the body after the drug is released. These implants require surgical removal once their purpose is fulfilled, which can be a limitation in certain cases.

Materials such as **silicone** and **polymethylmethacrylate (PMMA)** are commonly used for non-biodegradable implants. Silicone is favored for its flexibility and inert nature, making it suitable for implants requiring long-term placement. PMMA, known for its mechanical strength, is often used in orthopedic and dental applications.

An example of a non-biodegradable implant is **Norplant**, a contraceptive implant that delivers the hormone levonorgestrel over several years. The implant consists of silicone rods that release the hormone through diffusion, providing long-term contraceptive protection.

Non-biodegradable implants are particularly useful in applications requiring extended drug delivery durations and where surgical removal is feasible. They are often used in conditions like chronic pain management, contraception, and certain cancers.

Examples of Implantable Systems

Implantable systems like the **Gliadel wafer** and **Norplant** highlight the versatility of these technologies. The Gliadel wafer, a biodegradable implant, offers localized chemotherapy for brain cancer, reducing systemic side effects. Norplant, a non-biodegradable system, provides a long-term contraceptive solution with minimal maintenance.

By selecting the appropriate type of implantable system based on the therapeutic need, clinicians can tailor drug delivery to maximize efficacy and patient convenience. These systems exemplify the advancements in controlled drug delivery technologies, addressing diverse medical challenges with precision and innovation.

6.2.3 Osmotic Pumps

Osmotic pumps represent a sophisticated drug delivery technology that utilizes osmotic pressure to achieve controlled and sustained drug release. These systems are highly precise, offering predictable drug delivery rates independent of external factors such as pH or motility. Their ability to deliver a consistent dose over extended periods makes them ideal for managing chronic diseases and delivering sensitive drugs like peptides.

Mechanism of Osmotic-Driven Drug Release

The working principle of osmotic pumps involves the generation of osmotic pressure within a drug reservoir. These systems consist of a semipermeable membrane that allows water to enter the reservoir from surrounding bodily fluids. As water permeates through the membrane, it dissolves or suspends the drug inside, creating an osmotic gradient. The resulting pressure forces the drug solution or suspension out through a delivery orifice, ensuring a controlled and consistent release rate.

Osmotic pumps are designed to deliver drugs at zero-order kinetics, meaning the release rate remains constant over time. This mechanism is particularly advantageous for maintaining steady plasma drug levels, reducing dosing frequency, and enhancing therapeutic efficacy.

Types of Osmotic Pumps

Several types of osmotic pump systems have been developed, each tailored to specific applications and drug properties:

1. **Elementary Osmotic Pumps (EOP)**

   These are the simplest form of osmotic pumps. The system comprises a drug core coated with a semipermeable membrane and a single delivery orifice. Water enters the core, dissolving the drug, which is then released through the orifice at a controlled rate. EOPs are particularly suitable for water-soluble drugs and are commonly used in oral formulations.

2. **Push-Pull Osmotic Pumps**

   Push-pull systems are designed for delivering drugs with low water solubility. These systems consist of two compartments: one containing the drug and the other containing a swelling polymer. As water enters, the polymer swells, pushing the drug solution out through the delivery orifice. This design ensures effective delivery of poorly soluble drugs and offers flexibility in formulation.

3. **Controlled Porosity Osmotic Pumps**

   In these systems, the semipermeable membrane contains pores that control the rate of water ingress and drug release. These pores are formed using water-soluble excipients that dissolve upon contact with bodily fluids, creating a porous membrane. Controlled porosity systems are highly adaptable and can be used for both oral and implantable formulations.

Applications of Osmotic Pumps

Osmotic pumps have found extensive applications in pharmaceutical therapy due to their versatility and precision.

- **Peptides and Protein Delivery**: Osmotic pumps are well-suited for delivering biologically sensitive molecules like peptides, which require controlled release to maintain stability and therapeutic activity.
- **Chronic Disease Management**: Conditions like diabetes, hypertension, and arthritis benefit from osmotic pump formulations, as they provide consistent drug levels and reduce dosing frequency.
- **Implantable Systems**: In cancer therapy, osmotic pumps can be used to deliver chemotherapeutic agents locally to the tumor site, minimizing systemic toxicity.

6.2.4 Advantages and Limitations of Implantable Systems

Implantable drug delivery systems are a significant advancement in pharmaceutical technology, offering a controlled and consistent release of drugs over extended periods. While these systems provide numerous therapeutic benefits, they also come with certain challenges that must be addressed for optimal application.

Advantages

One of the primary advantages of implantable systems is their ability to provide **long-term therapy**. These devices are designed to deliver drugs consistently over weeks, months, or even years, eliminating the need for frequent dosing. This feature is particularly beneficial for managing chronic conditions such as cancer, hormonal imbalances, and severe pain, where maintaining steady therapeutic levels is crucial for efficacy.

Reduced dosing frequency is another significant benefit of implantable systems. For patients with chronic diseases, adhering to a daily or multiple-dose regimen can be challenging. Implantable systems alleviate this burden by requiring minimal patient intervention, improving compliance and overall treatment outcomes.

Implantable systems also enable **localized drug delivery**, minimizing systemic exposure and reducing the risk of side effects. For example, in cancer therapy, implantable devices can deliver chemotherapeutic agents directly to the tumor site, enhancing efficacy while sparing healthy tissues. Additionally, their biocompatible materials ensure minimal immune response and high tolerability within the body.

Limitations

Despite their advantages, implantable systems have certain limitations that can affect their widespread adoption. One of the most significant challenges is the need for **surgical procedures** for insertion and, in some cases, removal of the device. These procedures carry inherent risks, including tissue damage, bleeding, and anesthesia-related complications.

Another limitation is the **risk of infection**. Since these devices are implanted within the body, they create an entry point for pathogens, increasing the likelihood of localized or systemic infections. Stringent aseptic techniques during implantation and the use of antimicrobial coatings can mitigate this risk, but it remains a concern, particularly in immunocompromised patients.

High cost is another barrier associated with implantable systems. The advanced materials, sophisticated engineering, and surgical requirements contribute to the overall expense, making these systems less accessible to patients in low-resource settings. Additionally, their development and regulatory approval involve significant time and financial investment, further driving up costs.

6.3 Applications and Case Studies

6.3.1 Applications of Mucosal Drug Delivery Systems

Mucosal drug delivery systems are innovative pharmaceutical technologies designed to enhance drug absorption through mucosal surfaces. These systems leverage the high vascularity and permeability of mucosal membranes to provide rapid and efficient drug delivery. Their versatility allows for applications across a range of therapeutic areas, from pain management to hormone replacement therapy and vaccination.

One significant application of mucosal drug delivery systems is in **pain management**. Buccal fentanyl formulations are widely used for the treatment of breakthrough pain, particularly in cancer patients. The buccal route ensures rapid absorption of the opioid through the rich vascular network in the buccal mucosa, bypassing hepatic first-pass metabolism.

This results in faster onset of analgesic action compared to conventional oral formulations, providing quick relief from acute pain episodes.

Another important area is **hormone replacement therapy (HRT)**. Buccal estradiol formulations are used to manage symptoms of menopause, such as hot flashes and osteoporosis. These systems offer precise and sustained delivery of estradiol, ensuring consistent therapeutic levels while reducing systemic side effects commonly associated with oral administration. The buccal route also improves patient compliance by eliminating the need for frequent dosing and providing a non-invasive alternative to injectable therapies.

Mucosal drug delivery systems are also emerging as promising platforms for **vaccination**. Vaccines delivered via mucosal routes, such as nasal or buccal sprays, offer several advantages, including ease of administration and the potential to induce both systemic and mucosal immunity. For example, intranasal influenza vaccines have demonstrated efficacy in providing protective immune responses while improving patient convenience and compliance. These systems are particularly valuable in mass vaccination programs, where rapid and non-invasive administration is critical.

6.3.2 Applications of Implantable Systems

Implantable drug delivery systems are transformative technologies that offer precise, controlled, and long-term drug administration. Their applications span multiple therapeutic areas, addressing complex medical needs where traditional drug delivery methods may fall short. These systems provide localized or systemic drug release, ensuring improved efficacy, reduced side effects, and enhanced patient compliance.

A prominent application of implantable systems is in **cancer therapy**, where localized drug delivery minimizes systemic toxicity and enhances therapeutic outcomes. An excellent example is the **Gliadel wafer**, a biodegradable implant used in the treatment of brain tumors. This implant delivers the chemotherapeutic agent carmustine directly to the tumor site, bypassing the blood-brain barrier and maintaining high local drug concentrations. The wafer gradually dissolves, releasing the drug over several weeks, reducing the need for systemic chemotherapy and its associated side effects.

Another significant application is in **contraception**. Hormonal implants, such as **Norplant** or **Nexplanon**, provide long-term birth control by releasing hormones like levonorgestrel or etonogestrel. These non-biodegradable implants are placed subdermally and can remain effective for up to five years. They offer a convenient and reliable contraceptive option, particularly for women seeking alternatives to daily oral pills or other short-term methods.

Emerging applications of implantable systems are expanding their scope in areas like neurological disorders and chronic diseases. In **Parkinson's disease**, implantable pumps are being developed to deliver dopamine or dopamine agonists directly to the brain, bypassing systemic barriers and providing consistent symptomatic relief. These systems hold promise for reducing the fluctuations in motor function associated with traditional oral therapies.

For **diabetes management**, implantable insulin delivery systems are under development to address the challenges of maintaining precise glucose control. These implants release insulin in response to glucose levels, mimicking the physiological insulin secretion of the pancreas. By eliminating the need for multiple daily injections or continuous subcutaneous infusions, these systems aim to improve the quality of life for individuals with diabetes.

CHAPTER VII

Transdermal and Gastroretentive Drug Delivery Systems

7.1 Transdermal Drug Delivery Systems (TDDS)

7.1.1 Introduction to Transdermal Drug Delivery Systems

Transdermal Drug Delivery Systems (TDDS) represent a revolutionary advancement in pharmaceutical technology, enabling the non-invasive delivery of drugs through the skin for systemic therapeutic effects. The transdermal route bypasses many of the challenges associated with oral and injectable drug administration, making it a preferred choice for a range of therapeutic applications. TDDS provides a method to achieve controlled and sustained drug release, improving both efficacy and patient compliance.

The skin, while serving as a natural barrier to external agents, offers a convenient route for drug delivery. TDDS leverages the unique properties of the skin, particularly its large surface area and rich vascularization, to facilitate the absorption of drugs directly into the bloodstream. Unlike oral administration, where drugs undergo degradation in the gastrointestinal tract and first-pass metabolism in the liver, transdermal systems bypass these processes, leading to improved bioavailability.

One of the key advantages of TDDS is its **non-invasive nature,** which eliminates the discomfort and risks associated with needles. This makes it particularly suitable for patients who require long-term therapy, such as those with chronic pain or hormonal deficiencies. Transdermal patches, for example, offer a convenient way to deliver drugs over extended periods, reducing the need for frequent dosing and enhancing patient adherence to treatment regimens.

TDDS also provides a **controlled and sustained release** of drugs, maintaining consistent plasma drug levels and minimizing fluctuations that can occur with traditional dosing methods. For instance, nicotine patches used in smoking cessation therapy deliver a steady dose of nicotine, helping to reduce withdrawal symptoms without the spikes and troughs associated with oral or inhaled formulations. Similarly, hormone replacement therapy using transdermal estradiol patches ensures stable hormone levels, improving therapeutic outcomes while minimizing side effects.

The use of TDDS is not limited to systemic delivery; it can also be tailored for localized therapy. Drugs such as lidocaine and capsaicin, delivered via transdermal patches, provide targeted pain relief at the site of application. This localized approach reduces systemic exposure and potential side effects, making it a safer option for patients with localized conditions.

Despite its advantages, the transdermal route poses certain challenges. The primary barrier to drug absorption is the stratum corneum, the outermost layer of the skin, which restricts the passage of most molecules. Advances in formulation technology, such as the use of permeation enhancers and microneedle systems, have addressed these challenges by improving the delivery of both hydrophilic and large-molecule drugs.

7.1.2 Mechanisms of Drug Permeation Through the Skin

The effectiveness of transdermal drug delivery systems relies heavily on the mechanisms by which drugs permeate through the skin to reach systemic circulation. The skin, particularly its outermost layer, the stratum corneum, serves as a formidable barrier, regulating the absorption of substances while protecting the body from external agents. Understanding the structure of the skin and the pathways available for drug permeation is crucial for designing effective transdermal formulations.

The **stratum corneum** is the skin's primary barrier, consisting of corneocytes (dead keratinized cells) embedded in a lipid matrix. This structure resembles a "brick-and-mortar" arrangement, with the corneocytes acting as bricks and the lipids as mortar. Its hydrophobic nature poses a significant challenge for drug permeation, especially for hydrophilic and large-molecule drugs. Below the stratum corneum lies the viable epidermis, followed by the dermis, which contains capillaries responsible for systemic drug absorption.

Drugs can permeate the skin via three primary pathways:

1. **Transcellular Pathway**
   In this route, drugs pass directly through the corneocytes, traversing the hydrophilic interior of the cells. While this pathway offers a direct route, it requires drugs to overcome both hydrophilic and lipophilic barriers

within the corneocyte and the lipid matrix, making it less commonly used.

2. **Intercellular Pathway**

The intercellular route involves the diffusion of drugs through the lipid matrix surrounding the corneocytes. This pathway is the most common and effective for many drugs, as the lipid matrix provides a continuous hydrophobic environment conducive to the transport of lipophilic molecules.

3. **Transappendageal Pathway**

This route utilizes appendages such as hair follicles and sweat glands to bypass the stratum corneum. Although these structures occupy a small surface area of the skin (approximately 0.1%), they provide an important route for hydrophilic and large-molecule drugs that may struggle to penetrate the stratum corneum directly.

Several factors influence drug permeation through the skin, including drug properties, skin condition, and environmental factors. Drug properties such as molecular size, lipophilicity, and solubility are critical determinants of permeability. Small, lipophilic molecules with balanced hydrophilic-lipophilic characteristics (Log P values between 1 and 3) exhibit optimal permeation through the stratum corneum.

The condition of the skin also plays a significant role. Intact, healthy skin provides a robust barrier, while damaged or hydrated skin can enhance permeability. Hydration of the stratum corneum increases its porosity, facilitating the transport of hydrophilic drugs. Conversely, conditions like hyperkeratosis or scarring can impede drug absorption.

Environmental factors such as temperature and humidity further affect skin permeability. Higher temperatures increase lipid fluidity, enhancing drug diffusion through the intercellular pathway. Similarly, high humidity levels hydrate the stratum corneum, improving its permeability.

7.1.3 Components of Transdermal Drug Delivery Systems (TDDS)

Transdermal Drug Delivery Systems (TDDS) are intricate pharmaceutical formulations composed of multiple layers, each with a specific function to ensure efficient, controlled, and sustained drug delivery through the skin. The design and composition of these layers play a critical role in determining the system's performance, bioavailability, and patient acceptability.

Layers of TDDS: Functions and Materials Used

1. **Drug Reservoir**

   The drug reservoir is the core component of a transdermal system, where the active pharmaceutical ingredient (API) is stored. This layer can exist in various forms, such as a gel, liquid, or solid matrix, depending on the system's design. The primary role of the drug reservoir is to serve as a stable source of the drug, ensuring a consistent release over the intended duration. The choice of material for the reservoir depends on the physicochemical properties of the drug, such as solubility and stability.

2. **Rate-Controlling Membrane**

   The rate-controlling membrane regulates the release of the drug from the reservoir into the skin. This membrane ensures that the drug is delivered at a predictable and steady rate, preventing fluctuations in plasma drug concentrations. Polymers such as ethylcellulose or polyethylene are commonly used for their durability and permeability. The design of this membrane is critical in achieving zero-order kinetics, where the drug release rate remains constant over time.

3. **Adhesive Layer**

   The adhesive layer ensures that the transdermal patch remains securely attached to the skin throughout its application. This layer must provide strong adhesion without causing irritation or discomfort. Pressure-sensitive adhesives, such as polyacrylates, silicones, or rubber-basedadhesives, are commonly used. In some systems, the adhesive layer also contains the drug, enabling direct drug delivery to the skin.

   Backing Layer

The backing layer provides structural support and protects the patch from external factors such as moisture, light, and mechanical damage. This layer is typically made of polyester, polypropylene, or polyethylene films, chosen for their flexibility, impermeability, and compatibility with other components. The backing layer also ensures that the drug does not leach out from the reservoir in the opposite direction, maintaining the system's integrity.

Role of Permeation Enhancers

Permeation enhancers are vital components in Transdermal Drug Delivery Systems (TDDS), used to overcome the natural barrier posed by the stratum corneum, the outermost layer of the skin. The skin's barrier function primarily exists to protect the body from external harmful agents, but it also poses a significant challenge to drug delivery. The stratum corneum consists mainly of lipid bilayers, which act as a barrier to many drugs, particularly hydrophilic compounds. Permeation enhancers, through their action, help bypass this barrier and facilitate the penetration of therapeutic agents into the deeper layers of the skin, ultimately allowing systemic absorption.

Mechanisms of Action

Permeation enhancers work by temporarily altering the lipid structure of the stratum corneum or by interacting with protein components. The effect is often reversible, meaning that after the enhancer's action, the skin barrier regains its normal structure and function. The mechanisms by which permeation enhancers work can vary depending on their chemical structure and interaction with the skin. Some enhancers, such as ethanol, can disrupt the lipid bilayers, creating micro pores in the skin's outer layer, which allows larger drug molecules to pass through. Others, such as dimethyl sulfoxide (DMSO), increase the solubility of the drug within the skin, enabling better drug absorption. Some permeation enhancers, such asterpenes and fatty acids, help to increase thefluidity of the lipid matrix of the skin, making it more permeable to drugs by reducing the packing density of the lipids.

Examples of Permeation Enhancers

Ethanol is one of the most commonly used permeation enhancers. It acts by disrupting the lipid bilayer of the stratum corneum, allowing greater movement of drug molecules across the skin barrier. It is particularly useful for hydrophilic drugs, which otherwise would struggle to penetrate the skin's lipophilic layers. Dimethyl sulfoxide (DMSO) is another well-known enhancer. DMSO is a solvent that increases the solubility of drugs in the skin, thus enhancing their ability to pass through the skin's barrier. In addition to these, terpenes—naturally occurring compounds found in essential oils—are also used as permeation enhancers. They increase the fluidity of the skin's lipid layers and create small, reversible defects in the lipid structure, improving drug absorption. Other fatty acids, such as oleic acid, are often used in combination with other enhancers to further improve skin permeability by altering the structure of the lipids in the stratum corneum.

Considerations in the Use of Permeation Enhancers

While permeation enhancers are crucial for improving drug absorption, they must be selected and used carefully to avoid potential adverse effects. One of the most important considerations is the concentration of the enhancer. If used in excessive amounts, permeation enhancers can compromise the skin's barrier integrity, leading toirritation, dermatitis, or eventoxicity. For example, although ethanol is effective at disrupting the lipid bilayer, high concentrations can lead to skin dryness and irritation. Similarly, DMSO, while very effective, can also increase the absorption of other substances, including potentially harmful chemicals, into the skin, which could pose safety risks.

Another critical factor is the compatibility of the permeation enhancer with the drug being delivered. Some enhancers may interfere with the drug's stability or cause chemical reactions that could alter the drug's efficacy. For instance, the use of certain oils or fatty acids could cause some drugs to degrade or crystallize, reducing their effectiveness.

Moreover, the effect on the skin's barrier properties needs to be considered. Ideally, permeation enhancers should temporarily disrupt the barrier to allow the drug to pass through but should not cause long-term damage to the skin. The reversibility of the enhancer's effect is important, as it ensures that the skin returns to its natural state after drug absorption.

Regulatory and Safety Considerations

Regulatory bodies such as the **FDA** and **EMA** require that the safety and efficacy of permeation enhancers be thoroughly assessed before they are used in commercial drug formulations. The use of certain enhancers, especially those that can cause irritation or toxicity, is strictly regulated. As a result, manufacturers must carry out extensive testing to ensure that the enhancers used in transdermal formulations are both effective and safe.

7.1.4 Types of Transdermal Systems

Transdermal drug delivery systems (TDDS) are classified into various types based on their design principles and the mechanisms by which the drug is delivered through the skin. Each type offers unique advantages and applications, making it suitable for specific therapeutic needs. The most commonly used types include reservoir systems, matrix systems, microreservoir systems, and adhesive matrix systems.

Reservoir System

The reservoir system is a transdermal design where the drug is stored in a liquid or gel reservoir, separated from the skin by a rate-controlling membrane. The membrane regulates the release of the drug, ensuring a consistent delivery rate over time.

The design principle of the reservoir system is ideal for drugs requiring precise control of release kinetics. For instance, **nitroglycerin transdermal patches** for angina pectoris use this system to provide steady therapeutic levels and minimize the risk of dose dumping. The system's primary advantage lies in its ability to maintain zero-order release kinetics, ensuring a constant drug release rate independent of the concentration in the reservoir.

However, reservoir systems require careful design to avoid rupture or leakage, which could lead to uncontrolled drug release. The manufacturing process is also relatively complex, contributing to higher costs compared to other systems.

Matrix System

In matrix systems, the drug is dispersed homogeneously within a polymer matrix, which controls the release by diffusion. Unlike reservoir systems, matrix systems lack a separate rate-controlling membrane, simplifying their design and reducing manufacturing costs.

The drug release rate in a matrix system depends on the diffusion of the drug through the polymer matrix. **Fentanyl transdermal patches**, widely used for chronic pain management, utilize this design. The matrix system is particularly advantageous for delivering lipophilic drugs, as the polymer structure enhances their diffusion.

Matrix systems are less prone to dose dumping than reservoir systems, but achieving consistent release rates can be challenging, especially for highly soluble drugs.

Microreservoir System

Microreservoir systems are a hybrid of reservoir and matrix designs. In this type, microscopic reservoirs containing the drug are dispersed within a polymer matrix. The release is regulated by the polymer matrix and, in some cases, an additional rate-controlling membrane.

This design offers the benefits of both reservoir and matrix systems, providing precise release control and improved stability. Microreservoir systems are used for delivering drugs with narrow therapeutic windows, where maintaining consistent plasma levels is critical. An example includes advanced hormone replacement therapies.

Adhesive Matrix System

The adhesive matrix system integrates the drug, adhesive, and matrix into a single layer, simplifying the overall design. The adhesive layer is in direct contact with the skin and delivers the drug through diffusion.

This system is particularly convenient for drugs requiring low doses and offers excellent patient comfort due to its thin and flexible design. **Clonidine patches**, used for hypertension management, are an example of adhesive matrix systems. These systems also reduce the risk of detachment and provide steady drug release over time.

7.1.5 Advantages and Disadvantages of Transdermal Drug Delivery Systems (TDDS)

Advantages

Transdermal drug delivery systems have revolutionized medication administration by providing a non-invasive and patient-friendly alternative to oral and injectable routes. A significant advantage of these systems is their ability to bypass the liver's first-pass metabolism. By delivering drugs directly into the bloodstream through the skin, transdermal systems enhance the bioavailability of drugs that would otherwise be extensively metabolized.

Another important benefit is their capacity to provide controlled and sustained drug release. This ensures stable plasma drug concentrations over extended periods, reducing the need for frequent dosing and enhancing patient compliance. For instance, transdermal patches used for conditions such as chronic pain or angina provide consistent therapeutic effects, minimizing the fluctuations that are often seen with traditional dosing methods.

The non-invasive nature of these systems eliminates the discomfort and risks associated with needles, making them ideal for long-term therapies or for patients with needle phobia. Moreover, the systems are easy to apply and remove, offering a discreet and convenient option for medication administration. In addition, therapy can be terminated quickly by removing the patch, stopping further drug delivery immediately.

Disadvantages

Despite their numerous advantages, transdermal drug delivery systems face several challenges. One of the primary limitations is their suitability for only certain types of drugs, particularly those that are lipophilic and have low molecular weights. The outermost layer of the skin, known as the stratum corneum, acts as a strong barrier, restricting the absorption of hydrophilic drugs and larger molecules.

Skin irritation and sensitization are common issues, often caused by the adhesives used in the patches or the permeation enhancers included in the formulations. These reactions can range from mild redness to severe allergic responses, potentially affecting patient adherence to the treatment.

The manufacturing process for transdermal systems is complex and involves advanced technology to ensure uniform drug distribution and consistent release rates. This complexity, combined with the need for stringent quality control measures, makes the production of these systems costly. This high cost can also make transdermal systems less accessible to patients in resource-limited settings.

Moreover, transdermal systems are generally not suitable for delivering high doses of drugs because the skin has a limited capacity for absorption. This restricts their use to medications that are effective at low doses over prolonged durations.

While transdermal drug delivery systems offer innovative solutions to many drug delivery challenges, their limitations highlight the need for careful selection and design to maximize their effectiveness and minimize potential drawbacks. Ongoing advancements in material science and technology are expected to address these issues and further expand the applicability of these systems.

7.1.6 Formulation and Development of Transdermal Drug Delivery Systems (TDDS)

The formulation and development of transdermal drug delivery systems involve a multidisciplinary approach, integrating principles of pharmaceutics, material science, and biopharmaceutics. A well-designed TDDS must ensure effective drug delivery through the skin, maintaining therapeutic levels in the systemic circulation while being safe and patient-friendly.

Criteria for Drug Selection

The selection of a suitable drug is the cornerstone of TDDS formulation. Drugs intended for transdermal delivery must possess specific physicochemical and pharmacokinetic properties to ensure effective absorption through the skin. Ideally, the molecular weight of the drug should be less than 500 Da to facilitate its passage through the stratum corneum, the primary barrier of the skin. The drug should also have balanced solubility characteristics, being both hydrophilic and lipophilic, as this dual nature aids in permeating the lipid-rich and aqueous layers of the skin.

Additionally, the drug's melting point and stability under formulation and storage conditions are critical. Drugs with a low therapeutic dose, typically less than 10 mg per day, are more suitable for transdermal delivery due to the skin's limited absorption capacity. Pharmacokinetic properties such as a short biological half-life and the need for sustained plasma levels also make a drug a good candidate for transdermal systems.

Role of Polymers, Enhancers, and Adhesives

Polymers play a pivotal role in TDDS, serving as the backbone of the system. They form the matrix or reservoir that controls the drug release rate. Polymers such as hydroxypropyl methylcellulose (HPMC), ethylcellulose, and polyvinylpyrrolidone (PVP) are widely used due to their compatibility and ability to modulate drug release profiles. The choice of polymer depends on the desired release kinetics and the drug's properties.

Permeation enhancers are incorporated to improve the drug's ability to traverse the stratum corneum. These agents, such as ethanol, oleic acid, and dimethyl sulfoxide, temporarily alter the skin barrier by disrupting lipid bilayers or modifying protein structures, thereby increasing permeability.

Adhesives are another critical component, ensuring the patch remains in contact with the skin throughout the application period. Adhesives such as polyacrylates and silicones provide both adherence and, in some designs, contribute to the drug's delivery by incorporating the active ingredient directly into the adhesive layer.

Evaluation Techniques

A rigorous evaluation process is essential to ensure the safety, efficacy, and stability of TDDS. **In vitro permeation studies** are performed using skin models or synthetic membranes to evaluate the rate and extent of drug permeation. These studies help optimize the formulation by identifying factors that influence drug release and absorption.

Adhesive strength testing ensures the patch adheres well to the skin without causing discomfort or detachment during use. This involves measuring parameters such as tack, peel strength, and shear resistance. Additional tests, such as **drug release kinetics**, moisture content analysis, and stability studies, assess the system's performance under various conditions.

7.1.7 Evaluation of Transdermal Drug Delivery Systems (TDDS)

The evaluation of transdermal drug delivery systems is a critical step in ensuring their safety, efficacy, and reliability. A comprehensive evaluation encompasses multiple parameters, including drug release, permeation, adhesion, and stability, to guarantee consistent performance under real-world conditions.

Testing for Drug Release and Permeation

Drug release studies are fundamental in evaluating TDDS, as they measure the rate and extent of drug liberation from the system. In vitro drug release studies are typically conducted using specialized equipment such as Franz diffusion cells. These cells consist of a donor compartment containing the transdermal patch and a receptor compartment filled with a medium that simulates physiological conditions. The amount of drug released into the medium over time is analyzed to determine release kinetics, ensuring the patch provides controlled and sustained delivery.

Permeation studies assess the drug's ability to penetrate the stratum corneum and reach systemic circulation. These studies often use excised human or animal skin as a biological barrier. Factors such as permeation enhancers and drug properties are optimized during these studies to maximize skin absorption without causing irritation.

Adhesion Testing

Adhesion is a vital characteristic of TDDS, as poor adherence can compromise drug delivery and patient compliance. Adhesion testing involves evaluating the patch's ability to stick to the skin over time under various conditions, including movement, moisture, and temperature changes. Tests such as peel strength and tack tests are performed to quantify the adhesive properties. Peel strength measures the force required to remove the patch, while tack tests assess the initial stickiness upon application.

Skin Irritation and Sensitization Studies

Since TDDS is applied directly to the skin, it is essential to ensure that the patch does not cause irritation or allergic reactions. Skin irritation studies are conducted using human volunteers or animal models to observe any redness, swelling, or discomfort after patch application. Sensitization studies assess the potential for long-term allergic reactions.

Stability Studies

Stability testing is crucial to ensure that the TDDS maintains its integrity, efficacy, and safety over its shelf life. Stability studies are performed under varying environmental conditions, including temperature, humidity, and light exposure. Parameters such as drug content, adhesive properties, and physical appearance are monitored periodically. For example, a transdermal patch may be tested under accelerated conditions of 40°C and 75% relative humidity to simulate long-term storage.

Overall Evaluation

The evaluation process for TDDS ensures that the formulation meets regulatory standards and performs effectively across a range of conditions. A robust evaluation program not only confirms the system's reliability but also provides valuable insights for optimizing design and improving patient outcomes. Through rigorous testing and quality assurance, TDDS continues to emerge as a promising and patient-centric approach to drug delivery.

7.2 Gastroretentive Drug Delivery Systems (GRDDS)

7.2.1 Introduction to Gastroretentive Drug Delivery Systems

Gastroretentive drug delivery systems (GRDDS) are advanced formulations designed to enhance the retention of drugs in the stomach, thereby improving their absorption and therapeutic efficacy. These systems address the challenge of short gastric residence times associated with conventional oral formulations, which can lead to suboptimal drug absorption, particularly for drugs with a narrow absorption window or those requiring localized gastric action.

The stomach's unique environment, including its acidic pH and limited motility during fasting states, makes it an ideal site for certain drugs. However, typical oral formulations quickly pass into the intestines, reducing the time available for gastric absorption. GRDDS counteract this issue by prolonging the drug's presence in the stomach, ensuring a sustained and localized release.

Drugs that benefit most from gastroretentive systems include those with poor solubility in intestinal fluids but good solubility in acidic environments, such as weakly basic drugs like ciprofloxacin. Additionally, GRDDS are valuable for drugs that target the stomach, such as antibiotics for Helicobacter pylori infections or nonsteroidal anti-inflammatory drugs (NSAIDs) formulated to minimize gastric irritation.

7.2.2 Mechanisms of Gastroretention

The success of GRDDS depends on their ability to remain in the stomach for extended periods. Various mechanisms have been developed to achieve effective gastroretention, with floating, swelling, and mucoadhesive systems being the most widely utilized.

Floating Systems

Floating systems are designed to achieve buoyancy in gastric fluids, allowing the formulation to remain in the stomach's upper region for prolonged periods. These systems typically have a low density, achieved through the inclusion of gas-generating agents like sodium bicarbonate or effervescent polymers. Upon contact with gastric acid, these agents release carbon dioxide, causing the system to float. Floating tablets or capsules are commonly used for drugs such as metformin, where sustained gastric retention enhances therapeutic outcomes.

Swelling Systems

Swelling systems rely on polymers that absorb gastric fluid and expand significantly in size. The increased size prevents the system from passing through the pyloric sphincter into the intestines. These systems use swellable polymers such as hydroxypropyl methylcellulose (HPMC) or carbopol, which form a gel-like structure in the stomach. Drugs like diclofenac have been formulated using swelling systems to ensure consistent release and prolonged gastric residence.

Mucoadhesive Systems

Mucoadhesive systems are designed to adhere to the gastric mucosa, ensuring the formulation remains in close contact with the stomach lining. These systems use polymers like chitosan or polyacrylic acid, which interact with the mucin layer of the stomach through hydrogen bonding or electrostatic interactions. This close contact facilitates localized drug delivery and enhances absorption for drugs such as amoxicillin, which targets bacterial infections in the stomach.

7.2 Gastroretentive Drug Delivery Systems (GRDDS)

7.2.1 Introduction to Gastroretentive Drug Delivery Systems

Gastroretentive drug delivery systems (GRDDS) are specialized oral formulations designed to extend the time a drug remains in the stomach, enhancing its absorption and therapeutic effect. These systems are particularly valuable for drugs that are absorbed primarily in the stomach or the proximal part of the small intestine, or for those requiring local action in the gastric region. By increasing gastric retention time, GRDDS ensure that the drug remains in the optimal site for absorption or action, thus improving its efficacy.

The principle behind GRDDS lies in countering the natural physiology of the stomach, which is characterized by rapid emptying into the intestines. Conventional oral formulations often fail to provide adequate therapeutic levels for drugs with a narrow absorption window due to their brief residence in the stomach. GRDDS overcome this limitation by employing mechanisms that maintain the formulation within the stomach for extended periods, ensuring sustained drug release and absorption.

These systems are especially advantageous for drugs that are poorly soluble at higher pH levels, such as weak bases that exhibit greater solubility in the acidic environment of the stomach. Examples include ciprofloxacin and ketoconazole. Additionally, GRDDS are used for drugs that target specific gastric conditions, such as antibiotics for eradicating Helicobacter pylori infections or NSAIDs formulated to reduce local gastric irritation.

7.2.2 Mechanisms of Gastroretention

Gastroretentive drug delivery systems (GRDDS) utilize various mechanisms to prolong the residence time of drugs in the stomach, enhancing their absorption and therapeutic effects. These mechanisms leverage the unique properties of gastric physiology and incorporate innovative formulation strategies to ensure the system remains in the stomach for extended periods. The primary mechanisms of gastroretention include buoyancy, swelling, and mucoadhesion, each offering distinct advantages depending on the drug's properties and therapeutic goals.

Floating Systems

Floating systems are among the most widely used approaches in GRDDS. These systems are designed to achieve buoyancy, enabling them to float on the surface of gastric fluids. Floating is achieved by incorporating low-density materials or gas-generating agents within the formulation. Effervescent agents such as sodium bicarbonate and citric acid react with gastric acid to release carbon dioxide, which creates a buoyant layer in the system. Non-effervescent polymers like hydroxypropyl methylcellulose (HPMC) and polyvinyl alcohol can also trap air during hydration, contributing to buoyancy.

Floating systems are particularly effective for drugs that are absorbed in the stomach or upper small intestine. By remaining in the gastric region, these systems facilitate sustained drug release and consistent therapeutic levels. An example is the use of floating formulations for metformin, ensuring prolonged glucose control in diabetic patients.

Swelling Systems

Swelling systems rely on the use of hydrophilic polymers that absorb gastric fluid and expand significantly in size. The increased bulk of the formulation prevents it from passing through the pyloric sphincter, ensuring prolonged retention in the stomach. Polymers such as carbopol, xanthan gum, and HPMC are commonly used in swelling systems.

When exposed to gastric fluids, these polymers form a gel-like structure that encapsulates the drug and allows for its controlled release. The swelling action not only ensures gastric retention but also provides a matrix for sustained drug diffusion. Drugs like diclofenac have been formulated using swelling systems to achieve prolonged action and minimize dosing frequency.

Mucoadhesive Systems

Mucoadhesive systems are designed to adhere to the gastric mucosa, ensuring the formulation remains in close contact with the stomach lining. These systems employ bioadhesive polymers such as chitosan, polyacrylic acid, and alginate, which interact with the mucin layer of the stomach. The interaction is facilitated by hydrogen bonding, electrostatic forces, or van der Waals interactions.

By adhering to the gastric mucosa, mucoadhesive systems provide localized drug delivery and enhance absorption for drugs targeting the stomach or upper small intestine. They are particularly effective for drugs used in treating Helicobacter pylori infections or gastric ulcers. For instance, amoxicillin formulations using mucoadhesive systems ensure that the antibiotic remains in the stomach for extended durations, improving its therapeutic efficacy.

7.2.3 Types of Gastroretentive Drug Delivery Systems (GRDDS)

Gastroretentive drug delivery systems (GRDDS) employ various strategies to prolong the retention of formulations in the stomach. These systems are categorized based on their mechanisms of action, with each type designed to address specific drug properties and therapeutic requirements. The primary types of GRDDS include floating systems, mucoadhesive systems, expandable systems, and high-density systems.

Floating Systems

Floating systems are designed to remain buoyant on the surface of gastric fluids. This is achieved using either effervescent or non-effervescent mechanisms. Effervescent systems incorporate gas-generating agents like sodium bicarbonate, which react with gastric acid to release carbon dioxide. The gas reduces the system's density, causing it to float. Non-effervescent systems, on the other hand, use polymers such as hydroxypropyl methylcellulose (HPMC) that swell and trap air, enabling buoyancy. These systems are ideal for drugs like metformin that require prolonged gastric retention for improved therapeutic outcomes.

Mucoadhesive Systems

Mucoadhesive systems adhere to the gastric mucosa, ensuring the drug remains in close contact with the stomach lining. Polymers like chitosan, carbopol, and polyvinyl alcohol are commonly used to create bioadhesive formulations. These polymers form hydrogen bonds or electrostatic interactions with mucin, enhancing adhesion. This type of GRDDS is particularly effective for delivering drugs that target gastric infections or ulcers, such as amoxicillin.

Expandable Systems

Expandable systems use polymers that swell upon contact with gastric fluids, increasing the size of the formulation. This prevents it from passing through the pyloric sphincter. Polymers like xanthan gum and carbopol are commonly employed in these systems. The swollen structure forms a gel-like matrix that allows for sustained drug release. Expandable systems are ideal for drugs requiring long gastric residence times, such as diclofenac for extended pain relief.

High-Density Systems

High-density systems are designed to settle at the bottom of the stomach. These formulations have a density greater than that of gastric fluid, ensuring their retention in the stomach for extended periods. Substances like barium sulfate and zinc oxide are used to increase the density of these systems. High-density systems are suitable for drugs that are absorbed in the lower parts of the stomach or proximal small intestine.

Each type of GRDDS provides unique advantages, and the choice of system depends on the drug's properties and therapeutic goals. By tailoring the system to specific needs, GRDDS offer a versatile approach to enhancing drug efficacy and patient compliance.

7.2.4 Formulation and Development of Gastroretentive Drug Delivery Systems (GRDDS)

The formulation and development of gastroretentive drug delivery systems (GRDDS) are focused on achieving prolonged gastric retention and controlled drug release. This requires careful selection of materials and design strategies to ensure that the drug remains in the stomach for an extended period, allowing for optimal absorption and therapeutic effects. Polymers, hydrogels, and gas-generating agents play key roles in the development of these systems, each contributing to the different mechanisms of gastroretention.

Role of Polymers in Controlling Drug Release and Gastroretention

Polymers are essential components in the design of GRDDS, as they control the drug release rate and determine the system's retention time in the stomach. The selection of an appropriate polymer depends on the desired release profile, stability, and the drug's physicochemical properties. For instance, hydrophilic polymers such as hydroxypropyl methylcellulose (HPMC) and carbopol are commonly used in swelling and mucoadhesive systems. These polymers swell upon contact with gastric fluids, forming a gel-like structure that retains the drug and prolongs its release.

In floating systems, polymers play a crucial role in achieving buoyancy. Non-effervescent floating systems rely on polymers that swell and trap air, reducing the density of the formulation. This ensures that the system floats on the surface of the gastric fluid. In effervescent systems, polymers help control the release of gas-generating agents, which create buoyancy by releasing carbon dioxide when they react with gastric acid.

Use of Gas-Forming Agents in Floating Systems

Gas-forming agents are integral to the development of floating GRDDS. These agents, such as sodium bicarbonate or citric acid, react with the gastric acid to release carbon dioxide, which increases the volume of the system and allows it to float. The release of gas from the system helps maintain buoyancy in the stomach, preventing it from passing into the intestines prematurely. This mechanism is particularly useful for drugs that need to stay in the stomach for prolonged periods, such as those with poor solubility in the intestine or those targeting the stomach directly, like anti-ulcer drugs.

Designing Expandable and Mucoadhesive Formulations

Expandable systems rely on the use of hydrophilic polymers that swell upon contact with stomach fluids, increasing the size of the system and preventing it from passing through the pyloric sphincter. Polymers like xanthan gum and polycarbophil are commonly used in these systems. The swelling action forms a gel that retains the drug and provides controlled release over time. These systems are designed to ensure that the drug stays in the stomach long enough for absorption to occur.

Mucoadhesive systems, on the other hand, use polymers that adhere to the gastric mucosa, ensuring that the formulation remains in close contact with the stomach lining. Polymers like chitosan, carbopol, and polyvinyl alcohol are used to create mucoadhesive formulations. These polymers interact with the mucin layer of the stomach, ensuring prolonged retention. Mucoadhesive systems are particularly useful for localized drug delivery in the stomach or upper gastrointestinal tract.

In conclusion, the formulation of GRDDS requires careful selection and combination of polymers, hydrogels, and gas-generating agents to create systems that offer sustained drug release and prolonged gastric retention. By employing these materials and strategies, GRDDS can significantly improve the bioavailability of drugs, particularly those with poor absorption or those targeting the stomach directly.

7.2.5 *Evaluation of Gastroretentive Drug Delivery Systems (GRDDS)*

The evaluation of gastroretentive drug delivery systems (GRDDS) involves both in vitro and in vivo testing to assess their effectiveness in terms of drug release, gastric retention, and overall performance. The evaluation process ensures that the GRDDS meets the necessary criteria for controlled drug release and prolonged gastric retention, which are critical for maximizing therapeutic efficacy.

In Vitro Tests

In vitro evaluation of GRDDS primarily focuses on determining the floating duration, swelling properties, and drug release profile. Floating duration is a key parameter for floating systems, as it measures how long the system remains buoyant in gastric fluids. This test is typically conducted using a simulated gastric fluid at the desired pH level. The system's ability to float for an extended period indicates its potential for prolonged gastric retention.

Swelling index is another important parameter, particularly for swelling-based systems. This test measures the extent to which the formulation swells when exposed to gastric fluids. A higher swelling index indicates that the system will remain in the stomach longer, providing controlled drug release over time.

The drug release profile is assessed by conducting dissolution tests. These tests involve placing the GRDDS in a medium that simulates gastric conditions, and then measuring the amount of drug released over a specific period. The release kinetics provide valuable insights into how the drug is being released from the system and whether it follows the desired release pattern, such as zero-order or controlled release.

In Vivo Tests

In vivo evaluation of GRDDS focuses on gastric retention time and the overall effectiveness of the system in the human body. Gastric retention time is critical for ensuring that the formulation remains in the stomach for the intended period. Imaging techniques such as radiographic imaging or magnetic resonance imaging (MRI) are often used to monitor the position of the GRDDS within the stomach over time. These imaging methods provide real-time data on the system's ability to stay in the stomach and its behavior during digestion.

In vivo testing also involves assessing the therapeutic efficacy of the GRDDS by measuring parameters such as plasma drug concentrations or clinical outcomes in animal models or human volunteers. The results help to determine whether the system delivers the drug effectively to the target site and maintains therapeutic levels over the required duration.

Overall, the evaluation of GRDDS is a multi-faceted process that combines in vitro testing for release and retention properties with in vivo testing to assess gastric retention time and therapeutic effectiveness. These evaluations are essential to ensure the system functions as intended, providing prolonged and controlled drug release for improved therapeutic outcomes.

7.2.6 Applications of Gastroretentive Drug Delivery Systems (GRDDS)

Gastroretentive drug delivery systems (GRDDS) offer significant advantages in the management of various therapeutic conditions by ensuring that drugs remain in the stomach for extended periods. This extended gastric retention enhances drug absorption, especially for drugs that are poorly absorbed in the small intestine or those requiring localized action in the stomach. GRDDS are particularly valuable for drugs with a narrow absorption window, poor solubility in alkaline pH, and those targeting gastric conditions such as ulcers or infections.

Examples of GRDDS Applications

One prominent example of GRDDS in use is the floating tablet system designed for metformin, a drug used in the management of type 2 diabetes. Metformin is best absorbed in the stomach, but its absorption decreases significantly as it moves into the alkaline environment of the small intestine. By formulating metformin as a floating tablet, the drug remains in the stomach longer, where the environment is more conducive to its absorption. The floating system ensures that metformin stays in the stomach, allowing for more consistent blood glucose control with reduced dosing frequency.

Another important application is the treatment of **Helicobacter pylori** infections, which are commonly associated with gastric ulcers. Antibiotics such as amoxicillin, used to eradicate H. pylori, can be more effective when delivered directly to the stomach. GRDDS, particularly mucoadhesive or floating systems, ensure that the drug remains in contact with the gastric mucosa for longer periods, enhancing its effectiveness in treating infections located within the stomach. These systems also help in reducing systemic side effects by targeting the drug precisely where it is needed.

Drugs with Poor Solubility in Alkaline pH

GRDDS are especially beneficial for drugs that exhibit poor solubility in the alkaline environment of the small intestine but are more soluble in the acidic conditions of the stomach. Many drugs, such as certain weak acids and some antibiotics, experience reduced bioavailability when they pass through the alkaline pH of the intestines. By employing GRDDS, these drugs can be retained in the stomach for longer periods, ensuring that they dissolve and are absorbed effectively in the stomach's acidic environment.

For instance, **ketoconazole**, an antifungal medication, has limited solubility in higher pH environments, making it a suitable candidate for formulation in a GRDDS. By keeping ketoconazole in the stomach for an extended period, GRDDS ensure that the drug is absorbed optimally before it moves into the small intestine, where absorption may otherwise be compromised.

7.3 Comparative Analysis of Transdermal Drug Delivery Systems (TDDS) and Gastroretentive Drug Delivery Systems (GRDDS)

Transdermal drug delivery systems (TDDS) and gastroretentive drug delivery systems (GRDDS) are both innovative approaches to controlled drug release, yet they operate through distinct mechanisms and cater to different therapeutic needs. Both systems aim to provide sustained and controlled drug release, enhancing bioavailability and improving patient compliance. However, they differ in their route of delivery, applications, and the challenges associated with their formulation and use. Understanding these differences is crucial for selecting the appropriate system for specific therapeutic needs.

Similarities and Differences in Design

Both TDDS and GRDDS are designed to provide controlled and sustained drug release, minimizing the fluctuations in plasma drug levels associated with conventional dosage forms. However, the mechanisms of action are fundamentally different. TDDS deliver drugs through the skin, bypassing the first-pass metabolism in the liver. This system typically includes a drug reservoir, a rate-controlling membrane, and an adhesive backing layer. In contrast, GRDDS are designed to remain in the stomach for extended periods, ensuring that drugs are released and absorbed in the optimal environment, especially for drugs with a narrow absorption window.

The design of TDDS focuses on the skin's permeability, and formulations often include permeation enhancers to aid drug absorption. In contrast, GRDDS rely on mechanisms such as buoyancy (floating systems), swelling, or mucoadhesion to ensure retention in the stomach. The key difference lies in the target site: TDDS primarily aim for systemic drug delivery, whereas

GRDDS are designed for either systemic delivery (via prolonged gastric retention) or local gastric action.

Applications

The applications of TDDS and GRDDS differ according to the drug's properties and the required therapeutic effect. TDDS are ideal for drugs that need to be delivered continuously into the bloodstream, such as nicotine patches for smoking cessation, hormone replacement therapy (estradiol), and pain management (fentanyl). These systems are particularly useful for drugs that require a steady, controlled release over a prolonged period.

In contrast, GRDDS are most useful for drugs that are primarily absorbed in the stomach or upper small intestine, or those requiring local gastric action. For instance, GRDDS are employed in the delivery of drugs like metformin (for diabetes) and antibiotics for H. pylori treatment, where retention in the stomach maximizes absorption or efficacy. Drugs that are poorly soluble in the alkaline environment of the small intestine, like ketoconazole, also benefit from GRDDS as they can remain in the stomach longer, where they dissolve more efficiently.

Challenges

Despite their advantages, both systems present challenges. One of the major challenges for TDDS is skin irritation or sensitivity to adhesives, which can limit the wear time of the patch. Additionally, drug absorption through the skin is limited by the skin's permeability, especially for larger or hydrophilic molecules. Ensuring effective permeation enhancers without compromising patient comfort is a critical consideration in the formulation of TDDS.

For GRDDS, challenges include variability in gastric emptying times due to individual patient factors such as age, diet, and gastrointestinal health. Moreover, the formulation of GRDDS must address issues related to the drug's solubility, stability, and release kinetics in the stomach. There is also the challenge of ensuring that the drug stays in the stomach long enough for absorption while avoiding premature release or expulsion.

Selection Criteria for Specific Therapeutic Needs

The selection of either TDDS or GRDDS largely depends on the drug's properties and the therapeutic needs. TDDS are suitable for drugs that require a continuous release into the bloodstream, particularly for chronic conditions requiring consistent dosing. These systems are often selected for their non-invasive nature and ease of use. They are best suited for lipophilic drugs, or those that are effective when released into the systemic circulation over time.

GRDDS, on the other hand, are better suited for drugs that are absorbed in the stomach or upper small intestine or those that need to act locally within the stomach. Drugs that have a narrow absorption window or are sensitive to pH changes benefit the most from GRDDS. These systems are also ideal for drugs that require prolonged gastric residence time or are intended for local action, such as treating gastric ulcers or infections.

CHAPTER VIII

Nasal and Pulmonary Drug Delivery Systems

8.1 Introduction to Nasal and Pulmonary Drug Delivery Systems

8.1.1 Definition and Overview

Nasal and pulmonary drug delivery systems refer to methods that utilize the nasal cavity and the lungs as routes for the administration of therapeutic agents. These systems are non-invasive and offer several advantages in terms of convenience, efficacy, and speed of onset, particularly for drugs that need to be rapidly absorbed into the bloodstream or targeted directly to the respiratory system.

The nasal route involves the administration of drugs through the nasal mucosa, where they are absorbed into the bloodstream. This route can be used for both systemic and localized effects, making it versatile. The pulmonary route, on the other hand, delivers drugs directly to the lungs, where they can act locally (such as in the case of inhaled bronchodilators for asthma) or be absorbed systemically. The main advantage of these routes is their ability to bypass the gastrointestinal tract, thus avoiding the first-pass metabolism in the liver.

When compared to other delivery routes like oral or injectable administration, both nasal and pulmonary drug delivery systems offer certain benefits. These include rapid onset of action due to the large surface area and rich blood supply in these areas. For instance, the nasal cavity provides a direct pathway to the bloodstream, which can lead to faster therapeutic effects. Pulmonary delivery, particularly via inhalation, can deliver drugs efficiently to the lungs, offering targeted treatment for respiratory diseases and conditions.

In addition to systemic delivery, both nasal and pulmonary routes are increasingly being explored for localized treatments, especially for conditions affecting the respiratory system, such as chronic obstructive pulmonary disease (COPD), asthma, and cystic fibrosis. The non-invasive nature of these systems also makes them more acceptable to patients compared to injections, improving patient compliance.

Despite these advantages, there are challenges associated with nasal and pulmonary drug delivery systems, such as limited drug absorption due to the physiological barriers in the nasal and lung tissues. Furthermore, the formulation of drugs for these routes requires careful consideration of factors such as particle size, stability, and drug solubility. However, advancements in technology are continually improving the effectiveness and efficiency of nasal and pulmonary drug delivery systems.

8.1.2 Importance in Modern Drug Delivery

Nasal and pulmonary drug delivery systems have gained considerable attention in modern drug delivery due to their unique advantages, including rapid onset of action, the ability to bypass first-pass metabolism, and targeted delivery. These benefits make them highly effective, particularly in scenarios where quick therapeutic effects are necessary, or when targeted treatment is desired.

One of the primary advantages of nasal and pulmonary drug delivery systems is the rapid onset of action. The nasal cavity and the lungs provide large surface areas with rich blood supply, which allows for faster absorption of drugs into the bloodstream. This rapid absorption is particularly beneficial in situations where fast therapeutic effects are crucial. For instance, in the case of emergency treatments for conditions like asthma or chronic obstructive pulmonary disease (COPD), drugs delivered via the nasal or pulmonary route can act swiftly to relieve symptoms and provide immediate relief.

Another significant benefit of these systems is their ability to bypass first-pass metabolism, a phenomenon where drugs administered orally are metabolized in the liver before reaching the systemic circulation. By avoiding this metabolic process, drugs delivered via the nasal or pulmonary routes can achieve higher bioavailability. This means that a larger amount of the drug reaches the bloodstream in its active form, enhancing its therapeutic effect. For example, drugs like fentanyl and other analgesics delivered through the nasal route provide faster pain relief with lower doses compared to oral formulations.

The ability of nasal and pulmonary drug delivery systems to achieve targeted delivery further enhances their effectiveness. For instance, inhalation therapy can directly target the lungs, making it the ideal choice for treating respiratory conditions such as asthma, COPD, or pulmonary infections. Similarly, nasal delivery allows for targeted drug delivery to the nasal mucosa and sinuses, where local treatments for conditions like rhinitis or sinusitis can be administered effectively.

These drug delivery systems are also important in the management of chronic diseases. For example, inhalers for asthma or COPD patients allow for the sustained release of bronchodilators or corticosteroids, offering long-term symptom control with minimal side effects. Nasal sprays for hormone replacement therapy, such as for estrogen or testosterone, also provide an alternative to oral tablets, enhancing patient compliance and avoiding the gastrointestinal side effects of oral drugs.

Nasal and pulmonary routes have also been explored for their potential in vaccination. In recent years, the nasal route has been considered for the delivery of vaccines, such as the flu vaccine. This non-invasive method not only makes vaccinations more accessible but can also promote a localized immune response in the mucosal areas, offering additional protection against respiratory infections.

8.2.1 Nasal System

The nasal cavity plays a crucial role in drug delivery systems that utilize the nasal route for administering therapeutics. The structure of the nasal cavity is uniquely designed to aid in the absorption of drugs while also protecting the body from harmful substances. The nasal cavity is lined with mucosa, which consists of various layers of epithelial cells, including ciliated cells that help in the movement of mucus. The mucosa is highly vascularized, allowing for rapid drug absorption into the bloodstream. Additionally, the olfactory region, located at the top of the nasal cavity, is also of particular interest for drug delivery due to its proximity to the brain, which allows for drugs to bypass the blood-brain barrier and act directly on central nervous system targets.

Several factors affect the efficiency of drug delivery through the nasal system. One of the most significant factors is mucociliary clearance, which is the body's natural defense mechanism for expelling foreign particles and pathogens. The ciliated cells in the nasal epithelium move mucus in a coordinated manner, which can clear drugs from the nasal cavity before they are absorbed. Therefore, drug formulations must be designed to overcome this barrier, often by increasing residence time in the nasal cavity.

Enzymatic activity in the nasal mucosa also plays a role in drug absorption. Certain enzymes in the nasal cavity may degrade drugs, reducing their efficacy before they can be absorbed. Formulations for nasal drug delivery must be designed to protect the drug from enzymatic breakdown, which can be achieved by using enzyme inhibitors or encapsulating the drug in a protective coating.

The pH of the nasal cavity is another important factor in drug delivery. The nasal mucosa is naturally acidic, and the pH can influence the solubility and ionization of drugs, affecting their permeability across the mucosal barrier. For instance, drugs that are more soluble in acidic conditions may be absorbed more efficiently, while drugs that require a specific pH for absorption may need to be formulated with buffers or other agents to adjust the pH of the nasal formulation.

8.2.2 Pulmonary System

The pulmonary system plays a vital role in respiratory functions, and its anatomy is highly adapted for drug delivery via the lungs. The system consists of the bronchi, bronchioles, and alveoli, with each part playing a distinct role in air conduction and gas exchange. The bronchi branch out from the trachea and divide into smaller bronchioles that eventually lead to the alveoli, the tiny air sacs where gas exchange occurs. The alveoli are lined with a thin layer of epithelial cells, known as the alveolar epithelium, which forms the blood-gas barrier. This barrier allows for efficient oxygen exchange while also being a crucial site for drug absorption when drug delivery systems target the lungs.

The structure of the pulmonary system, particularly the large surface area provided by the alveoli, is essential for effective drug absorption. The alveolar membrane has an enormous surface area, approximately the size of a tennis court, which facilitates the rapid exchange of gases like oxygen and carbon dioxide between the lungs and the bloodstream. This vast surface area is also highly advantageous for drug absorption. Drugs delivered via the pulmonary route can diffuse across the alveolar epithelium into the bloodstream and be rapidly absorbed.

Mechanisms of drug absorption in the pulmonary system involve diffusion through the alveolar epithelium and the blood-gas exchange process. Drugs, especially those that are small and lipophilic, can easily diffuse across the respiratory membrane, which is composed of the alveolar epithelium, the basement membrane, and the capillary endothelium. Once across the respiratory membrane, the drug enters the bloodstream and is transported throughout the body, similar to how gases are exchanged in the lungs.

The efficiency of drug absorption in the lungs depends on several factors, including the drug's physicochemical properties (such as molecular size and solubility), the particle size of the inhaled drug formulation, and the condition of the lung tissue. The particle size is critical as it determines where the drug will deposit within the respiratory tract. Small particles tend to reach the deeper parts of the lungs (the alveoli), while larger particles may be deposited in the upper respiratory tract, such as the trachea and bronchi.

8.3 Mechanisms of Drug Absorption in Nasal and Pulmonary Delivery

The nasal and pulmonary routes of drug delivery involve distinct but related mechanisms for drug absorption. These routes are increasingly being used for both systemic and localized drug delivery due to their advantages in avoiding first-pass metabolism and providing rapid onset of action. The primary mechanism for drug absorption in both nasal and pulmonary delivery is diffusion, but other factors like active transport, particle size, and drug formulation also play significant roles in determining how effectively a drug is absorbed.

In both the nasal and pulmonary systems, the drug molecules move from a higher concentration in the formulation to a lower concentration in the bloodstream or target tissues. This movement, called passive diffusion, occurs across the epithelial layers lining the nasal cavity or the lungs. In the case of nasal delivery, the drug is absorbed across the nasal mucosa, while in pulmonary delivery, it crosses the alveolar epithelium. The efficiency of this process is influenced by several factors, including the drug's solubility, molecular size, and the permeability of the epithelial layers.

For systemic absorption through the nasal route, drugs are absorbed via the capillaries present in the nasal mucosa, which are richly vascularized. Once absorbed, the drugs enter the systemic circulation, allowing for rapid onset of therapeutic effects. However, the nasal route also provides an opportunity for local treatment, such as for nasal congestion or sinus infections, where the drug acts directly on the mucosal tissues. In these cases, absorption occurs at the site of application, delivering targeted effects with minimal systemic exposure.

Similarly, for pulmonary drug delivery, absorption occurs in the alveoli, where the drug particles diffuse across the alveolar membrane and into the bloodstream. The alveolar membrane is highly permeable, facilitating the rapid diffusion of small, lipophilic drugs. However, larger or hydrophilic drugs may require additional strategies, such as nanoparticle formulations or other enhancement techniques, to increase their absorption. Pulmonary drug delivery is particularly beneficial for local treatment of respiratory conditions, such as asthma or chronic obstructive pulmonary disease (COPD), where drugs act directly on the lung tissue, or for systemic treatment of conditions that require rapid drug absorption.

In addition to diffusion, active transport mechanisms also play a role in drug absorption in both nasal and pulmonary routes. Active transport involves the movement of drugs across cell membranes against their concentration gradient, using specific transport proteins. This mechanism is particularly important for the absorption of larger molecules or those that are not easily absorbed by passive diffusion alone. Active transport can help enhance the bioavailability of drugs that would otherwise be poorly absorbed through passive diffusion.

Several factors influence drug absorption in both nasal and pulmonary drug delivery systems. Particle size is one of the most critical factors; smaller particles are more likely to be absorbed through the mucosal barriers and reach the systemic circulation or target tissues more efficiently. For nasal delivery, optimal particle sizes typically range between 5–10 microns to ensure effective deposition in the nasal cavity and efficient absorption through the mucosal lining. In pulmonary drug delivery, particles in the size range of 1–5 microns are ideal for deep lung penetration and alveolar absorption.

Solubility is another crucial factor affecting drug absorption. Drugs that are highly soluble in the aqueous environment of the nasal cavity or pulmonary system are absorbed more readily. However, poorly soluble drugs may require formulation strategies to enhance solubility, such as the use of solubilizing agents or carriers like cyclodextrins. The formulation type also plays a role in determining the release and absorption of the drug. For example, liquid formulations such as nasal sprays or inhalable aerosols provide rapid absorption, while solid formulations like powders or capsules may require more time to dissolve and release the drug.

8.4 Formulation Considerations

8.4.1 Nasal Drug Delivery Systems

Nasal drug delivery systems are increasingly used for both local and systemic therapies due to their ability to provide rapid onset of action and bypass the first-pass metabolism that occurs with oral administration. Various types of nasal formulations are available, including sprays, drops, gels, and powders. Each of these formulations has its own unique advantages, depending on the therapeutic goals, the nature of the drug, and the desired release profile.

Spray formulations are among the most common nasal delivery systems. They allow for even distribution of the drug across the nasal mucosa, ensuring optimal absorption. Nasal sprays are particularly useful for drugs that need to be rapidly absorbed into the bloodstream. The spray droplets are small enough to be inhaled into the nasal cavity, where they are deposited on the mucosal lining. The main advantage of nasal sprays is their ease of use, quick administration, and ability to provide controlled doses.

Nasal drops, another common formulation, are typically used for local treatment in the nasal cavity, such as in the case of nasal congestion or sinus infections. While nasal drops provide effective deposition in the nasal cavity, they may not be as well suited for systemic drug delivery compared to sprays. However, they offer a more direct method of drug delivery to the mucosal surfaces, making them suitable for localized treatments.

Gels are another type of nasal formulation that offers prolonged retention time on the mucosal surfaces. They are often used when extended drug release or better local action is desired. The gel-like consistency allows for sustained contact with the nasal lining, which can enhance drug absorption and improve therapeutic efficacy. In addition, gels can be formulated with mucoadhesive agents to improve their retention and stability in the nasal cavity.

Powders, although less common than sprays or drops, are also used in nasal drug delivery. They are generally administered using a dry powder inhaler, which delivers the drug in a fine particulate form. Powders can provide higher drug concentrations, and their use in systemic therapies, such as insulin or other hormones, is an area of growing interest. The main advantage of powders is that they are not affected by the solubility and dissolution challenges faced by liquid formulations, making them useful for drugs that have low solubility.

In all of these nasal drug delivery formulations, mucoadhesive agents and permeation enhancers play an important role in improving the efficiency of drug absorption. Mucoadhesive agents, such as chitosan or carbopol, enhance the formulation's ability to adhere to the mucosal surfaces, increasing the residence time of the drug in the nasal cavity. This helps to maintain therapeutic drug levels for longer periods and improves the overall bioavailability of the drug. On the other hand, permeation enhancers, like ethanol or dimethyl sulfoxide (DMSO), help increase the permeability of the nasal mucosa, allowing the drug to cross the mucosal barrier more effectively. These enhancers can overcome the natural barriers that limit the absorption of larger or less permeable drugs.

8.4.2 Pulmonary Drug Delivery Systems

Pulmonary drug delivery systems are used to deliver drugs directly to the lungs for both local and systemic effects. The lungs offer a large surface area and highly vascularized tissue, which makes them ideal for rapid drug absorption. Pulmonary systems include aerosols, nebulizers, dry powder inhalers (DPIs), and metered-dose inhalers (MDIs), each with its unique formulation requirements and applications.

One of the primary formulation requirements for pulmonary systems is particle size. The drug particles must be small enough to reach the deep lung tissues for effective absorption. Ideally, the particle size for pulmonary drug delivery should be between 1 and 5 microns. Particles larger than this are likely to be deposited in the upper respiratory tract, while smaller particles may be exhaled without reaching the lung tissues. Therefore, controlling the particle size is crucial for ensuring that the drug is deposited in the optimal region of the lungs.

Another important factor for pulmonary formulations is stability. The formulation should be stable under various environmental conditions, including temperature and humidity. Instability can lead to changes in the drug's physical properties, which can affect its performance. For example, instability could result in the clumping of particles or the loss of drug efficacy. As such, it is essential to use stabilizing agents, such as surfactants or preservatives, in the formulation to maintain its integrity and ensure consistent performance.

Aerosolization is another critical consideration for pulmonary systems. The drug formulation needs to be efficiently aerosolized to create a fine mist or powder that can be easily inhaled into the lungs. In liquid formulations, this is typically achieved through the use of nebulizers or MDIs, which release the drug in aerosol form. For dry powder formulations, DPIs are used to deliver the drug as a fine powder, which is then inhaled. The formulation must be designed to ensure efficient aerosolization without compromising the stability or size of the drug particles.

Propellants and excipients are also crucial components of inhalation formulations. In MDIs, propellants such as hydrofluoroalkanes (HFAs) are used to expel the drug from the inhaler. These propellants must be non-toxic, efficient in releasing the drug, and compatible with the drug substance. In contrast, DPIs do not require propellants but rely on the patient's inhalation to generate airflow that disperses the powder. The excipients in DPIs often include lactose or other carrier agents that help in the uniform distribution of the drug powder and improve the inhaler's handling properties.

For nebulizers, which are typically used in clinical settings, the formulation must be liquid-based, and the nebulizer should be able to efficiently convert the liquid into a fine mist. Nebulizers are commonly used for drugs like bronchodilators and corticosteroids in the treatment of respiratory conditions such as asthma and chronic obstructive pulmonary disease (COPD). In addition to stability and aerosolization, the formulation should also be free of particulate matter that could clog the nebulizer and affect the drug's delivery.

8.5 Devices for Nasal and Pulmonary Drug Delivery

8.5.1 Nasal Devices

Nasal drug delivery systems rely on various devices designed to deliver the drug effectively to the nasal cavity. These devices are used to ensure accurate dosing, enhance drug absorption, and provide convenience for patients. The choice of device depends on the type of drug being delivered and the specific needs of the patient. Commonly used nasal devices include spray pumps, nebulizers, and atomizers, each having its own advantages and applications.

Spray pumps are one of the most widely used devices for nasal drug delivery. These pumps work by atomizing the drug solution, turning it into fine droplets that can be easily absorbed through the nasal mucosa. Nasal spray pumps are often used for drugs that require rapid systemic absorption, such as decongestants, antihistamines, and nasal vaccines. They are also commonly used for delivering corticosteroids and other treatments for conditions like allergic rhinitis. One of the key benefits of spray pumps is their ability to provide a precise and consistent dose of medication with each use, ensuring reliable delivery to the nasal cavity. Furthermore, the drug is quickly absorbed into the bloodstream, bypassing the first-pass metabolism that occurs with oral drugs.

Nebulizers are another type of nasal device, although they are typically more commonly used for pulmonary drug delivery. However, nasal nebulizers are designed specifically for use in the nasal cavity, often to treat conditions such as chronic rhinosinusitis. These devices work by converting a liquid drug formulation into a fine mist that can be inhaled or deposited directly into the nasal passages. Unlike nasal spray pumps, nebulizers are usually used for drugs that require a more extended contact time with the nasal mucosa or for higher doses. Nebulizers are often preferred in clinical settings or for patients who may have difficulty using other devices, such as those with respiratory conditions or children. The mist produced by a nebulizer allows for more uniform distribution and is especially beneficial for patients requiring frequent or high doses.

Atomizers are another important class of devices used for nasal drug delivery. Similar to spray pumps, atomizers use a mechanical process to convert a liquid drug into a fine mist. However, atomizers typically create finer droplets compared to spray pumps. This characteristic makes them ideal for drugs that need to be distributed more evenly within the nasal cavity or for formulations that require deeper penetration into the nasal mucosa. Atomizers are commonly used for delivering vaccines, antibiotics, and other treatments where the drug needs to be uniformly distributed to maximize efficacy. The design of atomizers ensures that the drug is released in a consistent spray pattern, making them useful for delivering precise doses.

The selection of a nasal device depends on several factors, including the type of drug, the patient's condition, and the therapeutic goal. For example, a spray pump may be more appropriate for quick, localized relief, while a nebulizer may be necessary for more prolonged or higher-dose treatments. Additionally, the ease of use and comfort of the device are important considerations, especially for patients who need frequent treatments, such as those with chronic conditions. Devices that are easy to operate, portable, and capable of providing precise dosages are preferred to ensure adherence to the prescribed treatment.

8.5.2 Pulmonary Devices

Pulmonary drug delivery systems are designed to deliver medications directly to the lungs, offering both local and systemic therapeutic effects. The main devices used for pulmonary drug delivery are nebulizers, metered-dose inhalers (MDIs), and dry powder inhalers (DPIs). Each of these devices works by different mechanisms and is suited to specific drug types and patient needs. Understanding the mechanisms of each device and their respective advantages and limitations is essential for effective drug administration.

Nebulizers are devices that convert liquid medications into a fine mist or aerosol, which can then be inhaled directly into the lungs. Nebulizers are commonly used in clinical settings for patients with respiratory conditions like asthma, chronic obstructive pulmonary disease (COPD), and cystic fibrosis. These devices are particularly beneficial for patients who have difficulty using other inhalation devices, such as children or elderly patients. The main advantage of nebulizers is their ability to deliver large doses of medication without the need for forceful inhalation, making them suitable for patients with compromised lung function. However, nebulizers can be bulky, require power sources, and typically take longer to administer a dose compared to other devices, which may reduce patient compliance in some cases. Additionally, nebulizers require cleaning and maintenance to ensure their proper functioning and to avoid contamination.

Metered-Dose Inhalers (MDIs) are pressurized canisters that deliver a pre-measured dose of medication in the form of an aerosol. MDIs are compact, easy to use, and widely used for the treatment of asthma and COPD. They are designed to deliver a consistent and precise dose with each actuation. The drug is expelled from the inhaler as a fine mist, which can be inhaled into the lungs. The primary advantage of MDIs is their portability and convenience, allowing patients to administer medication anywhere and at any time. However, using an MDI effectively requires good coordination between pressing the canister and inhaling the medication. This may be challenging for some patients, such as young children or those with manual dexterity issues. Inhalation technique plays a critical role in ensuring proper drug deposition in the lungs. MDIs also use propellants, such as hydrofluoroalkanes (HFAs), which are environmentally friendly alternatives to older chlorofluorocarbon (CFC)-based propellants.

Dry Powder Inhalers (DPIs) are devices that deliver medication in a dry powder form, which is inhaled into the lungs by the patient's own breath. DPIs are often used for chronic respiratory conditions, such as asthma and COPD. The main advantage of DPIs is that they do not require a propellant, unlike MDIs. Instead, the patient's inhalation powers the device, making the drug release dependent on the inhalation strength. This feature makes DPIs more environmentally friendly and eliminates the need for a propellant. DPIs also provide a quick and easy method of drug administration. However, they require sufficient inhalation effort from the patient. If the patient does not inhale deeply enough, the drug may not reach the lungs effectively. Additionally, the drug must be in a very fine powder form to ensure it can reach the deep lungs, which requires careful formulation of the drug powder. DPIs are also generally more sensitive to humidity, which can affect the quality of the powder and the drug's delivery.

8.6 Applications of Nasal and Pulmonary Drug Delivery

8.6.1 Nasal Drug Delivery Applications

Nasal drug delivery has gained significant attention due to its ability to provide rapid and effective drug absorption, bypassing the first-pass metabolism typically associated with oral drug administration. The nasal cavity, with its extensive blood supply and large surface area, is an ideal site for drug absorption. Nasal drug delivery systems are used in a variety of therapeutic areas, offering both systemic and localized effects.

One prominent application of nasal drug delivery is in **vaccines**. Nasal sprays have become increasingly popular for delivering flu vaccines. Unlike traditional injections, nasal vaccines offer a non-invasive and patient-friendly alternative. They are particularly beneficial for individuals who have a fear of needles or for those who need repeated doses. Nasal vaccines can also stimulate both local and systemic immune responses, enhancing overall immunity. This method of vaccine delivery is not only effective but also convenient, making it an appealing option for mass vaccination programs, especially in situations requiring rapid deployment.

In addition to vaccines, **migraine treatment** has benefited from the advancements in nasal drug delivery. Drugs like **sumatriptan**, commonly used for treating acute migraines, can be delivered nasally to provide rapid relief. Nasal delivery of sumatriptan ensures that the drug is absorbed quickly into the bloodstream, leading to faster onset of action compared to oral administration. This is especially important in migraine treatment, where the rapid onset of relief is critical for preventing the progression of symptoms. Nasal sprays for migraines allow for more consistent and reliable drug absorption, bypassing gastrointestinal issues that might delay oral drug absorption.

Another key area for nasal drug delivery is **hormone replacement therapy (HRT)**. Nasal formulations of hormones, such as **estradiol**, are used to treat conditions like menopause or estrogen deficiency. These nasal sprays provide a convenient alternative to oral HRT, offering similar therapeutic effects while avoiding potential gastrointestinal side effects. Nasal delivery of hormones also allows for a more direct route of absorption, providing faster relief compared to other methods.

8.6.2 Pulmonary Drug Delivery Applications

Pulmonary drug delivery systems offer an effective way to treat respiratory diseases by directly targeting the lungs. The lungs provide a large surface area for absorption and are richly vascularized, allowing for quick systemic absorption or localized treatment. Pulmonary drug delivery is commonly used for treating conditions such as asthma, chronic obstructive pulmonary disease (COPD), and pulmonary hypertension. These systems are particularly beneficial for patients requiring rapid relief or long-term management of chronic respiratory conditions.

One of the most common applications of pulmonary drug delivery is in the treatment of **asthma**. Asthma is a chronic condition characterized by inflammation and constriction of the airways, leading to difficulty breathing. **Bronchodilators**, such as beta-agonists and anticholinergic drugs, are frequently delivered via inhalers to provide quick relief from bronchoconstriction. Pulmonary drug delivery allows for fast action, with the medication directly reaching the airways, where it is needed most. Devices like metered-dose inhalers (MDIs) and dry powder inhalers (DPIs) are commonly used to deliver these bronchodilators. The advantage of inhaled bronchodilators is their ability to act rapidly, offering relief within minutes, and allowing for targeted treatment with minimal systemic side effects.

In addition to bronchodilators, **COPD**, another chronic respiratory disease, benefits from pulmonary drug delivery. COPD is characterized by chronic inflammation and progressive airflow limitation. Inhaled corticosteroids and bronchodilators are the mainstay of treatment for COPD. By delivering drugs directly to the lungs, these medications can reduce inflammation and open the airways, improving breathing and quality of life. Inhalers and nebulizers are commonly used for administering COPD medications, ensuring that drugs are deposited directly in the lungs for maximum therapeutic effect.

Another important application of pulmonary drug delivery is in the management of **pulmonary hypertension**, a condition characterized by high blood pressure in the arteries of the lungs. **Prostacyclin analogs**, such as iloprost and epoprostenol, are used to relax the pulmonary blood vessels, reducing blood pressure and improving heart function. These prostacyclin analogs are often delivered via nebulizers or inhalers, allowing for rapid drug delivery directly to the lungs. Inhaled prostacyclin analogs offer advantages over intravenous or oral formulations by minimizing systemic side effects and providing more targeted treatment.

8.7 Advantages and Limitations

8.7.1 Advantages of Nasal and Pulmonary Drug Delivery

Nasal and pulmonary drug delivery systems offer several significant advantages, making them increasingly popular in modern therapeutic strategies. One of the key benefits of these systems is their **rapid absorption**. Both the nasal and pulmonary routes provide a large surface area for drug absorption, with rich vascularization that allows for quick entry into the bloodstream. This rapid absorption makes these systems ideal for drugs that require fast action, such as those used in the treatment of acute conditions like asthma attacks or pain management. By bypassing the gastrointestinal tract, these systems help drugs enter the systemic circulation much faster compared to oral medications.

Another major advantage is the ability of nasal and pulmonary drug delivery systems to **bypass first-pass metabolism**. When drugs are administered orally, they first pass through the liver, where they are metabolized before entering the bloodstream. This process can reduce the bioavailability of certain drugs. However, by delivering drugs through the nasal or pulmonary routes, the medication is absorbed directly into the bloodstream, bypassing the liver and avoiding first-pass metabolism. This leads to higher bioavailability and more effective drug action, particularly for drugs that are poorly absorbed or extensively metabolized when taken orally.

These drug delivery systems also offer the convenience of **non-invasive administration**. Patients can administer the drug themselves without the need for injections or other invasive procedures. This is particularly beneficial for individuals who may have a fear of needles or who require frequent medication. Non-invasive systems like nasal sprays and inhalers also improve **patient compliance**. Because these systems are easy to use and often require less frequent dosing compared to oral or injectable medications, patients are more likely to adhere to their prescribed treatment regimens. This ease of use can significantly improve treatment outcomes, especially in chronic conditions such as asthma or COPD, where ongoing management is necessary.

Furthermore, nasal and pulmonary drug delivery systems are effective for **localized treatment**. For conditions affecting the respiratory system, such as asthma, allergies, and chronic bronchitis, these systems allow drugs to be delivered directly to the site of action in the lungs or nasal passages. This localized drug delivery is highly effective in reducing symptoms without affecting other areas of the body. For example, corticosteroids delivered via inhalers or nasal sprays directly target the lungs or nasal mucosa, providing fast relief from inflammation without causing systemic side effects.

8.7.2 Limitations of Nasal and Pulmonary Drug Delivery

While nasal and pulmonary drug delivery systems offer several advantages, they also come with certain limitations that can affect their overall effectiveness and patient compliance. One of the primary challenges with these delivery systems is **nasal irritation**. The nasal mucosa can become irritated due to the repeated administration of drugs, particularly when nasal sprays or inhalers are used frequently. This irritation can lead to discomfort, dryness, or even inflammation in the nasal passages, which may discourage patients from continuing treatment. In some cases, prolonged use of nasal formulations can result in more severe side effects, such as nasal congestion or damage to the mucosal lining.

Another significant limitation is the **variability in lung deposition**. Pulmonary drug delivery relies heavily on the deposition of drug particles in the lungs. However, the efficiency of this deposition can vary based on factors such as the patient's inhalation technique, lung function, and the size of the drug particles. For example, if a patient does not inhale deeply or correctly when using an inhaler, the drug may not reach the deep lung tissues where it is needed most. Furthermore, certain drugs require specific particle sizes to ensure proper deposition in the lungs, and achieving the right size during formulation can be challenging. As a result, the effectiveness of pulmonary drug delivery can vary from patient to patient, depending on how well they can use the device and how their lungs respond.

Device dependence is another limitation of nasal and pulmonary drug delivery systems. These systems often rely on devices such as metered-dose inhalers (MDIs), dry powder inhalers (DPIs), or nebulizers, which require proper technique to ensure effective drug delivery. Inhalers, for example, demand coordination between pressing the canister and inhaling the drug, which may be difficult for some patients, especially the elderly or young children. Improper use of these devices can lead to inadequate drug delivery and reduced therapeutic outcomes. Additionally, not all patients may be able to afford or have access to the necessary devices, particularly those living in low-resource settings, which can further limit the widespread use of these delivery systems.

8.8 Evaluation of Nasal and Pulmonary Drug Delivery Systems

8.8.1 Nasal Delivery Evaluation

Evaluating the performance of nasal drug delivery systems is essential to ensure their efficacy, safety, and optimal performance. Several methods are used to assess the drug release, permeation, and bioavailability of drugs administered through the nasal route. These evaluations help determine the effectiveness of the formulation and device, as well as how well the drug can reach its intended site of action.

One key method of evaluating nasal drug delivery systems is **in vitro diffusion testing**. This involves simulating the conditions in the nasal cavity to measure how the drug diffuses across the nasal mucosa. These studies are typically carried out using a membrane that mimics the nasal barrier. Drug release rates can be assessed by monitoring how quickly the drug crosses the membrane over a set period. This test helps in determining whether the formulation releases the drug at the desired rate, which is crucial for controlled or sustained-release nasal systems.

Another important consideration is **mucociliary clearance**, which refers to the natural process by which mucus and particles are removed from the nasal passages. Mucociliary clearance plays a crucial role in nasal drug delivery as it can influence the residence time of the drug in the nasal cavity. If a drug formulation is cleared too quickly, it may not have sufficient time to be absorbed into the bloodstream. To evaluate this, in vivo studies are often conducted to measure the rate of clearance of the drug from the nasal cavity. Additionally, formulations that enhance the drug's ability to remain in the nasal cavity, such as those with mucoadhesive properties, are often tested for their ability to prolong retention time and improve absorption.

Bioavailability is another important aspect of nasal drug delivery evaluation. Nasal formulations are designed to bypass the first-pass metabolism that occurs with oral administration, providing higher bioavailability for certain drugs. To evaluate bioavailability, researchers compare the systemic drug concentration after nasal administration to that achieved with other delivery routes, such as oral or intravenous delivery. This comparison helps determine how much of the drug reaches the bloodstream and is available to produce therapeutic effects. Bioavailability studies often include both animal and human testing to assess the pharmacokinetics of the drug.

8.8.2 Pulmonary Delivery Evaluation

The evaluation of pulmonary drug delivery systems is critical for ensuring that the drug reaches its target site in the lungs and is delivered effectively. Several in vitro and in vivo testing methods are used to assess the performance of these systems. These tests help determine the drug's aerosol performance, its deposition in the lungs, and its overall pharmacokinetics.

One of the first and most important steps in pulmonary delivery evaluation is **particle size analysis**. The size of the drug particles is a critical factor in determining where the drug will deposit in the lungs. Particles that are too large may be deposited in the upper airways, while smaller particles can reach the deeper regions of the lungs, such as the alveoli, where drug absorption occurs. In vitro methods, such as laser diffraction or cascade impaction, are commonly used to measure the particle size distribution of the aerosolized drug. These tests provide valuable information about the drug's ability to penetrate the lungs and its suitability for deep lung deposition.

Lung deposition studies are another key aspect of evaluating pulmonary drug delivery. These studies are typically performed using animals or human volunteers, where the drug is administered via inhalation, and the distribution of the drug in the lungs is measured. One commonly used technique involves gamma scintigraphy, where a radiolabeled drug is inhaled, and its deposition is tracked using imaging techniques. This allows researchers to visualize where the drug particles are deposited in the lungs and how efficiently the drug reaches its intended target. Lung deposition studies help ensure that the drug is reaching the lower respiratory tract, where it can exert its therapeutic effect.

Drug release profiles are also important in evaluating pulmonary drug delivery systems. These profiles provide information on how the drug is released from the formulation and absorbed into the bloodstream over time. In vitro studies, such as dissolution testing in simulated lung conditions, are often used to assess the drug release characteristics. These studies help determine whether the drug is released at a controlled rate and if the formulation provides the desired therapeutic effects. Additionally, in vivo pharmacokinetic studies are conducted to measure the drug's absorption, distribution, metabolism, and excretion in the body. By analyzing the pharmacokinetic data, researchers can evaluate the efficiency of the drug delivery system and compare it to other routes of administration.

8.9 Challenges and Future Trends in Nasal and Pulmonary Delivery

8.9.1 Challenges

Nasal and pulmonary drug delivery systems, although highly effective, face several challenges that must be addressed to optimize their clinical use. One of the primary challenges is **bioavailability**. While these systems offer the advantage of bypassing first-pass metabolism, ensuring consistent and adequate drug absorption remains a challenge. Factors such as the drug's physicochemical properties, including solubility and particle size, can affect its absorption efficiency. For example, drugs that are poorly soluble or have a large molecular size may not be absorbed effectively, limiting their therapeutic benefits. Furthermore, the absorption rate can vary depending on the specific area of the nasal or pulmonary passages where the drug is deposited. Achieving consistent drug absorption across different patients and conditions remains a significant hurdle.

Another challenge is **stability**. Nasal and pulmonary formulations are often sensitive to environmental factors such as temperature, humidity, and light. This can lead to degradation or reduced potency of the drug, especially for drugs that are unstable in aerosolized forms. In addition, many drugs delivered through these systems are sensitive to enzymatic degradation within the nasal or pulmonary mucosa. Protecting these drugs from degradation while ensuring their effective delivery and stability within the body is an ongoing concern for researchers and formulators.

Patient variability is another major challenge in nasal and pulmonary drug delivery. The effectiveness of these systems can vary significantly between individuals due to differences in anatomy, physiology, and technique. For example, variations in nasal passage structure or lung function can impact the deposition and absorption of the drug. Inhalation techniques also vary among patients, with some individuals unable to perform the required technique effectively. Inadequate inhalation or improper use of devices can result in suboptimal drug delivery, reducing the therapeutic efficacy. Additionally, patient-related factors such as age, respiratory diseases (e.g., asthma or COPD), and nasal conditions can further affect the performance of these delivery systems.

Furthermore, **irritation** remains a significant issue, particularly with nasal systems. Frequent use of nasal sprays or inhalers can lead to irritation of the nasal mucosa or respiratory tract. This can result in discomfort, dryness, or even damage to the mucosal lining, which may discourage patients from continuing their treatment. Reducing irritation while maintaining effective drug delivery is a critical challenge in the development of these systems.

CHAPTER IX

Nanotechnology in Drug Delivery

9.1 INTRODUCTION TO NANOTECHNOLOGY IN DRUG DELIVERY

Definition and Scope

Nanotechnology is the study and application of materials and devices at the nanoscale, which ranges between 1 and 100 nanometers. This scale is incredibly small, with one nanometer being equivalent to one-billionth of a meter. At this size, materials exhibit unique physical, chemical, and biological properties. These properties differ significantly from those observed in their bulk counterparts. The high surface area-to-volume ratio is a defining feature of nanoscale materials. This characteristic enhances their interaction with biological systems, making them particularly useful in drug delivery applications.

Nanotechnology has emerged as a transformative approach in modern medicine, especially in the pharmaceutical industry. Its primary focus is on developing systems that can improve the efficacy and safety of drugs. By manipulating materials at the atomic and molecular levels, scientists can design carriers capable of precise drug delivery to specific sites within the body. This targeted delivery reduces systemic exposure to the drug, minimizing potential side effects. It also improves the therapeutic outcomes, especially for complex diseases such as cancer and neurological disorders.

The scope of nanotechnology in drug delivery is vast and continuously evolving. One of the significant advantages is its ability to solubilize poorly water-soluble drugs. Approximately 40% of drugs currently in development exhibit poor water solubility, which limits their absorption and bioavailability. Nanotechnology-based carriers, such as nanoparticles, liposomes, and niosomes, address this challenge by enhancing the solubility and stability of these drugs. For instance, nanoparticles composed of biodegradable polymers can encapsulate hydrophobic drugs, protecting them from degradation while ensuring their gradual release at the target site.

Additionally, the versatility of nanotechnology enables its application across various drug delivery routes. These include oral, intravenous, transdermal, and pulmonary administration. For example, liposomes are widely used for intravenous drug delivery due to their biocompatibility and ability to encapsulate both hydrophilic and hydrophobic drugs. Pulmonary delivery systems using nanoparticles have shown promise in treating respiratory conditions like asthma and chronic obstructive pulmonary disease.

Nanotechnology also plays a crucial role in developing personalized medicine. By tailoring drug delivery systems to the specific needs of an individual, nanotechnology ensures optimal therapeutic efficacy. Advanced techniques such as ligand-conjugation allow nanoparticles to target specific receptors expressed on diseased cells. For instance, targeting overexpressed folate receptors in cancer cells has shown significant promise in reducing tumor growth without harming normal tissues.

The unique properties of nanotechnology extend beyond drug delivery to diagnostics and theranostics. Theranostics combines therapy and diagnostics within a single platform, enabling real-time monitoring of treatment efficacy. Nanoparticles engineered for theranostics can carry imaging agents along with therapeutic drugs. For example, quantum dots are used for imaging tumors while simultaneously delivering anticancer agents.

Despite its advantages, the integration of nanotechnology into mainstream healthcare comes with challenges. These include the high cost of development, scalability issues, and regulatory hurdles. The production of nanoscale materials requires sophisticated equipment and expertise, which increases manufacturing expenses. Moreover, ensuring the consistent quality of nanotechnology-based products during large-scale production remains a significant challenge. Regulatory agencies like the FDA and EMA demand rigorous evaluation of nanotechnology-based drugs for their safety and efficacy, which further adds to the development timeline.

Nanotechnology in drug delivery is a rapidly advancing field with immense potential to revolutionize healthcare. By addressing the limitations of conventional drug delivery systems, it opens new avenues for treating diseases that were previously deemed incurable. As research progresses, the integration of nanotechnology into clinical practice is expected to become more seamless, leading to better therapeutic outcomes for patients worldwide.

9.1.2 CONCEPTS AND APPROACHES FOR TARGETED DELIVERY

Targeted drug delivery is a fundamental aspect of nanotechnology that focuses on directing therapeutic agents to specific sites within the body while minimizing their interaction with non-target tissues. This approach significantly improves drug efficacy and reduces systemic side effects. Targeted delivery systems utilize the unique properties of nanomaterials to achieve precision in drug delivery. Two primary mechanisms, passive targeting and active targeting, are widely employed in this context.

Passive Targeting

Passive targeting takes advantage of the natural physiological and anatomical differences between diseased and healthy tissues. One of the most well-known principles underlying passive targeting is the Enhanced Permeability and Retention (EPR) effect. This effect is particularly relevant in cancer therapy, where tumors exhibit leaky vasculature and impaired lymphatic drainage. These features allow nanoparticles to accumulate preferentially in the tumor microenvironment. The EPR effect is highly dependent on the size and surface properties of the nanoparticles. Particles in the size range of 10 to 200 nanometers are optimal for exploiting this effect. For example, liposomal formulations like Doxil leverage the EPR effect to deliver doxorubicin directly to tumors, minimizing its cardiotoxicity.

Active Targeting

Active targeting involves the use of specific molecular interactions to direct the drug delivery system to its target site. This approach relies on the conjugation of targeting ligands, such as antibodies, peptides, or small molecules, to the surface of nanoparticles. These ligands bind selectively to receptors overexpressed on diseased cells. Ligand-receptor interactions enhance the specificity of drug delivery, ensuring that therapeutic agents reach only the intended site of action.

For instance, nanoparticles functionalized with folic acid can target cancer cells overexpressing folate receptors. Similarly, trastuzumab, an antibody targeting HER2 receptors, is conjugated to nanoparticles for treating HER2-positive breast cancer. The high affinity and specificity of these interactions enable precise drug delivery, reducing the required dosage and minimizing off-target effects.

Combination of Passive and Active Targeting

In many cases, a combination of passive and active targeting is employed to enhance drug delivery efficiency. Nanoparticles are first guided to the target tissue through passive mechanisms like the EPR effect. Once in proximity to the diseased site, active targeting ensures their interaction with specific cells. This dual strategy improves drug retention and uptake by target cells, leading to better therapeutic outcomes.

Smart and Stimuli-Responsive Targeting

Advances in nanotechnology have led to the development of smart drug delivery systems that respond to specific stimuli. These systems release their therapeutic payload in response to internal triggers such as pH, temperature, or enzymes, or external triggers like light and magnetic fields. For example, pH-sensitive nanoparticles release their drug content in acidic tumor environments, while thermosensitive liposomes release drugs upon exposure to hyperthermia. These systems offer unparalleled control over drug release, ensuring maximum efficacy with minimal side effects.

Challenges in Targeted Delivery

Despite the potential of targeted delivery systems, several challenges hinder their widespread application. The heterogeneity of target tissues, particularly tumors, can limit the effectiveness of both passive and active targeting. Variations in receptor expression levels and physiological barriers, such as the blood-brain barrier, further complicate targeted delivery. Additionally, the stability of nanoparticles in the bloodstream and their potential immunogenicity pose significant hurdles.

9.1.3 ADVANTAGES AND DISADVANTAGES

Nanotechnology-based drug delivery systems have revolutionized the pharmaceutical industry by offering novel solutions to overcome the limitations of traditional drug delivery methods. These systems utilize the unique properties of nanomaterials to enhance drug performance, improve patient outcomes, and target complex diseases. However, despite their significant advantages, they also pose certain challenges that must be addressed for their widespread adoption.

Advantages of Nanotechnology-Based Drug Delivery Systems

One of the most notable advantages of nanotechnology in drug delivery is the improvement in drug bioavailability. Many drugs, particularly those that are poorly water-soluble, exhibit low bioavailability when administered through conventional routes. Nanotechnology offers solutions such as nanoparticles and liposomes that enhance solubility and stability, ensuring better absorption and therapeutic efficacy. For example, paclitaxel, an anticancer drug with poor water solubility, is formulated into nanoparticles to enhance its bioavailability.

Targeted delivery is another critical advantage. Nanocarriers can be designed to deliver drugs to specific tissues or cells, reducing systemic toxicity and improving treatment outcomes. This precision is achieved through mechanisms such as the Enhanced Permeability and Retention (EPR) effect and ligand-mediated active targeting. For instance, liposomal doxorubicin minimizes cardiotoxicity by delivering the drug directly to tumor cells.

Controlled and sustained release of drugs is a key feature of nanotechnology-based systems. By modulating the release profile, these systems maintain therapeutic drug levels over extended periods, reducing the frequency of administration and improving patient compliance. Biodegradable polymeric nanoparticles, for instance, are engineered to release drugs gradually as the polymer matrix degrades in the body.

Nanotechnology also enables multimodal therapies by combining therapeutic and diagnostic functions within a single platform. This integration, known as theranostics, allows real-time monitoring of treatment efficacy. Quantum dots and gold nanoparticles are examples of theranostic agents used for simultaneous imaging and therapy in oncology.

Disadvantages of Nanotechnology-Based Drug Delivery Systems

Despite these advantages, there are several challenges associated with nanotechnology in drug delivery. One of the primary concerns is the high cost of development. The synthesis and characterization of nanocarriers require sophisticated equipment and highly skilled personnel. This increases the overall cost of drug development, which can translate into higher prices for the end user.

Scalability remains a significant obstacle. While many nanotechnology-based systems demonstrate excellent results in laboratory settings, their production on a commercial scale often encounters difficulties. Maintaining consistency in particle size, shape, and surface properties during large-scale manufacturing is technically challenging and resource-intensive.

Regulatory hurdles are another major disadvantage. Nanotechnology-based drugs are subject to rigorous evaluation by regulatory agencies such as the FDA and EMA. These evaluations require comprehensive data on safety, efficacy, and environmental impact, which can prolong the development timeline and increase costs.

The potential toxicity and long-term effects of nanomaterials raise safety concerns. Some nanoparticles may accumulate in tissues, leading to unintended side effects. For example, metallic nanoparticles, such as silver and gold, are known to pose risks if not adequately metabolized or excreted. Addressing these issues requires extensive preclinical and clinical testing.

9.2 LIPOSOMES IN DRUG DELIVERY

Introduction to Liposomes

Liposomes are spherical vesicles composed of one or more concentric phospholipid bilayers surrounding an aqueous core. They are widely utilized in drug delivery systems due to their unique ability to encapsulate both hydrophilic and hydrophobic drugs, enabling versatile applications in pharmaceuticals. The structural integrity and biocompatibility of liposomes make them an ideal candidate for delivering drugs to targeted tissues, improving therapeutic efficacy while minimizing systemic toxicity.

The structure of a liposome is similar to that of a cell membrane, consisting of phospholipids arranged in a bilayer. Phospholipids have a hydrophilic head and hydrophobic tail, allowing them to self-assemble into bilayers in aqueous environments. The hydrophilic drugs are encapsulated in the aqueous core, while hydrophobic drugs are incorporated within the lipid bilayer. This dual capability makes liposomes a versatile carrier for a wide range of pharmaceutical agents.

Liposomes can vary significantly in size, ranging from a few nanometers to several micrometers, depending on their formulation and preparation method. Small unilamellar vesicles (SUVs) typically measure less than 100 nanometers and are commonly used for targeted delivery due to their ability to penetrate tissues and access specific sites. Larger multilamellar vesicles (MLVs), which contain multiple bilayers, are employed in applications where prolonged drug release is required.

One of the key advantages of liposomes is their biocompatibility and biodegradability. Phospholipids used in liposome preparation are naturally occurring substances, making them non-toxic and less likely to provoke immune responses. This property is particularly important for intravenous drug delivery, where compatibility with the bloodstream is essential.

Liposomes can also be engineered to enhance their functionality. For example, surface modifications with polyethylene glycol (PEG) result in "stealth" liposomes that evade detection by the immune system. This modification increases their circulation time, allowing more effective drug delivery to target tissues. Additionally, ligands such as antibodies or peptides can be attached to the surface of liposomes for active targeting, ensuring precise delivery to specific cells or tissues.

Over the years, liposomes have been utilized in various therapeutic applications, including cancer therapy, vaccine delivery, and the treatment of infectious diseases. For instance, Doxil, a liposomal formulation of doxorubicin, is widely used in cancer treatment. It leverages the Enhanced Permeability and Retention (EPR) effect to accumulate in tumor tissues, reducing the adverse effects associated with conventional doxorubicin therapy.

Despite their numerous advantages, liposomes face challenges in large-scale production and stability. The formulation process requires precise control over parameters such as size, charge, and drug encapsulation efficiency. Moreover, liposomes are prone to degradation and leakage during storage, necessitating the use of stabilizers or advanced preservation techniques.

9.2.2 FORMULATION AND PREPARATION TECHNIQUES

The formulation and preparation of liposomes involve methods that enable precise control over their size, structure, and drug encapsulation efficiency. The choice of preparation technique depends on the intended application, type of drug, and desired liposomal characteristics such as particle size, bilayer composition, and surface modifications. Below are the key methods commonly used in developing liposomal drug delivery systems.

Thin-Film Hydration Technique

The thin-film hydration technique is one of the most widely employed methods for liposome preparation. This method begins with dissolving phospholipids and other lipophilic components in an organic solvent, typically chloroform or methanol. The solvent is then evaporated under reduced pressure, often using a rotary evaporator, to form a thin lipid film on the inner walls of a round-bottom flask. After complete solvent removal, an aqueous solution containing the drug is added to the flask. Hydration of the lipid film occurs under gentle agitation, resulting in the formation of multilamellar vesicles (MLVs). These vesicles can be further processed using sonication or extrusion to reduce their size and achieve uniformity.

Reverse-Phase Evaporation Technique (REV)

The reverse-phase evaporation technique is particularly useful for encapsulating hydrophilic drugs. In this method, phospholipids are first dissolved in an organic solvent. An aqueous phase containing the drug is then added to the solvent, creating a water-in-oil emulsion. The emulsion is subjected to sonication to achieve fine dispersion. The organic solvent is gradually removed under reduced pressure, leading to the formation of a gel-like phase. Upon further solvent evaporation, the gel collapses into unilamellar vesicles. REV is highly efficient in encapsulating water-soluble drugs, offering better drug entrapment compared to the thin-film hydration technique.

Extrusion Technique

The extrusion technique is primarily used to control the size and uniformity of liposomes. In this method, liposomes prepared by thin-film hydration or reverse-phase evaporation are passed through polycarbonate membranes with defined pore sizes using an extruder. The process reduces the size of the vesicles and results in the formation of unilamellar liposomes with consistent particle size. This technique is particularly useful for preparing small unilamellar vesicles (SUVs), which are ideal for applications requiring precise targeting and penetration.

Sonication Technique

Sonication is a commonly used method to reduce the size of liposomes and convert multilamellar vesicles (MLVs) into small unilamellar vesicles (SUVs). This process involves exposing the liposomal suspension to ultrasonic waves, which break down larger vesicles into smaller, more uniform particles. Two types of sonicators, bath and probe sonicators, are typically used. While sonication is simple and effective, it can generate heat and free radicals, potentially affecting the stability of the encapsulated drug.

Microfluidization

Microfluidization is an advanced technique used for the large-scale production of liposomes with high reproducibility and controlled particle size. This method involves forcing lipid and aqueous phases through narrow microchannels under high pressure. The intense mixing in these channels results in the formation of uniform and stable liposomes. Microfluidization is particularly suitable for industrial applications due to its scalability and efficiency.

Factors Influencing Liposomal Formulation

Several factors affect the formulation and preparation of liposomes, including lipid composition, drug properties, and process parameters. The choice of phospholipids and cholesterol concentration determines the stability and fluidity of the liposomal bilayer. Hydrophilic drugs are primarily encapsulated in the aqueous core, while hydrophobic drugs are embedded within the lipid bilayer. Particle size and surface charge also play a crucial role in determining the circulation time and cellular uptake of liposomes.

Challenges in Liposome Preparation

While the aforementioned techniques are effective, challenges remain in ensuring consistent quality during large-scale production. Achieving uniform particle size, optimizing drug encapsulation efficiency, and maintaining stability during storage are critical aspects that require precise control. Advances in automated manufacturing processes and stabilization techniques continue to address these challenges, making liposomal drug delivery systems increasingly reliable.

9.2.3 APPLICATIONS OF LIPOSOMES

Liposomes have emerged as versatile carriers in drug delivery due to their ability to encapsulate both hydrophilic and hydrophobic drugs, biocompatibility, and potential for surface modification. Over the years, their application has expanded across various therapeutic areas, addressing challenges in drug solubility, stability, and targeted delivery. Below are the major applications of liposomes in modern medicine, highlighting their role in transforming therapeutic outcomes.

Cancer Therapy

One of the most significant applications of liposomes is in cancer therapy. Liposomes are utilized to deliver chemotherapeutic agents directly to tumor tissues, reducing systemic toxicity and improving therapeutic efficacy. This is achieved through passive targeting mechanisms such as the Enhanced Permeability and Retention (EPR) effect. Tumor tissues, characterized by leaky vasculature and poor lymphatic drainage, allow liposomes to accumulate preferentially in the tumor microenvironment.

A notable example is **Doxil**, a liposomal formulation of doxorubicin. Doxil encapsulates the chemotherapeutic agent within a polyethylene glycol

(PEG)-coated liposome, also known as a stealth liposome. This coating prolongs the circulation time of the liposomes by evading immune detection, enabling higher drug concentration at the tumor site. As a result, Doxil has shown significant efficacy in treating various cancers, including ovarian cancer and Kaposi's sarcoma, while reducing side effects like cardiotoxicity commonly associated with doxorubicin.

Treatment of Infectious Diseases

Liposomes are also extensively used in the treatment of infectious diseases. They enhance the therapeutic index of antimicrobial agents by improving their solubility, stability, and delivery to infected tissues. For instance, **AmBisome**, a liposomal formulation of amphotericin B, is used to treat systemic fungal infections and leishmaniasis. Amphotericin B is known for its nephrotoxicity, but encapsulating it in liposomes reduces its toxicity while maintaining its antifungal efficacy. AmBisome has become a gold standard for treating severe fungal infections, particularly in immunocompromised patients.

Liposomes are also being explored for their ability to deliver antiviral drugs. Their capacity to encapsulate nucleic acids and other molecules makes them promising carriers for treating viral infections, including HIV and hepatitis.

Vaccine Delivery

Liposomes are increasingly being used as adjuvants and delivery systems in vaccines. Their ability to encapsulate antigens and protect them from enzymatic degradation enhances the immune response. Liposomal vaccines have shown promise in improving immunogenicity and reducing the required dose of antigens.

For example, liposomes are employed in certain COVID-19 vaccine formulations to stabilize and deliver the active components effectively. Additionally, research into liposomal vaccines for diseases like influenza, tuberculosis, and malaria is progressing rapidly. These vaccines utilize liposomes to present antigens to the immune system in a controlled manner, eliciting a robust and long-lasting immune response.

Applications in Dermatology

In dermatology, liposomes are used to deliver drugs and cosmetic agents to the skin. Their ability to penetrate the stratum corneum and deliver active ingredients to deeper layers of the skin has made them a preferred choice for treating conditions like psoriasis, eczema, and acne. Liposomal formulations are also used in anti-aging and skin rejuvenation products due to their enhanced delivery efficiency and reduced skin irritation.

Gene Therapy and Molecular Medicine

Liposomes play a crucial role in gene therapy by delivering nucleic acids, such as DNA and RNA, to target cells. Their biocompatibility and low immunogenicity make them ideal for delivering genetic material. Cationic liposomes, which have a positive charge, are particularly effective in binding to negatively charged nucleic acids and facilitating their delivery into cells. Liposomal gene delivery systems are being explored for treating genetic disorders, cancer, and viral infections.

Other Therapeutic Applications

Liposomes are also being utilized in targeted delivery for cardiovascular diseases, neurological disorders, and inflammatory conditions. Their ability to cross biological barriers, such as the blood-brain barrier, makes them valuable in treating central nervous system disorders. Liposomes encapsulating drugs like corticosteroids are used for managing inflammatory diseases, providing sustained release and reduced systemic side effects.

9.2.3.1 Classification of Liposomes

Liposomes can be classified based on various parameters, including the number of bilayers, size, charge, and method of preparation. This classification helps in tailoring liposomes for specific therapeutic applications and optimizing their performance in drug delivery systems.

Classification Based on the Number of Bilayers

1. **Unilamellar Vesicles (ULVs):**
   These liposomes consist of a single phospholipid bilayer enclosing an aqueous core. Unilamellar vesicles are further divided into:

   - **Small Unilamellar Vesicles (SUVs):**
     SUVs have a size range of 20–100 nm. They are ideal for targeted delivery due to their small size, which allows them to penetrate tissues and access specific sites.
   - **Large Unilamellar Vesicles (LUVs):**
     LUVs are larger, typically ranging from 100 nm to several micrometers. They are used for encapsulating larger drug quantities and are suitable for sustained drug release applications.

2. **Multilamellar Vesicles (MLVs):**
MLVs contain multiple concentric phospholipid bilayers, resembling an onion-like structure. These vesicles are larger, usually in the range of 0.5–10 micrometers, and are employed for prolonged drug release.

Classification Based on Size

1. **Small Liposomes:**
Liposomes smaller than 100 nm are considered small and are suitable for applications requiring enhanced permeability and retention, such as cancer therapy.
2. **Large Liposomes:**
Liposomes larger than 100 nm are used when higher drug encapsulation volumes are required, such as in vaccine delivery or long-term treatments.

Classification Based on Charge

1. **Neutral Liposomes:**
These liposomes have no net charge and are often used to reduce interactions with biological membranes, providing stability during circulation.
2. **Cationic Liposomes:**
Positively charged liposomes are used to deliver nucleic acids like DNA and RNA due to their ability to bind to negatively charged molecules.
3. **Anionic Liposomes:**
Negatively charged liposomes are less common but are used for specific applications requiring repulsion from other negatively charged components in biological systems.

Classification Based on Composition and Function

1. **Conventional Liposomes:**
These are made from natural or synthetic phospholipids without any additional surface modifications. They are primarily used in early-stage research or simple drug delivery systems.
2. **Stealth Liposomes:**
These liposomes are coated with polyethylene glycol (PEG), which helps

them evade immune detection. Stealth liposomes, such as those used in Doxil, are widely used in cancer therapy.

3. **Targeted Liposomes:**
These liposomes are functionalized with ligands, such as antibodies or peptides, to enable active targeting of specific cells or tissues.

4. **Thermosensitive Liposomes:**
Designed to release their drug content upon exposure to heat, these liposomes are used in combination with hyperthermia treatments.

5. **pH-Sensitive Liposomes:**
These liposomes release their payload in response to acidic environments, making them suitable for tumor-targeting applications.

Classification Based on Method of Preparation

1. **Thin-Film Hydration Liposomes:**
These are prepared using the thin-film hydration method and are generally multilamellar vesicles.

2. **Reverse-Phase Evaporation Liposomes:**
Liposomes produced using the reverse-phase evaporation technique, suitable for hydrophilic drug encapsulation.

3. **Extrusion Liposomes:**
Liposomes formed through the extrusion method, ensuring uniform size and structure.

9.3 NIOSOMES IN DRUG DELIVERY

Introduction to Niosomes

Niosomes are microscopic vesicles composed of non-ionic surfactants and cholesterol, forming a bilayer structure that encapsulates both hydrophilic and hydrophobic drugs. These vesicles are structurally similar to liposomes but differ in their composition, as niosomes use non-ionic surfactants instead of phospholipids. This composition renders niosomes a cost-effective alternative to liposomes, making them an attractive choice for drug delivery in resource-limited settings.

The non-ionic surfactants used in niosome preparation provide significant structural stability, enhancing the vesicles' robustness against environmental and storage conditions. Cholesterol is often included in the formulation to modulate the fluidity of the bilayer, improving its rigidity and stability. This stability ensures that the encapsulated drug remains protected until it reaches the target site.

Niosomes are capable of delivering a wide range of pharmaceutical agents due to their ability to encapsulate molecules of varying solubility. Hydrophilic drugs are housed within the aqueous core, while hydrophobic drugs are embedded in the bilayer. This dual capacity makes niosomes versatile carriers in drug delivery.

A key advantage of niosomes is their biodegradability and biocompatibility. Non-ionic surfactants used in their formation are generally less toxic compared to phospholipids or other surfactants, making niosomes suitable for therapeutic use. Moreover, their preparation is relatively simple and cost-effective, allowing for large-scale production without compromising quality.

Niosomes have demonstrated considerable utility in enhancing drug bioavailability and providing sustained or controlled drug release. Their size and surface properties can be easily modified to suit specific therapeutic needs. For example, the size of niosomes typically ranges from 10 nanometers to several micrometers, depending on the preparation method and intended application. Smaller niosomes are particularly effective in achieving targeted delivery due to their ability to penetrate biological barriers.

One of the notable applications of niosomes is in transdermal drug delivery. Niosomes enhance the permeation of drugs through the skin by improving drug solubility and stability, ensuring effective delivery to deeper layers. They are also used in delivering anticancer drugs, where their ability to target tumor tissues minimizes systemic toxicity and enhances therapeutic outcomes.

Despite their advantages, niosomes face challenges, such as stability issues during storage and scalability concerns. The oxidation of surfactants or cholesterol can affect their integrity, leading to drug leakage or reduced efficacy. However, advances in formulation techniques and stabilization strategies are addressing these limitations, making niosomes an increasingly reliable platform for drug delivery.

9.3.2 FORMULATION AND PREPARATION TECHNIQUES

The formulation and preparation of niosomes involve various techniques, each designed to optimize their size, structure, and drug encapsulation efficiency. These methods are influenced by the intended application, the type of drug to be delivered, and the desired stability of the formulation. Below are the most common techniques used for preparing niosomes, focusing on their principles and processes.

Ether Injection Method

The ether injection method is a widely used technique for preparing niosomes. This method involves dissolving surfactants and cholesterol in an organic solvent, typically diethyl ether. The organic phase is then injected slowly into an aqueous phase containing the drug, under constant stirring at a temperature above the phase transition temperature of the surfactant. The injection of the ether causes the organic solvent to evaporate, leading to the spontaneous formation of vesicles.

This method produces niosomes with uniform size and is particularly suitable for encapsulating both hydrophilic and hydrophobic drugs. However, one limitation is the potential presence of residual organic solvent, which must be carefully removed to ensure the safety of the formulation.

Thin-Film Hydration Method

The thin-film hydration method is another commonly used technique for niosome preparation. In this method, surfactants and cholesterol are dissolved in an organic solvent, which is then evaporated to form a thin lipid film on the inner walls of a flask. The lipid film is hydrated with an aqueous drug solution under agitation, resulting in the formation of multilamellar niosomal vesicles.

This technique is simple and allows for high drug encapsulation efficiency. The size of the vesicles can be controlled through processes such as sonication or extrusion, depending on the desired application.

Sonication Method

Sonication is a method used to reduce the size of niosomal vesicles, converting multilamellar vesicles into smaller unilamellar vesicles. This process involves exposing the niosomal suspension to ultrasonic waves, either in a bath or with a probe sonicator. The high-energy waves disrupt the larger vesicles, forming smaller, more uniform niosomes.

While sonication is effective in producing small vesicles, it may generate heat and free radicals, which can affect the stability of heat-sensitive drugs.

Reverse-Phase Evaporation Method

The reverse-phase evaporation method is particularly useful for encapsulating hydrophilic drugs. In this method, surfactants and cholesterol are dissolved in an organic solvent, and an aqueous phase containing the drug is added to create a water-in-oil emulsion. The emulsion is subjected to sonication to achieve fine dispersion. The organic solvent is then removed under reduced pressure, leading to the formation of niosomal vesicles.

This method offers high drug encapsulation efficiency and is suitable for producing unilamellar vesicles with controlled size.

Microfluidization Technique

Microfluidization is an advanced method that allows for the production of niosomes with consistent size and high reproducibility. In this process, the lipid and aqueous phases are forced through narrow microchannels under high pressure, creating intense mixing and shear forces. This results in the formation of small, uniform niosomes.

Microfluidization is particularly useful for large-scale production and industrial applications, where consistency and scalability are critical.

Factors Affecting Niosome Preparation

Several factors influence the efficiency and stability of niosomes, including the type of surfactant, cholesterol concentration, hydration time, and temperature. The choice of preparation method also determines the size, charge, and encapsulation efficiency of the niosomes. For example, ether injection typically produces smaller vesicles compared to the thin-film hydration method.

9.3.3 APPLICATIONS OF NIOSOMES

Niosomes have gained significant attention in pharmaceutical research and development due to their versatility, biocompatibility, and ability to encapsulate a wide range of therapeutic agents. Their structural properties allow them to deliver drugs effectively to target sites, improving therapeutic efficacy and minimizing systemic side effects. Below are the major applications of niosomes in drug delivery, along with examples and use cases.

Peptide and Protein Delivery

Peptides and proteins are challenging to deliver due to their susceptibility to enzymatic degradation and poor stability in the gastrointestinal tract. Niosomes offer a protective environment for these biomolecules, enhancing their stability and bioavailability.

For example, insulin, a peptide hormone used in diabetes management, has been encapsulated in niosomes for non-invasive delivery routes like transdermal and oral administration. Niosomal encapsulation protects insulin from enzymatic degradation and facilitates its absorption across biological barriers, offering an alternative to injectable formulations.

Gene Therapy

Niosomes are emerging as promising carriers for gene therapy due to their ability to encapsulate and deliver nucleic acids, such as DNA, RNA, and siRNA. Their non-ionic surfactant composition reduces the risk of immune reactions, making them safer than cationic lipid-based systems.

Cationic niosomes are particularly effective for binding to negatively charged genetic material, forming stable complexes that facilitate cellular uptake. For instance, niosomes have been employed to deliver siRNA targeting specific genes in cancer cells, effectively suppressing tumor growth.

Anti-Cancer Drug Delivery

Niosomes have shown great potential in delivering chemotherapeutic agents directly to tumor tissues, reducing systemic toxicity and improving drug efficacy. Their ability to encapsulate hydrophilic and hydrophobic drugs makes them versatile for cancer treatment.

For example, doxorubicin, a widely used anticancer drug, has been successfully formulated into niosomal systems. These formulations exploit passive targeting mechanisms such as the Enhanced Permeability and

Retention (EPR) effect, allowing the drug to accumulate in the tumor microenvironment. Additionally, functionalized niosomes with ligands targeting specific tumor receptors have shown improved specificity and reduced off-target effects.

Transdermal and Topical Delivery

Niosomes enhance drug permeation across the skin, making them ideal for transdermal and topical applications. They improve the solubility, stability, and absorption of drugs through the stratum corneum, providing sustained and localized drug release.

For example, niosomal formulations of diclofenac, a nonsteroidal anti-inflammatory drug (NSAID), have been developed for topical application to treat conditions like arthritis. These formulations improve drug penetration and provide prolonged relief from inflammation and pain.

Antimicrobial Therapy

Niosomes are used to deliver antimicrobial agents, including antibiotics, antifungals, and antivirals, to combat infections effectively. By encapsulating these agents, niosomes enhance their stability and bioavailability, reducing the required dosage and minimizing side effects.

For instance, niosomes loaded with ciprofloxacin, an antibiotic, have been developed for treating bacterial infections. Similarly, niosomal amphotericin B formulations are explored for fungal infections, offering an alternative to liposomal versions like AmBisome.

Vaccine Delivery

Niosomes have also been investigated as adjuvants and carriers in vaccine development. Their ability to encapsulate antigens and deliver them to immune cells enhances the immunogenicity of vaccines. Additionally, niosomes can be tailored to provide sustained antigen release, improving the efficacy of single-dose vaccines.

For example, niosomal vaccines for diseases like hepatitis B and influenza are under development, leveraging their stability and immunostimulatory properties.

Other Applications

Niosomes are also employed in targeted delivery for cardiovascular diseases, neurological disorders, and inflammatory conditions. Their ability to cross biological barriers, such as the blood-brain barrier, makes them valuable in treating central nervous system disorders. Niosomal formulations of corticosteroids are used for inflammatory diseases, providing sustained release and reduced systemic side effects.

9.4 NANOPARTICLES IN DRUG DELIVERY

9.4.1 TYPES OF NANOPARTICLES

Nanoparticles are submicron-sized particles ranging between 1 and 100 nanometers, used as carriers in drug delivery systems. Their small size and large surface area-to-volume ratio enable them to enhance drug solubility, stability, and bioavailability. Depending on their composition, nanoparticles can be classified into various types, each with distinct structural characteristics and applications. Below is a detailed classification of nanoparticles used in drug delivery.

Polymeric Nanoparticles

Polymeric nanoparticles are composed of natural or synthetic polymers and are widely used in drug delivery due to their biocompatibility and versatility. They are further classified into nanospheres and nanocapsules based on their structure:

- **Nanospheres:** In nanospheres, the drug is uniformly dispersed throughout the polymer matrix. This structure is suitable for sustained drug release as the drug is gradually released as the polymer degrades. For example, poly(lactic-co-glycolic acid) (PLGA)-based nanoparticles are extensively used in delivering anticancer and anti-inflammatory drugs.
- **Nanocapsules:** Nanocapsules are vesicular systems where the drug is enclosed in an oily or aqueous core surrounded by a polymeric shell. This design ensures controlled drug release and protects the encapsulated drug from degradation.

Polymeric nanoparticles can be engineered to target specific tissues or cells by functionalizing their surface with ligands, such as antibodies or peptides.

Metallic Nanoparticles

Metallic nanoparticles are made from metals such as gold, silver, and iron oxide. These nanoparticles are renowned for their unique optical, magnetic, and electronic properties, making them suitable for theranostics, which combines therapy and diagnostics.

- **Gold Nanoparticles (AuNPs):** Gold nanoparticles are used in cancer therapy, imaging, and drug delivery. Their surface can be functionalized with biomolecules for targeted delivery. For example, gold nanoparticles conjugated with anticancer drugs and targeting ligands can selectively destroy tumor cells when exposed to laser light (photothermal therapy).
- **Silver Nanoparticles (AgNPs):** Silver nanoparticles possess antimicrobial properties and are used in treating infections and wound healing.
- **Iron Oxide Nanoparticles:** These nanoparticles are employed in magnetic resonance imaging (MRI) as contrast agents and in hyperthermia therapy for cancer treatment.

Lipid-Based Nanoparticles

Lipid-based nanoparticles are composed of lipids and are biocompatible and biodegradable, making them suitable for delivering both hydrophilic and hydrophobic drugs. Examples include:

- **Solid Lipid Nanoparticles (SLNs):** SLNs consist of a solid lipid core stabilized by surfactants. They offer controlled drug release and improved drug stability. SLNs are used for delivering anticancer drugs and neurotherapeutics.
- **Nanostructured Lipid Carriers (NLCs):** NLCs are an advanced version of SLNs, incorporating liquid lipids into the solid core. This modification improves drug loading capacity and reduces drug expulsion during storage.
- **Liposomes and Lipid Nanocapsules:** These are also considered part of the lipid-based nanoparticle category, widely utilized in drug and vaccine delivery.

Hybrid Nanoparticles

Hybrid nanoparticles combine two or more types of materials, such as polymers, lipids, or metals, to leverage the advantages of each component. For example, polymer-coated metallic nanoparticles enhance stability and biocompatibility, while lipid-polymer hybrid nanoparticles improve drug encapsulation and controlled release.

Hybrid nanoparticles are particularly useful in theranostic applications, where they serve dual roles in therapy and imaging. For instance, hybrid nanoparticles combining gold and PLGA are used for targeted cancer therapy and imaging.

Other Types of Nanoparticles

1. **Carbon-Based Nanoparticles:** Carbon nanotubes (CNTs) and graphene-based nanoparticles are explored for delivering drugs and genetic material due to their high surface area and functionalization capabilities.
2. **Silica-Based Nanoparticles:** Mesoporous silica nanoparticles (MSNs) are widely used for drug delivery and imaging. Their porous structure provides a high drug-loading capacity.
3. **Protein-Based Nanoparticles:** These nanoparticles are derived from proteins such as albumin and gelatin. For example, albumin nanoparticles are used in the formulation of Abraxane, a nanoparticle-based chemotherapy drug.

9.4.2 FORMULATION AND PREPARATION TECHNIQUES

The formulation and preparation of nanoparticles are critical to achieving desired characteristics such as size, morphology, surface charge, and drug encapsulation efficiency. Different techniques are used based on the type of nanoparticle, the properties of the drug, and the intended application. Below are the commonly employed methods for preparing nanoparticles for drug delivery.

Solvent Evaporation Technique

The solvent evaporation technique is widely used for preparing polymeric nanoparticles. In this method, the drug and polymer are dissolved in an organic solvent, such as chloroform or dichloromethane. The solution is then emulsified into an aqueous phase containing a stabilizer, creating an oil-in-water emulsion. The organic solvent is removed by evaporation, leaving behind nanoparticles suspended in the aqueous phase.

The size and uniformity of the nanoparticles can be controlled by adjusting parameters such as emulsification speed, polymer concentration, and the ratio of organic to aqueous phases. This technique is particularly suitable for encapsulating hydrophobic drugs.

Nanoprecipitation Method

Nanoprecipitation, also known as the solvent displacement method, is a simple and efficient technique for preparing polymeric and lipid-based nanoparticles. In this method, the drug and polymer are dissolved in a water-miscible organic solvent, such as acetone or ethanol. This solution is then added dropwise to an aqueous phase containing a stabilizer under continuous stirring. The rapid diffusion of the organic solvent into the aqueous phase causes the polymer to precipitate, forming nanoparticles.

This method offers advantages such as ease of preparation, the ability to produce small and uniform nanoparticles, and the absence of high-energy processes. It is commonly used for drugs with poor water solubility.

Emulsion-Based Methods

Emulsion-based techniques are versatile and widely used for the preparation of both polymeric and lipid-based nanoparticles. Depending on the type of emulsion formed, these methods can be categorized as:

1. **Single Emulsion Method:**

   In this method, an oil-in-water (O/W) emulsion is created by dissolving the drug and polymer in an organic solvent, which is emulsified in an aqueous phase containing a stabilizer. The organic solvent is then removed through evaporation or extraction, leaving behind nanoparticles. This method is ideal for encapsulating hydrophobic drugs.

2. **Double Emulsion Method:**

   This method involves creating a water-in-oil-in-water (W/O/W) emulsion. It is particularly suitable for encapsulating hydrophilic drugs. The drug is dissolved in an aqueous phase, which is emulsified into an organic phase containing the polymer. This primary emulsion is then re-emulsified into an external aqueous phase. Solvent removal results in nanoparticles encapsulating the hydrophilic drug.

3. **Microemulsion Method:**

   Microemulsion techniques involve thermodynamically stable systems composed of oil, water, surfactants, and co-surfactants. The drug is dissolved in the oil phase, and the microemulsion is destabilized to precipitate nanoparticles. This method is primarily used for lipid-based nanoparticles, such as solid lipid nanoparticles (SLNs).

Spray Drying

Spray drying is a scalable technique for preparing nanoparticles, especially for heat-stable drugs and polymers. In this method, a solution or suspension containing the drug and polymer is sprayed into a hot drying chamber. The solvent evaporates rapidly, leaving behind solid nanoparticles. Spray drying is widely used in the pharmaceutical industry due to its efficiency and ability to produce nanoparticles in a dry powder form suitable for storage and reconstitution.

Ionic Gelation

Ionic gelation is commonly used for preparing nanoparticles from natural polymers, such as chitosan and alginate. In this method, the polymer solution is mixed with a cross-linking agent, causing the polymer chains to form a gel matrix and encapsulate the drug. This technique is simple, avoids the use of organic solvents, and is suitable for sensitive drugs like proteins and peptides.

High-Pressure Homogenization

High-pressure homogenization is used for preparing lipid-based nanoparticles, such as solid lipid nanoparticles (SLNs) and nanostructured lipid carriers (NLCs). In this method, a lipid phase containing the drug is melted and mixed with an aqueous phase to form a coarse emulsion. The emulsion is then subjected to high-pressure homogenization, resulting in the formation of nanoparticles with a uniform size distribution.

Supercritical Fluid Technology

Supercritical fluid technology is an advanced method for preparing nanoparticles using supercritical carbon dioxide (CO_2) as a solvent or anti-solvent. This technique allows the formation of nanoparticles with controlled size and morphology while avoiding the use of toxic organic solvents. It is particularly suitable for drugs with low thermal stability.

Factors Influencing Nanoparticle Preparation

The choice of preparation technique is influenced by factors such as the physicochemical properties of the drug, desired particle size, drug encapsulation efficiency, and stability. Process parameters, including temperature, stirring speed, and surfactant concentration, also play a critical role in determining the final characteristics of the nanoparticles.

9.4.3 APPLICATIONS OF NANOPARTICLES

Nanoparticles have revolutionized the field of drug delivery due to their unique properties, including small size, high surface area, and the ability to modify their surface for targeted delivery. Their versatility allows for a wide range of clinical applications, addressing challenges such as drug solubility, stability, bioavailability, and site-specific delivery. Below are the key applications of nanoparticles in clinical practice.

Brain-Targeting and Crossing the Blood-Brain Barrier (BBB)

The blood-brain barrier (BBB) is a highly selective membrane that restricts the entry of most drugs into the central nervous system (CNS). Nanoparticles provide a solution by enabling drugs to cross the BBB and reach the brain. Their small size and surface modification capabilities allow them to bypass this barrier through receptor-mediated endocytosis or transcytosis.

For example, nanoparticles conjugated with transferrin or lactoferrin ligands can target transferrin receptors on the BBB, facilitating the delivery of therapeutic agents to treat neurological conditions such as Alzheimer's disease, Parkinson's disease, and brain tumors. Polymeric nanoparticles and lipid-based systems like liposomes are commonly used for brain-targeting applications.

Controlled and Sustained Drug Release

Nanoparticles offer the ability to control the release profile of drugs, ensuring a sustained therapeutic effect over extended periods. This reduces the frequency of drug administration and improves patient compliance. For example, polymeric nanoparticles made from biodegradable materials like poly(lactic-co-glycolic acid) (PLGA) release drugs gradually as the polymer matrix degrades.

These systems are widely used for chronic conditions, such as cancer and diabetes, where consistent drug levels are crucial for effective treatment. Insulin-loaded nanoparticles have been developed for sustained release, providing an alternative to frequent injections.

Cancer Therapy

One of the most significant applications of nanoparticles is in cancer therapy. Nanoparticles enhance the delivery of chemotherapeutic agents directly to tumor tissues, reducing systemic toxicity and improving efficacy. This is achieved through passive targeting mechanisms like the Enhanced Permeability and Retention (EPR) effect and active targeting using surface-functionalized nanoparticles.

Gold nanoparticles, liposomes, and polymeric nanoparticles are commonly employed in cancer therapy. For instance, nanoparticle-based formulations like Doxil (liposomal doxorubicin) and Abraxane (albumin-bound paclitaxel) have shown improved therapeutic outcomes with reduced side effects. Additionally, nanoparticles enable multimodal cancer therapy, combining drug delivery with imaging and hyperthermia

Gene Therapy

Nanoparticles are promising carriers for gene therapy, addressing challenges such as the delivery of genetic material to target cells and protection against enzymatic degradation. Cationic nanoparticles, which bind to negatively charged nucleic acids, are particularly effective for delivering DNA, RNA, and siRNA.

For example, lipid nanoparticles are widely used for delivering mRNA in vaccines, as demonstrated by COVID-19 vaccines developed by Pfizer-BioNTech and Moderna. Polymeric nanoparticles and dendrimers are also explored for gene delivery in treating genetic disorders, cancer, and viral infections.

Treatment of Infectious Diseases

Nanoparticles enhance the efficacy of antimicrobial agents by improving their solubility, stability, and targeted delivery to infected tissues. Silver nanoparticles, for example, are used for their broad-spectrum antimicrobial properties. Similarly, lipid nanoparticles are employed to deliver antiviral drugs for conditions such as HIV and hepatitis.

Nanoparticles have also played a pivotal role in vaccine development. For instance, lipid nanoparticles were crucial in the formulation of mRNA-based COVID-19 vaccines, providing stability and efficient delivery of the genetic material to immune cells.

Targeted and Personalized Medicine

Nanoparticles enable precise targeting of specific cells or tissues, reducing off-target effects and enhancing therapeutic outcomes. Surface modifications with ligands, such as antibodies or peptides, allow nanoparticles to recognize and bind to specific receptors expressed on diseased cells.

For example, HER2-targeted nanoparticles are used in treating HER2-positive breast cancer. This personalized approach ensures that drugs are delivered only to the affected tissues, minimizing systemic side effects.

Applications in Diagnostics and Theranostics

Nanoparticles are increasingly used in diagnostics and theranostics, combining therapy and imaging into a single platform. Gold nanoparticles and quantum dots are employed in imaging techniques to detect tumors and other abnormalities. Magnetic nanoparticles, such as iron oxide nanoparticles, serve as contrast agents in magnetic resonance imaging (MRI) while also being used in hyperthermia therapy for cancer.

Theranostic nanoparticles enable real-time monitoring of treatment efficacy, offering a comprehensive approach to disease management.

Other Applications

- **Ocular Drug Delivery:** Nanoparticles are used to treat eye diseases by delivering drugs to the cornea or retina. For instance, polymeric nanoparticles enhance the bioavailability of drugs for glaucoma or diabetic retinopathy.
- **Cardiovascular Diseases:** Nanoparticles are employed to deliver drugs to reduce arterial plaque or prevent clot formation in heart disease.
- **Pulmonary Delivery:** Nanoparticles are used in inhalable formulations to treat respiratory conditions like asthma and chronic obstructive pulmonary disease (COPD).

9.5 MONOCLONAL ANTIBODIES IN DRUG DELIVERY

9.5.1 BASICS OF MONOCLONAL ANTIBODIES

Monoclonal antibodies (mAbs) are highly specific proteins engineered to bind to unique antigens with exceptional precision. Derived from a single clone of immune cells, these antibodies are uniform in structure and function, making them invaluable tools in modern medicine, particularly in targeted drug delivery. Their ability to recognize and bind to specific molecular targets allows for precise therapeutic interventions, minimizing off-target effects and enhancing treatment efficacy.

At their core, monoclonal antibodies mimic the natural immune response. The immune system uses antibodies to identify and neutralize foreign substances such as pathogens or abnormal cells. By engineering these antibodies in the laboratory, researchers can tailor them to target specific antigens associated with diseases, including cancer, autoimmune disorders, and infectious diseases.

Structure and Mechanism of Action

Monoclonal antibodies have a characteristic Y-shaped structure, comprising two heavy chains and two light chains. The tips of the Y form the antigen-binding site, which is highly specific to the target antigen. This specificity enables monoclonal antibodies to bind only to the intended molecule, sparing healthy cells from unintended interactions.

When a monoclonal antibody binds to its target antigen, it can exert therapeutic effects through several mechanisms:

1. **Blocking Pathogenic Pathways:** By binding to specific receptors or ligands, monoclonal antibodies can prevent the activation of harmful signaling pathways. For example, mAbs targeting growth factor receptors, such as HER2 in breast cancer, block the proliferation of cancer cells.

2. **Immune System Activation:** Monoclonal antibodies can recruit immune cells to attack and destroy the target cells. This mechanism, known as antibody-dependent cellular cytotoxicity (ADCC), is particularly effective in cancer therapy.

3. **Payload Delivery:** Monoclonal antibodies are often conjugated with drugs, toxins, or radioactive isotopes to deliver these agents directly to diseased cells. This targeted delivery minimizes systemic toxicity and enhances therapeutic outcomes.

Applications of Monoclonal Antibodies in Targeted Delivery

Monoclonal antibodies have become a cornerstone in the development of targeted therapies. Their applications extend across various medical fields:

1. **Cancer Therapy:** In oncology, monoclonal antibodies are used to target specific antigens expressed on tumor cells. For instance, trastuzumab (Herceptin) is a monoclonal antibody that targets the HER2 receptor in HER2-positive breast cancer. Similarly, rituximab (Rituxan) targets CD20, a protein found on B cells, and is used in treating non-Hodgkin lymphoma.

2. **Autoimmune Disorders:** Monoclonal antibodies are used to modulate the immune system in autoimmune diseases. Adalimumab (Humira), for example, targets tumor necrosis factor-alpha (TNF-α), a cytokine involved in inflammatory conditions such as rheumatoid arthritis and Crohn's disease.

3. **Infectious Diseases:** Monoclonal antibodies are being developed to combat infectious diseases by neutralizing pathogens or blocking their entry into host cells. Palivizumab (Synagis) is a monoclonal antibody used to prevent respiratory syncytial virus (RSV) infections in high-risk infants.

Advantages of Monoclonal Antibodies

The high specificity of monoclonal antibodies ensures precise targeting, reducing the risk of off-target effects. Their versatility allows them to be engineered for a wide range of therapeutic applications. Additionally, advancements in antibody engineering, such as humanization and bispecific antibody development, have enhanced their efficacy and reduced immunogenicity.

Limitations and Challenges

Despite their advantages, monoclonal antibodies face challenges such as high production costs, complex manufacturing processes, and potential immunogenic reactions. Furthermore, the development of resistance by target cells, especially in cancer therapy, poses a significant hurdle.

9.5.2 FORMULATION AND APPLICATIONS

Monoclonal antibodies (mAbs) have revolutionized targeted drug delivery, especially in cancer therapy, where their precision in recognizing and binding to specific antigens has enabled the development of highly effective treatment strategies. One of the most innovative applications of monoclonal antibodies is their use in antibody-drug conjugates (ADCs), a class of therapeutics that combines the targeting capabilities of antibodies with the potency of cytotoxic drugs.

Formulation of Antibody-Drug Conjugates (ADCs)

Antibody-drug conjugates are designed to deliver cytotoxic agents directly to diseased cells, minimizing damage to healthy tissues. The formulation of ADCs involves three critical components:

1. **Monoclonal Antibody:**
   The antibody serves as the targeting moiety, recognizing and binding to specific antigens expressed on the surface of target cells. For example, trastuzumab, a monoclonal antibody targeting the HER2 receptor, is widely used in ADC formulations for HER2-positive cancers.

2. **Linker Molecule:**
   The linker connects the antibody to the cytotoxic drug and plays a crucial role in the stability and efficacy of the ADC. The linker must remain stable in the bloodstream to prevent premature release of the drug but should release the cytotoxic agent efficiently once the ADC is internalized by the target cell. Commonly used linkers include cleavable

linkers, such as those sensitive to pH or enzymatic activity, and non-cleavable linkers, which rely on the degradation of the antibody for drug release.

3. **Cytotoxic Payload:**
   The payload is a highly potent drug designed to kill target cells upon release. Common cytotoxic agents include microtubule inhibitors (e.g., auristatins and maytansinoids) and DNA-damaging agents (e.g., calicheamicins). These drugs are often too toxic for systemic administration but are highly effective when delivered specifically to target cells via ADCs.

The formulation process involves conjugating the antibody to the drug using the linker. Key considerations include maintaining the structural integrity of the antibody, optimizing the drug-to-antibody ratio (DAR), and ensuring the overall stability and bioavailability of the ADC.

Applications of Monoclonal Antibodies in Targeted Cancer Therapy

1. **HER2-Positive Breast Cancer:**
   Trastuzumab, a monoclonal antibody targeting the HER2 receptor, is a cornerstone in the treatment of HER2-positive breast cancer. Its ability to block HER2-mediated signaling pathways reduces tumor growth and enhances patient survival.

Trastuzumab Emtansine (T-DM1): An antibody-drug conjugate that combines trastuzumab with the cytotoxic agent emtansine (DM1) is used for patients with HER2-positive metastatic breast cancer. The ADC specifically delivers DM1 to HER2-overexpressing tumor cells, sparing healthy tissues and reducing systemic toxicity.

1. **Non-Hodgkin Lymphoma:**
   Rituximab, a monoclonal antibody targeting the CD20 antigen on B cells, has transformed the treatment of B-cell malignancies such as non-Hodgkin lymphoma. Its use in combination with chemotherapy has significantly improved remission rates and overall survival.

Polatuzumab Vedotin: This ADC targets CD79b, a protein expressed on B cells, and delivers a potent microtubule inhibitor, vedotin, to treat diffuse large B-cell lymphoma (DLBCL).

3. **Triple-Negative Breast Cancer (TNBC):**
   Sacituzumab Govitecan is an ADC approved for TNBC, targeting the Trop-2 antigen and delivering a cytotoxic payload to kill tumor cells.
4. **Solid Tumors:**
   ADCs are being developed for various solid tumors, including ovarian, lung, and gastric cancers.

For example, **Enfortumab Vedotin** targets Nectin-4, a protein highly expressed in urothelial carcinoma, and delivers the cytotoxic agent monomethyl auristatin E (MMAE), resulting in effective tumor cell destruction.

Challenges and Future Directions

Despite their success, ADCs face challenges such as resistance mechanisms developed by tumor cells, off-target effects, and the complexity of manufacturing processes. Advances in linker technology, optimization of payload selection, and innovations in antibody engineering are addressing these limitations, paving the way for more effective and safer therapies.

9.6 FORMULATION TECHNIQUES FOR NANOTECHNOLOGY-BASED SYSTEMS

9.6.1 KEY PARAMETERS IN FORMULATION

The formulation of nanotechnology-based drug delivery systems involves careful optimization of various parameters to achieve desired therapeutic outcomes. These parameters influence the physicochemical properties, stability, drug-loading capacity, and overall efficacy of the nanoparticle systems. Understanding and controlling these factors are critical to the success of nanotechnology-based formulations.

Particle Size

Particle size plays a pivotal role in determining the behavior and functionality of nanoparticles in drug delivery. Nanoparticles typically range from 1 to 100 nanometers in size. This small size allows them to penetrate biological barriers, such as the blood-brain barrier or the tight junctions of tumor vasculature, enhancing targeted delivery.

Smaller nanoparticles have a higher surface area-to-volume ratio, which can improve drug dissolution and bioavailability. However, excessively small nanoparticles may be rapidly cleared by the renal system, reducing their circulation time. Conversely, larger nanoparticles may be retained in circulation longer but may struggle to penetrate target tissues effectively.

For example, nanoparticles between 10 and 200 nanometers are optimal for exploiting the Enhanced Permeability and Retention (EPR) effect, allowing preferential accumulation in tumor tissues.

Surface Charge

The surface charge of nanoparticles, often expressed as zeta potential, affects their stability, cellular uptake, and interaction with biological systems. Positively charged nanoparticles tend to have better cellular uptake due to the negative charge on cell membranes. However, highly positive charges may lead to cytotoxicity or unwanted interactions with serum proteins.

Negatively charged or neutral nanoparticles generally exhibit reduced protein adsorption, improving their circulation time in the bloodstream. Surface modifications, such as coating nanoparticles with polyethylene glycol (PEG), can be used to control surface charge and improve biocompatibility.

Stability

Stability is a crucial consideration in formulating nanotechnology-based systems. Nanoparticles must remain stable during storage, transport, and administration. Instability can lead to particle aggregation, drug leakage, or degradation, compromising therapeutic efficacy.

Factors such as particle size, surface charge, and encapsulation method significantly influence stability. Stabilizers and surfactants, such as Pluronic or Tween, are commonly added to formulations to prevent aggregation and enhance stability. Additionally, lyophilization or freeze-drying techniques are employed to improve the shelf-life of nanoparticles, especially for sensitive drugs.

Encapsulation Efficiency

Encapsulation efficiency refers to the percentage of drug successfully loaded into or onto the nanoparticles compared to the initial amount used during formulation. High encapsulation efficiency is critical for minimizing drug wastage and ensuring a sufficient therapeutic dose.

Encapsulation efficiency depends on factors such as the solubility of the drug, the type of nanocarrier, and the preparation method. For instance, hydrophobic drugs are better suited for lipid-based carriers, while hydrophilic drugs can be effectively encapsulated in polymeric or hydrophilic core-shell nanoparticles.

For example, lipid nanoparticles such as solid lipid nanoparticles (SLNs) or nanostructured lipid carriers (NLCs) are highly efficient in encapsulating lipophilic drugs, while polymeric nanoparticles made from materials like PLGA excel in encapsulating hydrophilic or hydrophobic drugs based on the polymer composition.

Additional Considerations

- **Drug Release Profile:** The formulation must allow for controlled and sustained drug release to achieve prolonged therapeutic effects. Modifying the composition or structure of nanoparticles can fine-tune the release kinetics.
- **Biocompatibility and Toxicity:** All components used in nanoparticle formulations must be biocompatible and non-toxic. Regulatory approval requires extensive evaluation of these properties.
- **Scalability:** The formulation process must be scalable for commercial production while maintaining consistent quality and properties.

9.6.2 CHARACTERIZATION TECHNIQUES

Characterization of nanotechnology-based systems is a critical step in ensuring their effectiveness, stability, and safety in drug delivery applications. Various techniques are employed to evaluate key properties such as particle size, surface charge, morphology, and structural integrity. These parameters influence the biological behavior and therapeutic efficacy of nanoparticles. Below are the most commonly used methods for characterizing nanoparticles.

Dynamic Light Scattering (DLS)

Dynamic light scattering (DLS), also known as photon correlation spectroscopy, is widely used to measure the hydrodynamic diameter and size distribution of nanoparticles in suspension. This technique works by analyzing the scattering of light as it interacts with nanoparticles undergoing Brownian motion in a liquid medium.

DLS provides information on:

- **Particle Size:** The average size and size distribution of nanoparticles in solution.

- **Polydispersity Index (PDI):** A measure of the uniformity of particle sizes, with lower values indicating a more uniform size distribution.

DLS is ideal for characterizing nanoparticles ranging from a few nanometers to several micrometers. However, it is sensitive to sample purity and can be affected by the presence of aggregates or impurities.

Zeta Potential Analysis

Zeta potential is a measure of the surface charge of nanoparticles in a colloidal suspension. It provides insight into the stability of the nanoparticle formulation, as surface charge influences the electrostatic repulsion between particles, preventing aggregation.

A high positive or negative zeta potential (e.g., > ±30 mV) indicates good colloidal stability, while values closer to zero suggest a higher likelihood of aggregation. This analysis is essential for ensuring long-term stability and optimal interaction with biological systems.

Zeta potential analysis is also used to evaluate the effectiveness of surface modifications, such as coating nanoparticles with polyethylene glycol (PEG) or other stabilizers.

Electron Microscopy

Electron microscopy techniques provide high-resolution images, enabling detailed visualization of the morphology and structure of nanoparticles. Common types include:

- **Transmission Electron Microscopy (TEM):** TEM uses an electron beam to produce detailed two-dimensional images of nanoparticles, allowing visualization of their shape, size, and internal structure. It is particularly useful for confirming the uniformity of particles and identifying core-shell structures.
- **Scanning Electron Microscopy (SEM):** SEM provides three-dimensional surface images of nanoparticles, giving insights into their surface topography and structural features. It is commonly used for larger nanoparticles and microparticles.
- **Cryo-TEM:** Cryo-TEM is a specialized technique where samples are vitrified in their hydrated state, preserving their native structure. This method is especially useful for characterizing lipid-based nanoparticles, such as liposomes and nanostructured lipid carriers (NLCs).

X-Ray Diffraction (XRD)

XRD is employed to determine the crystalline structure and phase composition of nanoparticles, particularly those composed of metals, ceramics, or solid lipids. It provides valuable information on the degree of crystallinity, which influences the stability and drug release properties of nanoparticles.

Fourier Transform Infrared Spectroscopy (FTIR)

FTIR is used to identify the chemical composition of nanoparticles and confirm the presence of functional groups. It is particularly useful for verifying surface modifications, such as the attachment of ligands or stabilizers to the nanoparticle surface.

Thermal Analysis

Thermal analysis techniques, such as Differential Scanning Calorimetry (DSC) and Thermogravimetric Analysis (TGA), are used to assess the thermal stability and phase transitions of nanoparticles. These methods are particularly useful for lipid-based and polymeric nanoparticles to evaluate their stability under different storage conditions.

Surface Area and Porosity Analysis

Techniques like Brunauer-Emmett-Teller (BET) analysis are used to measure the surface area and porosity of nanoparticles. These parameters are critical for applications where high surface area is required, such as drug adsorption and controlled release systems.

UV-Visible Spectroscopy

UV-Visible spectroscopy is a simple and widely used technique for confirming drug encapsulation and loading efficiency in nanoparticles. The absorbance spectra provide quantitative data on drug content within the formulation.

9.7 APPLICATIONS OF NANOTECHNOLOGY-BASED SYSTEMS

9.7.1 CANCER THERAPY

Nanotechnology has revolutionized cancer therapy by enabling the development of advanced drug delivery systems that overcome the limitations of conventional chemotherapy. Nanocarriers, such as liposomes, nanoparticles, and micelles, offer precise tumor targeting, improved drug solubility, enhanced bioavailability, and reduced systemic toxicity. These systems leverage both passive and active targeting mechanisms to maximize therapeutic efficacy while minimizing adverse effects.

Tumor Targeting Through Passive Mechanisms

One of the key advantages of nanotechnology in cancer therapy is the ability to exploit the **Enhanced Permeability and Retention (EPR)** effect for passive tumor targeting. Tumor tissues often have leaky vasculature and poor lymphatic drainage, allowing nanoparticles in the size range of 10 to 200 nanometers to accumulate preferentially in the tumor microenvironment.

Liposomes, such as **Doxil** (a liposomal formulation of doxorubicin), utilize the EPR effect to deliver chemotherapeutic agents directly to tumor sites. This approach minimizes exposure to healthy tissues, reducing side effects like cardiotoxicity while maintaining antitumor efficacy.

Active Targeting Mechanisms

Active targeting involves functionalizing the surface of nanocarriers with ligands, such as antibodies, peptides, or small molecules, that specifically bind to receptors overexpressed on tumor cells. This approach enhances the specificity and uptake of drugs by cancer cells.

For example, **trastuzumab-conjugated nanoparticles** are designed to target HER2 receptors, which are overexpressed in HER2-positive breast cancer. These nanoparticles deliver chemotherapeutic agents directly to the tumor cells, sparing normal tissues and improving treatment outcomes.

Similarly, folate-functionalized nanoparticles target folate receptors commonly overexpressed in ovarian and colorectal cancers. The ligand-receptor interaction ensures precise drug delivery, enhancing therapeutic efficacy.

Controlled and Sustained Drug Release

Nanocarriers provide the ability to control and sustain the release of chemotherapeutic drugs, maintaining therapeutic levels over extended periods. Polymeric nanoparticles made from biodegradable materials like **poly(lactic-co-glycolic acid) (PLGA)** release drugs gradually as the polymer degrades, reducing the frequency of administration and improving patient compliance.

For example, PLGA nanoparticles loaded with paclitaxel have demonstrated prolonged release and enhanced antitumor activity in preclinical studies.

Multimodal Therapy

Nanotechnology enables the integration of multiple therapeutic modalities into a single system, combining chemotherapy, photothermal therapy, and immunotherapy for synergistic effects.

- **Gold nanoparticles:** These are used in photothermal therapy, where they generate heat upon exposure to laser light, selectively destroying tumor cells.
- **Theranostic nanoparticles:** These combine therapeutic and diagnostic functions, allowing real-time imaging of tumors while delivering drugs.

Overcoming Drug Resistance

Drug resistance is a major challenge in cancer therapy. Nanocarriers can overcome this issue by co-delivering multiple drugs or gene therapies that target resistance mechanisms. For example, nanoparticles co-loaded with paclitaxel and siRNA targeting drug-resistance genes have shown promise in reversing resistance in ovarian cancer.

Applications in Metastatic Cancer

Nanotechnology-based systems are particularly effective in targeting metastatic cancer, where precise delivery to multiple sites is critical. Liposomes and polymeric nanoparticles are used to deliver drugs to metastatic lesions, improving survival rates and quality of life for patients.

9.7.2 INFECTIOUS DISEASES

Nanotechnology has emerged as a powerful tool in combating infectious diseases, offering innovative solutions to challenges such as drug resistance, poor bioavailability, and systemic toxicity of traditional antimicrobial therapies. Nanotechnology-based systems, including nano-antibiotics, antiviral nanoparticles, and nanocarriers, enhance the delivery, efficacy, and targeting of therapeutic agents, paving the way for more effective treatments against bacterial, viral, and fungal infections.

Nano-Antibiotics: Overcoming Bacterial Resistance

Drug-resistant bacterial infections pose a significant threat to global health, rendering many conventional antibiotics ineffective. Nano-antibiotics, which involve the use of nanoparticles or nanoparticle-conjugated antibiotics, address this issue by improving drug delivery, enhancing antibacterial activity, and minimizing resistance development.

- **Enhanced Efficacy:** Nanoparticles, such as silver and gold nanoparticles, exhibit intrinsic antibacterial properties by disrupting bacterial membranes, generating reactive oxygen species, and interfering with essential bacterial processes.

- **Targeted Delivery:** Antibiotics encapsulated in polymeric nanoparticles, such as those made from poly(lactic-co-glycolic acid) (PLGA), deliver drugs directly to infection sites, reducing systemic toxicity and required dosage.
- **Combination Therapies:** Nanocarriers can co-deliver antibiotics with adjuvants or antimicrobial peptides, synergistically overcoming resistance mechanisms in multidrug-resistant (MDR) bacteria.

For instance, silver nanoparticles have demonstrated broad-spectrum activity against MDR pathogens, including methicillin-resistant *Staphylococcus aureus* (MRSA) and carbapenem-resistant *Klebsiella pneumoniae*.

Antiviral Nanoparticles: Targeting Viral Infections

Nanotechnology plays a vital role in developing antiviral therapies, particularly against viruses like HIV, influenza, and SARS-CoV-2. Antiviral nanoparticles are designed to inhibit viral entry, replication, or release, offering targeted and efficient treatments.

- **Drug Delivery Systems:** Lipid-based nanoparticles, such as those used in mRNA COVID-19 vaccines, stabilize and deliver genetic material to immune cells, eliciting robust antiviral responses.
- **Intrinsic Antiviral Properties:** Metallic nanoparticles, such as gold and silver, exhibit antiviral activity by interacting with viral surface proteins, preventing the virus from binding to host cells.
- **Targeted Therapy:** Functionalized nanoparticles can deliver antiviral agents directly to infected cells. For example, dendrimers functionalized with ligands specifically target HIV-infected cells, reducing viral load and improving treatment outcomes.

Nanotechnology Against Fungal Infections

Nanoparticles improve the delivery and efficacy of antifungal drugs, addressing issues such as poor solubility and systemic toxicity. Liposomal formulations of amphotericin B, such as **AmBisome**, reduce nephrotoxicity while maintaining antifungal potency. Similarly, polymeric nanoparticles encapsulating azole antifungals enhance drug penetration into fungal biofilms, a common cause of persistent infections.

Addressing Drug Resistance in Infectious Diseases

Nanotechnology provides innovative strategies to combat drug resistance, a growing challenge in the treatment of bacterial, viral, and fungal infections. By co-delivering multiple drugs or combining drugs with resistance-modifying agents, nanoparticles can bypass resistance mechanisms and restore therapeutic efficacy.

For example, nanoparticles co-loaded with antibiotics and efflux pump inhibitors block bacterial resistance pathways, making the pathogens susceptible to the antibiotics.

Applications in Vaccine Development

Nanotechnology-based systems are integral to modern vaccine development, enhancing antigen stability, delivery, and immune response. Lipid nanoparticles used in mRNA vaccines for COVID-19 are a prime example, demonstrating how nanotechnology can revolutionize infectious disease prevention. Nanoparticles also serve as adjuvants, boosting immune responses to antigens in vaccines for diseases like hepatitis B and tuberculosis.

Diagnostic Applications

Nanotechnology aids in the rapid and accurate detection of infectious diseases. Nanoparticle-based biosensors and diagnostic assays detect pathogens with high sensitivity, enabling early diagnosis and treatment. Gold nanoparticles, for instance, are used in lateral flow assays for detecting antigens of infectious agents such as malaria and dengue viruses.

9.7.3 VACCINES AND IMMUNOTHERAPY

Nanotechnology has revolutionized vaccine development and immunotherapy by enabling precise delivery of antigens and modulating immune responses. Nano-vaccines, which utilize nanoparticles as carriers for antigens, have shown tremendous potential in improving vaccine efficacy, stability, and immunogenicity. These advancements have paved the way for enhanced prevention of infectious diseases and innovative therapies for cancer and autoimmune disorders.

Nano-Vaccines and Antigen Delivery

Nano-vaccines involve the use of nanoparticles to encapsulate, stabilize, and deliver antigens to specific immune cells, such as dendritic cells. These nanoparticles protect the antigens from degradation and enhance their uptake by antigen-presenting cells (APCs), leading to a stronger and more sustained immune response.

- **Lipid-Based Nanoparticles:** Lipid nanoparticles (LNPs) are widely used in mRNA vaccines, such as the COVID-19 vaccines developed by Pfizer-BioNTech and Moderna. LNPs protect the fragile mRNA from enzymatic degradation and facilitate its delivery to immune cells, eliciting robust humoral and cellular immune responses.
- **Polymeric Nanoparticles:** Biodegradable polymers like poly(lactic-co-glycolic acid) (PLGA) are used to deliver protein antigens or DNA vaccines. These nanoparticles provide controlled release of antigens, ensuring prolonged exposure and enhanced immune activation.
- **Inorganic Nanoparticles:** Metallic nanoparticles, such as gold and silica nanoparticles, are utilized to present antigens in a stable and highly immunogenic form. Their unique surface properties allow for functionalization with adjuvants or additional antigens to enhance immune responses.

Immunomodulation and Adjuvant Activity

Nanoparticles serve as adjuvants, boosting the immune response by activating innate immune pathways and enhancing antigen presentation. They can stimulate toll-like receptors (TLRs) and other immune pathways, mimicking natural infection processes to amplify vaccine efficacy.

For example, nanoparticles functionalized with TLR ligands, such as CpG oligonucleotides, have shown enhanced immunostimulatory effects in cancer immunotherapy and infectious disease vaccines.

Applications in Cancer Immunotherapy

Nanotechnology plays a pivotal role in cancer immunotherapy, where it is used to deliver tumor antigens or immunomodulatory agents to stimulate an anti-tumor immune response.

- **Nanoparticles for Immune Checkpoint Inhibition:** Nanoparticles are used to deliver immune checkpoint inhibitors, such as anti-PD-1 or anti-CTLA-4 antibodies, directly to the tumor microenvironment, minimizing systemic toxicity.
- **Cancer Vaccines:** Nanoparticle-based cancer vaccines deliver tumor-associated antigens to dendritic cells, activating T cells to recognize and destroy cancer cells.

Personalized Vaccines

Nanotechnology enables the development of personalized vaccines tailored to individual genetic or disease profiles. By encapsulating specific antigens or tumor neoantigens, nanoparticle-based vaccines provide customized solutions for cancer and other diseases, enhancing therapeutic outcomes.

Advantages of Nano-Vaccines

1. **Enhanced Stability:** Nano-vaccines protect antigens from degradation during storage and transport, improving shelf-life and reducing cold chain dependency.
2. **Targeted Delivery:** Nanoparticles can be functionalized to deliver antigens specifically to APCs, enhancing immune activation.
3. **Dose Sparing:** The efficient delivery and immunostimulatory effects of nanoparticles reduce the required dose of antigens, making vaccines more cost-effective.
4. **Multimodal Immunity:** Nano-vaccines elicit both humoral (antibody-mediated) and cellular (T-cell-mediated) immune responses, providing comprehensive protection.

Applications in Global Vaccination Programs

Nano-vaccines are particularly beneficial in addressing global health challenges, such as pandemics and endemic diseases. The success of mRNA-based COVID-19 vaccines underscores their potential to rapidly develop effective vaccines against emerging infectious diseases. Additionally, nanoparticle-based vaccines for malaria, tuberculosis, and HIV are under development, offering hope for diseases that have eluded conventional vaccine approaches.

9.8 FUTURE TRENDS IN NANOTECHNOLOGY FOR DRUG DELIVERY

9.8.1 EMERGING NANOCARRIERS

As nanotechnology continues to advance, new and innovative nanocarriers are being developed to address the limitations of existing drug delivery systems and to unlock new possibilities in precision medicine. Emerging nanocarriers, such as dendrimers, nanomicelles, and quantum dots, represent a cutting-edge approach to delivering therapeutic agents with enhanced efficacy, specificity, and safety.

Dendrimers

Dendrimers are highly branched, tree-like macromolecules with a central core and multiple layers, called generations. These structures provide a high degree of control over size, shape, and surface functionality, making dendrimers highly versatile for drug delivery applications.

- **Controlled Drug Delivery:** Dendrimers possess numerous surface functional groups, allowing them to conjugate or encapsulate multiple therapeutic agents. Their well-defined structure enables precise control over drug release profiles.
- **Multifunctionality:** The surface of dendrimers can be functionalized with targeting ligands, imaging agents, or solubility enhancers, creating multifunctional nanocarriers for theranostics.
- **Applications:** Dendrimers like polyamidoamine (PAMAM) dendrimers have been explored for delivering anticancer drugs, genetic material, and antimicrobial agents. They are particularly effective in crossing biological barriers, such as the blood-brain barrier, for treating central nervous system (CNS) disorders.

Nanomicelles

Nanomicelles are self-assembled nanostructures formed by amphiphilic molecules with a hydrophobic core and hydrophilic shell. These carriers are particularly effective for delivering poorly water-soluble drugs.

- **Enhanced Solubility and Stability:** The hydrophobic core of nanomicelles solubilizes lipophilic drugs, improving their stability and bioavailability.
- **Targeted Drug Delivery:** Nanomicelles can be functionalized with targeting ligands to achieve site-specific drug delivery. Their small size (10–100 nm) allows them to penetrate tissues effectively, especially in tumor microenvironments.
- **Applications:** Nanomicelles are used in cancer therapy, where they enhance the delivery of drugs like paclitaxel and doxorubicin. They are also explored for delivering genetic materials, such as siRNA and mRNA, in gene therapy applications.

Quantum Dots (QDs)

Quantum dots are semiconductor nanoparticles with unique optical and electronic properties. While traditionally used in imaging and diagnostics, their integration into drug delivery systems represents a promising frontier.

- **Imaging-Guided Therapy:** Quantum dots serve as fluorescent markers, enabling real-time tracking of drug delivery and biodistribution. This theranostic capability combines therapy and diagnostics, enhancing treatment precision.
- **Controlled Drug Release:** Quantum dots can be conjugated with therapeutic agents, allowing for triggered drug release in response to external stimuli, such as light or pH changes.
- **Applications:** Quantum dot-based systems are being investigated for cancer therapy, where they provide simultaneous imaging and targeted drug delivery. Additionally, their ability to cross biological barriers makes them suitable for CNS applications.

Hybrid Nanocarriers

Hybrid nanocarriers combine the advantages of different nanomaterials, such as polymers, lipids, and metals, to create systems with enhanced functionality.

- **Versatility:** Hybrid nanoparticles, such as lipid-polymer or polymer-metal hybrids, offer superior drug encapsulation, stability, and targeting capabilities.
- **Applications:** These carriers are used in cancer therapy, gene delivery, and vaccine development, offering a balance of biocompatibility and therapeutic efficacy.

Stimuli-Responsive Nanocarriers

Emerging nanocarriers are being designed to respond to specific stimuli, such as pH, temperature, or light, enabling precise control over drug release.

- **pH-Responsive Carriers:** Designed to release drugs in acidic environments, such as tumor microenvironments.
- **Thermosensitive Carriers:** Release drugs in response to heat, often used in combination with hyperthermia therapy.

- **Light-Activated Carriers:** Enable on-demand drug release upon exposure to specific wavelengths of light, providing spatial and temporal control.

9.8.2 SMART NANOTECHNOLOGY

Smart nanotechnology represents the next frontier in drug delivery, offering systems that can intelligently respond to specific internal or external triggers for precise and controlled therapeutic action. These advanced systems, often referred to as stimuli-responsive or programmable nanocarriers, are designed to improve drug targeting, minimize side effects, and enhance therapeutic outcomes. Their multifunctionality also enables theranostic applications, integrating therapy and diagnostics into a single platform.

Stimuli-Responsive Nanocarriers

Stimuli-responsive nanocarriers are engineered to release their therapeutic payloads in response to specific stimuli, such as pH, temperature, light, or magnetic fields. These triggers can either be internal, originating from the biological environment, or external, applied through external devices.

Internal Stimuli-Responsive Systems

1. **pH-Responsive Nanocarriers:**
   These systems exploit the acidic microenvironment of tumors or inflamed tissues to trigger drug release. Tumor tissues often have a pH of 6.5–6.8, compared to the neutral pH of healthy tissues. Nanocarriers made from pH-sensitive polymers degrade or change their structure under acidic conditions, releasing the drug specifically at the tumor site.

   Example: Doxorubicin-loaded pH-responsive liposomes release the drug in acidic tumor environments, reducing systemic toxicity.

2. **Enzyme-Responsive Nanocarriers:**
   These carriers are designed to release drugs in response to specific enzymes overexpressed in diseased tissues. For example, matrix metalloproteinases (MMPs), which are abundant in tumor tissues, can cleave peptide linkers in enzyme-responsive systems, enabling localized

drug release.

Example: Polymeric nanoparticles with MMP-cleavable linkers for anticancer drug delivery.

3. **Redox-Responsive Nanocarriers:**
   Tumors and other diseased cells often exhibit high levels of intracellular reducing agents, such as glutathione (GSH). Redox-responsive nanocarriers release their payload when exposed to these reducing environments.

Example: Disulfide bond-based nanocarriers break down in the presence of GSH, facilitating controlled drug release within cells.

External Stimuli-Responsive Systems

1. **Light-Activated Nanocarriers:**
   These systems release drugs upon exposure to specific wavelengths of light, providing precise spatial and temporal control. Light-responsive nanoparticles, such as those containing photosensitive polymers or photosensitizers, are particularly useful in treating localized diseases like skin cancer.

Example: Gold nanoparticles activated by near-infrared (NIR) light for localized photothermal therapy and drug release.

2. **Magnetic-Responsive Nanocarriers:**
   Magnetic nanoparticles, such as those made from iron oxide, respond to external magnetic fields. These carriers can be guided to specific locations in the body, and the magnetic field can trigger drug release at the target site.

Example: Magnetic nanoparticles used in hyperthermia therapy for cancer.

3. **Temperature-Sensitive Nanocarriers:**
   Thermosensitive systems release their payload in response to temperature changes. These carriers are often combined with hyperthermia therapy to enhance drug release in heated tumor tissues.

Example: Liposomes containing phase-transition materials that release drugs at elevated temperatures.

Programmable Delivery Systems

Smart nanocarriers can be programmed to release their payload in a sequential or sustained manner, mimicking the natural pharmacokinetics of drugs.

- **Multistage Delivery:** These systems release drugs in stages, optimizing treatment efficacy. For instance, the outer layer of a nanoparticle might dissolve in an acidic tumor environment, exposing an inner layer designed for intracellular delivery.
- **Time-Controlled Release:** Nanocarriers engineered with programmable polymers can release drugs over a specific timeframe, reducing dosing frequency and improving patient compliance.

Theranostics: A Fusion of Therapy and Diagnostics

Theranostic nanocarriers integrate therapeutic and diagnostic functionalities, enabling real-time monitoring of treatment efficacy while delivering drugs. These systems are especially valuable in cancer therapy, where they allow simultaneous tumor imaging and drug delivery.

- **Example:** Quantum dots conjugated with chemotherapeutic agents provide fluorescence imaging and targeted drug delivery.
- **Example:** Gold nanoparticles serve as contrast agents in imaging and photothermal agents in therapy.

Applications of Smart Nanotechnology

1. **Oncology:** Targeted delivery of anticancer drugs, minimizing systemic toxicity, and enabling imaging-guided therapies.
2. **Neurological Disorders:** Smart nanocarriers can cross the blood-brain barrier and respond to the microenvironment of brain diseases, such as Parkinson's or Alzheimer's.
3. **Infectious Diseases:** Stimuli-responsive systems ensure the localized delivery of antimicrobials to infected tissues.
4. **Chronic Conditions:** Programmable systems provide sustained drug release for long-term management of conditions like diabetes or arthritis.

CHAPTER X

Ocular Drug Delivery Systems

10.1 ANATOMY OF THE EYE AND INTRAOCULAR BARRIERS

10.1.1 Anatomy of the Eye

The eye is a complex organ designed for vision, with structures that work in harmony to capture and process light signals. Its anatomy can be broadly divided into external and internal structures, each playing a crucial role in maintaining ocular health and functionality. A detailed understanding of these structures is essential for the development of effective ocular drug delivery systems.

External Anatomy

1. **Cornea:**

   The cornea is the transparent, dome-shaped outer layer that covers the front of the eye. It serves as the primary refractive surface, bending light to focus it on the retina. The cornea is avascular and composed of five layers, with the epithelium being the outermost, acting as a barrier to drug penetration. Its lipophilic nature makes it a critical challenge in ocular drug delivery.

2. **Conjunctiva:**

   The conjunctiva is a thin, transparent membrane that lines the inner surface of the eyelids and extends to cover the sclera. It contains blood vessels, lymphatics, and mucus-secreting goblet cells, providing protection and lubrication to the eye. Drugs applied topically must navigate the conjunctival capillaries to avoid systemic absorption through the nasolacrimal duct.

3. **Sclera:**

   The sclera is the white, fibrous outer layer of the eye that provides structural support and protection. It is less permeable than the cornea but plays a role in posterior drug delivery when using innovative systems like microneedles.

Internal Anatomy

1. **Aqueous Humor:**
   The aqueous humor is a clear fluid filling the anterior chamber between the cornea and the lens. It maintains intraocular pressure and supplies nutrients to avascular tissues like the cornea and lens. The blood-aqueous barrier, formed by the ciliary epithelium, limits drug penetration into this compartment, posing a challenge for anterior segment therapies.

2. **Vitreous Humor:**
   The vitreous humor is a gel-like substance occupying the posterior chamber of the eye. It maintains the eye's shape and provides a medium for light transmission. Delivering drugs to the vitreous humor requires invasive methods, such as intravitreal injections or implants, due to the presence of intraocular barriers.

3. **Retina:**
   The retina is a light-sensitive tissue lining the inner back of the eye. It contains photoreceptor cells (rods and cones) that convert light into neural signals. The retina is divided into two layers: the neural retina and the retinal pigment epithelium (RPE). The RPE forms part of the blood-retinal barrier, limiting drug penetration into retinal tissues.

4. **Choroid:**
   The choroid lies between the retina and sclera, providing oxygen and nutrients to the outer retina. It contains a dense network of blood vessels, making it a significant site for drug absorption in posterior segment therapies. However, the blood-retinal barrier limits systemic drug entry into this region.

10.1.2 *PHYSIOLOGICAL BARRIERS TO DRUG DELIVERY*

The eye's unique anatomy and physiology are designed to protect it from external insults, but these features also pose significant challenges for drug delivery. Several physiological barriers, including pre-corneal barriers, corneal barriers, and intraocular barriers, limit the bioavailability and effectiveness of ocular drugs. Understanding these barriers is essential for designing efficient drug delivery systems.

Pre-Corneal Barriers

The pre-corneal environment includes dynamic protective mechanisms that reduce the residence time of drugs applied to the eye, limiting absorption.

1. **Tear Film Dynamics:**
   The tear film, a thin layer covering the cornea, is vital for maintaining eye health and transparency. However, it acts as a significant barrier to drug delivery.

   - **Drainage:** The tear film rapidly drains excess fluid into the nasolacrimal duct, reducing the contact time of topical drugs. Within minutes, most of the administered dose is removed, leaving less than 5% available for absorption.
   - **Blinking:** Blinking spreads the tear film across the eye surface but also facilitates drug clearance. Frequent blinking significantly reduces drug retention.
   - **Lacrimation:** Reflex tearing occurs in response to irritation from the drug formulation, further diluting and washing away the drug.

Corneal Barriers

The cornea is a multi-layered structure with selective permeability, making it a major obstacle to drug delivery.

1. **Epithelium as a Lipophilic Barrier:**
   The corneal epithelium, the outermost layer, consists of tightly packed epithelial cells with tight junctions. This layer is highly lipophilic, allowing only small, lipophilic molecules to pass through. Hydrophilic drugs face significant resistance and often require permeation enhancers or prodrug strategies for effective delivery.
2. **Stroma and Endothelium as Hydrophilic Barriers:**

   - **Stroma:** Beneath the epithelium lies the stroma, a hydrophilic layer made of collagen fibrils. While the stroma permits the passage of hydrophilic drugs, it resists lipophilic compounds, creating a dual-barrier effect when combined with the epithelium.
   - **Endothelium:** The innermost layer, the endothelium, regulates corneal hydration. Although it is less dense than the epithelium, it

still acts as a barrier for drug molecules, especially large ones.

Intraocular Barriers

Once drugs penetrate the corneal barriers, intraocular barriers further limit their distribution within the eye, particularly to posterior segments.

1. **Blood-Aqueous Barrier:**
   The blood-aqueous barrier is formed by tight junctions in the ciliary epithelium and iris vasculature. It regulates the exchange of substances between the bloodstream and the aqueous humor, preventing systemic drugs from entering the anterior chamber. This barrier makes treating conditions like glaucoma challenging, as topical drugs must overcome it for therapeutic efficacy.

2. **Blood-Retinal Barrier:**
   The blood-retinal barrier comprises two components:

   - **Inner Barrier:** Formed by tight junctions between endothelial cells of retinal capillaries.
   - **Outer Barrier:** Formed by tight junctions in the retinal pigment epithelium (RPE).
     Together, these barriers limit the entry of systemic drugs into retinal tissues, protecting the retina from potentially harmful substances. However, this protection also makes it difficult to deliver drugs for treating retinal disorders, such as age-related macular degeneration or diabetic retinopathy.

10.2 CHALLENGES IN OCULAR DRUG DELIVERY

Delivering drugs to the eye poses significant challenges due to its unique anatomy, physiology, and protective barriers. These challenges result in limited drug bioavailability, rapid clearance, and difficulties in reaching target tissues, particularly in the posterior segment. Understanding these issues is critical for developing advanced ocular drug delivery systems that address these limitations effectively.

Drug Absorption and Retention

1. **Limited Bioavailability:**
   The bioavailability of topical ocular drugs is notoriously low, with less than 5% of the administered dose reaching the target tissues. This is primarily due to the rapid clearance mechanisms of the eye, including tear film drainage, blinking, and lacrimation.
2. **Short Residence Time:**
   Topical formulations, such as eye drops, are quickly washed away by tear turnover and blinking, leaving insufficient time for the drug to penetrate the cornea and reach therapeutic concentrations. The average residence time of eye drops is only a few minutes, necessitating frequent re-administration.

Systemic Side Effects

Ocular drugs, particularly topical formulations, can be absorbed into the systemic circulation through the nasolacrimal duct. This unintended absorption not only reduces the drug available for ocular tissues but also increases the risk of systemic side effects.

- **Examples:** Beta-blockers used in glaucoma treatment may cause systemic side effects like bradycardia or hypotension due to their absorption through the nasolacrimal duct.

Formulation Stability

Many ocular drugs face stability issues during formulation and storage, which can compromise their efficacy and safety.

1. **Degradation:**
   The aqueous environment of the eye can lead to the hydrolysis or oxidation of certain drugs, reducing their therapeutic effectiveness.
2. **Solubility Issues:**
   Poor solubility of many drugs limits their availability in aqueous formulations. Enhancers or solubilizers are often required, which may cause irritation or other side effects.
3. **Shelf Life:**
   Ensuring the stability of drugs during storage, especially in the presence of preservatives, remains a significant challenge.

Patient Compliance

1. **Frequent Dosing Requirements:**
   The short residence time of conventional eye drops requires patients to administer them multiple times a day, leading to poor compliance, especially in chronic conditions like glaucoma.

2. **Ease of Administration:**
   Elderly patients or those with dexterity issues may struggle with self-administration of eye drops, further affecting adherence to treatment regimens.

Challenges with Posterior Segment Delivery

Treating diseases of the posterior segment, such as diabetic retinopathy, macular degeneration, and retinal vein occlusion, is particularly challenging due to the presence of multiple barriers.

1. **Blood-Retinal Barrier:**
   This barrier prevents most drugs from reaching the retina via systemic circulation, necessitating invasive delivery methods such as intravitreal injections.

2. **Targeting Retinal Tissues:**
   Achieving localized and sustained drug delivery to the retina without affecting surrounding tissues is difficult. Current methods often involve repeated invasive procedures, which carry risks of infection and patient discomfort.

10.3 STRATEGIES TO OVERCOME OCULAR BARRIERS

Developing effective drug delivery systems for the eye requires innovative strategies to overcome its unique physiological barriers. One such approach is the use of prodrugs, which enhance drug permeability, stability, and therapeutic efficacy by modifying the chemical structure of active drugs.

10.3.1 PRODRUG APPROACH

Definition and Mechanism

A prodrug is a pharmacologically inactive compound that undergoes enzymatic or chemical transformation in the body to release the active drug. In ocular drug delivery, the prodrug approach is used to improve drug penetration across barriers such as the corneal epithelium and to enhance the drug's bioavailability in target tissues.

The key mechanism involves chemical modification of the parent drug, such as esterification or amidation, to alter its physicochemical properties. These modifications increase lipophilicity, enabling the prodrug to cross lipophilic barriers like the corneal epithelium. Once absorbed, the prodrug is metabolized by esterases or other enzymes present in ocular tissues to release the active drug.

Examples of Prodrugs in Ocular Therapy

1. **Dipivefrin (Propine):**

   - Dipivefrin is a prodrug of epinephrine used to treat open-angle glaucoma.
   - The addition of pivaloyl groups increases its lipophilicity, allowing it to penetrate the cornea more effectively than epinephrine.
   - Once inside the eye, dipivefrin is hydrolyzed by esterases in the cornea to release epinephrine, which reduces intraocular pressure by decreasing aqueous humor production and enhancing its outflow.

2. **Latanoprost:**

   - Latanoprost is a prostaglandin analog used to lower intraocular pressure in glaucoma.
   - As a prodrug, it is hydrolyzed by corneal esterases into its active form, latanoprost acid, which increases uveoscleral outflow of aqueous humor.

3. **Travoprost:**

   - Similar to latanoprost, travoprost is a prostaglandin analog that relies on enzymatic activation after corneal penetration.

4. **Brimonidine Prodrug:**

   - Researchers are developing prodrug versions of brimonidine, an alpha-2 adrenergic agonist, to enhance corneal penetration and reduce systemic absorption.

Advantages of the Prodrug Approach

1. **Improved Corneal Penetration:**

   - Prodrugs enhance lipophilicity, enabling efficient crossing of the lipophilic corneal epithelium.

2. **Reduced Systemic Absorption:**

   - By targeting drug activation within ocular tissues, systemic side effects are minimized.

3. **Enhanced Stability:**

   - Chemical modifications improve the stability of the drug in the pre-corneal environment, reducing degradation by tear film enzymes.

4. **Prolonged Action:**

   - Some prodrugs exhibit sustained release of the active drug, reducing dosing frequency and improving patient compliance.

Challenges and Considerations

- The enzymatic activity required for prodrug activation may vary among individuals, affecting therapeutic efficacy.
- Developing a suitable prodrug requires extensive research into the drug's chemistry, enzymatic pathways, and ocular pharmacokinetics.
- The modification should not compromise the drug's therapeutic efficacy or safety.

10.3.2 PERMEATION ENHANCERS

Permeation enhancers play a significant role in overcoming the physiological barriers of the eye, particularly in enhancing the penetration of hydrophilic drugs across the corneal epithelium. These substances temporarily modify the structural integrity of the ocular barrier without causing permanent damage, facilitating improved drug absorption and bioavailability. Their ability to increase drug permeability makes them indispensable in ocular drug delivery systems, especially for drugs that face challenges in crossing the lipophilic and hydrophilic layers of the cornea.

Mechanism of Action

The primary mechanism by which permeation enhancers work is by disrupting the tight junctions present in the epithelial cells of the cornea. Tight junctions are protein complexes that create a barrier to the paracellular transport of hydrophilic molecules. By temporarily loosening these junctions, permeation enhancers allow drugs to pass through the paracellular spaces.

In addition to disrupting tight junctions, some permeation enhancers alter the lipid bilayer of the epithelial membrane. This mechanism increases the permeability of both hydrophilic and lipophilic drugs. Certain enhancers also interact with mucins on the ocular surface, facilitating better drug penetration by reducing the viscosity of the tear film or by enhancing the retention of drugs on the corneal surface.

The effectiveness of permeation enhancers depends on their concentration, molecular structure, and interaction with ocular tissues. For example, at optimal concentrations, they achieve significant enhancement without causing irritation or toxicity. However, excessively high concentrations can lead to adverse effects such as inflammation or damage to the ocular tissues.

Examples of Permeation Enhancers

Cyclodextrins are widely used permeation enhancers in ocular drug delivery. These cyclic oligosaccharides form inclusion complexes with hydrophobic drug molecules, improving their solubility and permeability. By encapsulating the drug, cyclodextrins protect it from degradation and enhance its bioavailability. For instance, hydroxypropyl-beta-cyclodextrin has been used in formulations to increase the ocular penetration of hydrophilic drugs like dexamethasone.

Bile salts, such as sodium taurocholate and sodium deoxycholate, act as effective permeation enhancers by interacting with the lipid bilayer of the corneal epithelium. This interaction disrupts the lipid structure, facilitating drug passage through the membrane. Bile salts are particularly effective for hydrophilic drugs that require enhanced permeability. Their application, however, requires careful optimization to minimize potential irritation.

Surfactants, including non-ionic surfactants like polysorbates and cationic surfactants like benzalkonium chloride, are commonly used in ocular formulations. These substances reduce surface tension and interact with cell membranes to increase permeability. Polysorbates, for example, have been shown to enhance the penetration of both hydrophilic and lipophilic drugs. Benzalkonium chloride, widely used as a preservative in eye drops, also serves as a permeation enhancer. However, prolonged use of cationic surfactants can cause irritation or damage to the ocular surface.

Applications

Permeation enhancers have found extensive applications in improving the delivery of hydrophilic drugs to both the anterior and posterior segments of the eye. For example, formulations containing cyclodextrins have been used to improve the ocular bioavailability of antifungal agents like natamycin, which otherwise face challenges in penetrating the corneal epithelium. Similarly, bile salts have been incorporated into formulations for enhancing the delivery of antibiotics like ciprofloxacin to treat bacterial infections of the eye.

In the treatment of posterior segment diseases, permeation enhancers enable the penetration of drugs through the blood-aqueous and blood-retinal barriers. For example, certain surfactants are used to facilitate the delivery of anti-VEGF drugs for treating age-related macular degeneration. These applications demonstrate the versatility and importance of permeation enhancers in addressing the challenges of ocular drug delivery.

10.3.3 MUCOADHESIVE SYSTEMS

Mucoadhesive systems are an innovative approach in ocular drug delivery designed to prolong the residence time of drugs on the ocular surface. These systems utilize bioadhesive polymers that adhere to the mucin layer of the tear film, providing sustained drug release and enhancing drug bioavailability. By overcoming the rapid clearance of conventional formulations, mucoadhesive systems offer improved therapeutic outcomes for anterior eye conditions.

Mechanism

The efficacy of mucoadhesive systems lies in their ability to form strong interactions with the mucin layer, a glycoprotein-rich component of the tear film. Mucins create a hydrophilic, gel-like network on the corneal and conjunctival surfaces, which acts as a barrier to drug penetration.

Bioadhesive polymers interact with this network through various mechanisms, including hydrogen bonding, electrostatic interactions, and van der Waals forces.

When a mucoadhesive formulation is applied to the eye, the bioadhesive polymer binds to the mucin layer, anchoring the drug on the ocular surface. This prolongs the drug's contact time, allowing for gradual absorption through the cornea or conjunctiva. Additionally, the polymer matrix can act as a reservoir, releasing the drug in a controlled manner over an extended period. This dual mechanism—enhanced retention and controlled release—significantly improves drug bioavailability.

The effectiveness of mucoadhesive systems depends on the properties of the polymer used. Key factors include molecular weight, degree of hydration, and charge. For instance, positively charged polymers show stronger adhesion due to electrostatic interactions with the negatively charged mucin layer.

Examples of Bioadhesive Polymers

Chitosan, a natural polymer derived from chitin, is widely used in mucoadhesive formulations. Its positive charge enhances adhesion to the negatively charged mucin layer, while its biocompatibility and biodegradable nature make it ideal for ocular applications. Chitosan-based eye drops have been developed to deliver antibiotics like ciprofloxacin, demonstrating improved retention and therapeutic efficacy.

Hyaluronic acid, another commonly used bioadhesive polymer, is a hydrophilic polysaccharide found naturally in the extracellular matrix of tissues. It is well-known for its viscoelastic and water-retaining properties, making it suitable for formulating artificial tears and drug delivery systems. Hyaluronic acid-based eye drops are particularly effective for treating dry eye syndrome, as they provide lubrication while enhancing drug retention.

Other polymers, such as carbopol, polyvinyl alcohol (PVA), and hydroxypropyl methylcellulose (HPMC), are also employed in mucoadhesive systems. These polymers exhibit excellent bioadhesion and are often used to deliver anti-inflammatory drugs, antihistamines, and other therapeutic agents.

Applications

Mucoadhesive systems are used to treat a wide range of anterior segment conditions, including dry eye syndrome, conjunctivitis, and keratitis. They are particularly effective in chronic conditions that require frequent dosing of conventional eye drops. By extending the drug's residence time, these systems reduce the frequency of administration, improving patient compliance.

For example, chitosan-based formulations have been developed to deliver anti-inflammatory drugs for treating allergic conjunctivitis. Similarly, hyaluronic acid-based systems are used in postoperative care to manage inflammation and enhance wound healing.

In addition to their use in conventional formulations, mucoadhesive polymers are being incorporated into advanced delivery systems such as nanoparticles and in situ gelling systems. These combinations offer enhanced bioadhesion and controlled drug release, further improving therapeutic outcomes.

10.3.4 IN SITU GELLING SYSTEMS

In situ gelling systems are an advanced approach in ocular drug delivery that address the challenges of rapid drug clearance and poor bioavailability. These systems transition from a liquid state to a gel-like consistency upon exposure to specific physiological triggers such as pH, temperature, or ions. This transition enhances drug retention on the ocular surface and enables controlled drug release, improving therapeutic efficacy and patient compliance.

Mechanism of In Situ Gel Formation

In situ gelling systems are formulated as liquids to facilitate easy application to the eye. Upon instillation, they undergo a phase transition to form a gel-like structure in response to physiological stimuli.

1. **pH-Responsive Gelling Systems:**

   pH-responsive gels are formulated using polymers that remain in a liquid state at acidic pH levels and gel when exposed to the neutral or slightly alkaline pH of the tear fluid (approximately pH 7.4). Polymers such as carbopol exhibit this behavior, undergoing conformational changes and forming a gel matrix in response to the pH change.

2. **Temperature-Responsive Gelling Systems:**

   Temperature-sensitive systems utilize polymers that transition to a gel state at physiological temperatures (around 35–37°C). Poloxamers, also known as Pluronic, are widely used in these formulations. At lower temperatures, they remain as a liquid, but at body temperature, they form a gel due to changes in the hydrophilic-hydrophobic balance of the polymer chains.

3. **Ion-Responsive Gelling Systems:**
Ion-sensitive systems rely on the interaction between ions in the tear fluid and polymers in the formulation. For example, gellan gum forms a gel in the presence of divalent cations such as calcium ions found in tears.

In all these systems, the gel formation slows down drug clearance and creates a reservoir for sustained drug release. This mechanism ensures prolonged contact time with the ocular surface, enhancing drug absorption and therapeutic outcomes.

Advantages of In Situ Gelling Systems

1. **Improved Retention Time:**
The transition to a gel state significantly increases the residence time of the formulation on the ocular surface. This reduces the frequency of administration compared to conventional eye drops, improving patient compliance.

2. **Controlled Drug Release:**
The gel matrix acts as a depot, releasing the drug gradually over time. This ensures sustained therapeutic levels and reduces the risk of side effects associated with peak drug concentrations.

3. **Ease of Administration:**
As liquids, in situ gelling systems are easy to instill and spread evenly across the ocular surface. This improves patient comfort and eliminates issues associated with pre-formed gels or solid inserts.

4. **Versatility in Drug Loading:**
These systems can be used to deliver a wide range of drugs, including hydrophilic, lipophilic, and macromolecular drugs.

5. **Minimized Systemic Absorption:**
By enhancing local drug retention, in situ gels reduce the amount of drug lost through nasolacrimal drainage, minimizing systemic exposure and side effects.

Applications of In Situ Gelling Systems
In situ gelling systems are used to manage a variety of ocular conditions.

- **Glaucoma Treatment:** Pilocarpine-loaded in situ gels improve intraocular pressure control by prolonging drug action, reducing the need for frequent dosing.
- **Dry Eye Syndrome:** Artificial tears with in situ gelling properties provide sustained hydration and protection for the ocular surface.
- **Post-Surgical Care:** Antibiotics and anti-inflammatory drugs delivered through in situ gels enhance wound healing and reduce infection risks after ocular surgeries.
- **Anterior Segment Diseases:** Anti-allergic and anti-inflammatory drugs in in situ gels are used to manage conjunctivitis and keratitis.

10.4 FORMULATIONS AND DEVICES FOR OCULAR DELIVERY

10.4.1 OCULAR INSERTS

Ocular inserts are advanced drug delivery devices designed to address the limitations of conventional eye drops by providing sustained and controlled release of drugs to the ocular surface. These inserts are thin, flexible, and often made from biocompatible polymers that ensure patient safety and efficacy. They are placed in the conjunctival sac or on the surface of the eye, where they slowly release the drug over an extended period, enhancing therapeutic outcomes and reducing the need for frequent dosing.

One of the key features of ocular inserts is their ability to provide sustained drug release. Unlike eye drops, which are rapidly washed away due to tear turnover and blinking, inserts remain in place and maintain a consistent drug concentration on the ocular surface. This property is especially beneficial for chronic conditions like glaucoma, where maintaining therapeutic levels over a long period is critical. For example, the Ocusert Pilo system, which is an ocular insert containing pilocarpine, is used for the treatment of glaucoma. This insert releases pilocarpine at a controlled rate, effectively reducing intraocular pressure for up to seven days.

The design of ocular inserts varies depending on the intended use and drug delivery requirements. Reservoir systems, for instance, consist of a drug reservoir enclosed within a polymeric membrane that controls the release rate. On the other hand, matrix systems incorporate the drug within the polymer matrix itself, allowing for gradual drug release as the polymer degrades or swells. These design features ensure flexibility in adapting the insert to different drugs and therapeutic needs.

One significant advantage of ocular inserts is the reduction in dosing frequency. Frequent administration of eye drops is not only inconvenient but also leads to poor patient compliance, particularly in elderly patients or those with chronic conditions. Ocular inserts, by providing sustained release, reduce the need for frequent application, improving adherence to treatment regimens. Additionally, these devices minimize drug wastage, as the controlled release ensures that the administered drug is efficiently utilized by the eye.

Despite their advantages, ocular inserts face challenges that must be addressed for broader clinical acceptance. One of the primary issues is patient discomfort. The insertion of a foreign device into the eye can cause irritation or a foreign body sensation, especially in sensitive individuals. This discomfort may lead to poor patient acceptance and adherence to treatment. Additionally, some patients may find it difficult to insert or remove the device correctly, especially without prior training. Another challenge is the potential for displacement or expulsion of the insert during blinking or due to physical activity, which can compromise its effectiveness.

To overcome these challenges, researchers are working on developing smaller, softer, and more flexible inserts that conform better to the ocular surface. Materials such as hydrogels, which are highly biocompatible and have excellent moisture retention properties, are being explored to enhance comfort and adherence. Advances in insert design also aim to incorporate biodegradability, allowing the insert to dissolve naturally over time, eliminating the need for removal.

10.4.3 MICRONEEDLES FOR OCULAR DELIVERY

Microneedles are a revolutionary advancement in ocular drug delivery, offering a minimally invasive method for delivering drugs to various segments of the eye, including the posterior region. These devices consist of tiny needles, typically in the range of hundreds of micrometers in length, designed to penetrate the outer layers of the eye without causing significant pain or discomfort. By bypassing the barriers that limit the efficacy of conventional delivery methods, microneedles ensure precise and localized drug delivery to target tissues.

The concept of microneedles revolves around their ability to create microchannels through the ocular barriers, such as the cornea or sclera. These microchannels facilitate the direct delivery of drugs into specific compartments, such as the vitreous humor or retina, bypassing systemic circulation and minimizing off-target effects. Microneedles can be fabricated from a variety of materials, including metals, polymers, and biodegradable substances. Biodegradable microneedles are particularly advantageous, as they dissolve after delivering their payload, eliminating the need for device removal and reducing the risk of long-term complications.

One of the most promising applications of microneedles is the treatment of posterior eye diseases, such as age-related macular degeneration and diabetic retinopathy. These conditions require precise delivery of therapeutic agents, such as anti-VEGF drugs, to the retina or choroid. Conventional methods, such as intravitreal injections, are effective but associated with risks like infection and retinal detachment. Microneedles provide an alternative by enabling targeted delivery with minimal invasiveness. Studies have demonstrated the ability of microneedles to deliver nanoparticles, small molecules, and biologics to posterior tissues, achieving therapeutic concentrations with fewer side effects.

Microneedles also hold potential for delivering vaccines and gene therapies directly to ocular tissues. Their ability to deliver macromolecules, including DNA and RNA, makes them a promising tool for advancing the treatment of genetic and infectious ocular diseases. For example, microneedles have been explored for delivering DNA-based vaccines for conditions like cytomegalovirus retinitis. The precise delivery enabled by microneedles ensures enhanced efficacy and reduced systemic exposure.

Despite their numerous advantages, the adoption of microneedles faces challenges such as manufacturing complexity and potential safety concerns. Ensuring consistent microneedle fabrication with precise dimensions and mechanical strength is critical for maintaining their efficacy and safety. Furthermore, the risk of inflammation or tissue damage due to repeated applications must be carefully evaluated in clinical settings. Addressing these challenges through advancements in materials science and device engineering will be pivotal in translating microneedles from research to routine clinical use.

10.4.4 HYDROGELS

Hydrogels are polymeric networks capable of absorbing large amounts of water or biological fluids while maintaining their structural integrity. These materials have emerged as a versatile platform for ocular drug delivery due to their biocompatibility, tunable properties, and ability to provide prolonged drug release. By forming a soft, gel-like matrix, hydrogels adhere to the ocular surface or integrate into tissues, ensuring sustained therapeutic effects.

The mechanism of hydrogels in ocular drug delivery is primarily based on their swelling properties. When applied to the eye, hydrogels absorb tear fluid and swell, forming a hydrated matrix that entraps the drug. This matrix allows for the controlled diffusion of the drug over an extended period. The swelling behavior is influenced by factors such as polymer composition, crosslinking density, and environmental conditions like pH and temperature. For instance, temperature-sensitive hydrogels remain in a liquid state at room temperature but transition to a gel state upon reaching physiological temperatures, enhancing their retention on the ocular surface.

Hydrogels are widely used to deliver drugs for treating anterior segment diseases, such as dry eye syndrome, keratitis, and post-surgical inflammation. Hyaluronic acid, a naturally occurring polysaccharide, is one of the most commonly used materials in ocular hydrogels. It provides excellent moisture retention and biocompatibility, making it ideal for formulating artificial tears and therapeutic eye drops. For example, hyaluronic acid-based hydrogels are used to deliver anti-inflammatory agents and lubricants, offering relief in dry eye conditions and enhancing wound healing after surgeries.

Carbopol, another popular polymer used in hydrogels, is known for its bioadhesive properties and ability to form stable gels. Carbopol-based formulations are employed to deliver drugs like antibiotics and anti-glaucoma agents, ensuring prolonged contact time and improved therapeutic outcomes. These formulations are particularly effective for patients with chronic conditions, as they reduce the frequency of administration and improve adherence to treatment.

In addition to conventional drugs, hydrogels are being explored for advanced applications such as gene therapy and stem cell delivery. Hydrogels can encapsulate and protect sensitive biomolecules, such as DNA,

RNA, or proteins, ensuring their stability and controlled release. They also serve as scaffolds for delivering stem cells to damaged ocular tissues, facilitating tissue regeneration and repair.

While hydrogels offer numerous benefits, challenges such as achieving precise drug release kinetics and ensuring long-term stability remain. Innovations in polymer chemistry, such as the development of stimuli-responsive hydrogels, are addressing these limitations by enabling hydrogels to release drugs in response to specific triggers like pH or temperature changes.

10.5 APPLICATIONS OF OCULAR DRUG DELIVERY SYSTEMS

Ocular drug delivery systems have revolutionized the treatment of a wide range of eye diseases by providing targeted and sustained drug delivery to specific ocular tissues. These advanced systems address the limitations of conventional eye drops and injections, enhancing therapeutic efficacy, reducing side effects, and improving patient compliance. Their applications span various therapeutic areas, from chronic conditions like glaucoma to acute infections and post-surgical care.

10.5.1 THERAPEUTIC AREAS

Glaucoma Management

Glaucoma is a progressive eye disease characterized by increased intraocular pressure, which can lead to optic nerve damage and vision loss if untreated. Conventional eye drops, such as prostaglandin analogs and beta-blockers, are effective in reducing intraocular pressure but suffer from poor patient compliance due to the need for frequent administration.

Ocular inserts have emerged as a promising solution for glaucoma management. These inserts provide sustained release of drugs, ensuring consistent intraocular pressure control. For instance, prostaglandin analogs like latanoprost and beta-blockers like timolol can be delivered via inserts such as Ocusert. These inserts release the drug at a controlled rate over days or weeks, reducing the frequency of administration and improving patient adherence. The use of inserts also minimizes systemic absorption, reducing the risk of side effects such as hypotension or bradycardia.

Infections and Inflammations

Ocular infections and inflammations, such as bacterial conjunctivitis, keratitis, and uveitis, require rapid and effective treatment to prevent complications. Antibiotics and corticosteroids are the mainstay of therapy, but their efficacy is often limited by poor ocular penetration and short residence time on the eye surface.

Nanoformulations, such as liposomes, nanoparticles, and nanomicelles, have significantly improved the delivery of these drugs. These systems enhance drug penetration through the corneal barrier, ensuring therapeutic levels at the site of infection or inflammation. For example, liposomal formulations of ciprofloxacin provide sustained drug release, reducing the dosing frequency for bacterial keratitis. Similarly, corticosteroids encapsulated in nanoparticles achieve better anti-inflammatory effects by targeting inflamed tissues with minimal systemic exposure.

Retinal Disorders

Retinal disorders, such as age-related macular degeneration (AMD), diabetic retinopathy, and retinal vein occlusion, are leading causes of vision loss worldwide. Effective treatment requires precise delivery of drugs to the posterior segment of the eye, which is challenging due to the presence of the blood-retinal barrier.

Anti-VEGF drugs, such as ranibizumab and aflibercept, are commonly used to treat AMD by inhibiting abnormal blood vessel growth in the retina. These drugs are typically delivered through intravitreal injections, which, while effective, are invasive and associated with risks such as infection and retinal detachment. Advanced drug delivery systems, such as biodegradable implants and microneedles, offer less invasive and sustained-release alternatives. For example, biodegradable implants releasing anti-VEGF drugs over several months provide consistent therapeutic effects while reducing the need for repeated injections.

Post-Surgical Care

Ocular surgeries, including cataract removal, corneal transplants, and glaucoma procedures, often require post-operative management to control inflammation, prevent infections, and promote healing. Conventional eye drops, while effective, require frequent application and may fail to achieve consistent drug levels.

Sustained-release systems, such as hydrogels and in situ gelling systems, are highly effective in post-surgical care. These systems provide prolonged release of antibiotics and anti-inflammatory agents, ensuring consistent therapeutic levels and reducing the risk of complications. For instance, carbopol-based hydrogels have been used to deliver corticosteroids after cataract surgery, improving patient outcomes by reducing dosing frequency and ensuring better control of inflammation.

10.6 EVALUATION OF OCULAR DRUG DELIVERY SYSTEMS

Evaluating ocular drug delivery systems is a critical step in their development to ensure efficacy, safety, and stability. Both in vitro and in vivo methods are employed to assess the performance of these systems. In vitro evaluation focuses on controlled laboratory conditions to analyze drug release, permeation, and other key properties before proceeding to in vivo testing. These studies provide crucial insights into how the drug interacts with ocular tissues and the surrounding environment.

10.6.1 IN VITRO EVALUATION

Drug Release Studies

Drug release studies are fundamental in evaluating the sustained release and controlled delivery capabilities of ocular formulations. These studies help determine how effectively a drug is released over time and whether it achieves the desired therapeutic levels.

Diffusion cells, such as Franz diffusion cells or modified USP apparatus, are commonly used for this purpose. These devices simulate the drug release from the formulation into an appropriate medium, mimicking the ocular environment. The medium often consists of simulated tear fluid, which replicates the physiological pH and ionic composition of natural tears.

In a typical experiment, the drug-loaded formulation, such as a hydrogel or nanoparticle suspension, is placed in the donor compartment of the diffusion cell. The receptor compartment contains the simulated tear fluid, maintained at 34–37°C to mimic ocular conditions. A semi-permeable membrane separates the two compartments, allowing the drug to diffuse into the receptor medium. Samples are collected at regular intervals and analyzed using high-performance liquid chromatography (HPLC) or UV-visible spectroscopy to quantify the drug concentration.

These studies provide data on parameters like release kinetics, burst release, and cumulative drug release over time. For instance, in hydrogels, a zero-order release profile is often desirable as it indicates consistent drug delivery. Drug release data are also used to optimize formulation parameters, such as polymer concentration and crosslinking density, to achieve the desired therapeutic effect.

Permeation Studies

Permeation studies are conducted to evaluate the ability of a drug to penetrate ocular tissues, particularly the cornea. These studies are crucial for understanding the formulation's efficacy in overcoming ocular barriers and delivering drugs to the target site.

Excised corneal tissues from animals, such as rabbits, are widely used as models in permeation studies. The excised cornea is mounted between the donor and receptor compartments of a diffusion cell, with the formulation applied to the donor side. The receptor compartment contains a physiological medium, such as phosphate-buffered saline (PBS), maintained at 34–37°C.

The study measures the amount of drug that permeates through the cornea over time, providing data on permeability coefficients and flux rates. The results help in comparing different formulations and selecting the most effective one. For instance, nanoformulations like liposomes or nanoparticles are often compared against conventional eye drops to demonstrate superior permeation properties.

Advanced techniques, such as confocal laser scanning microscopy (CLSM), can be used alongside permeation studies to visualize drug distribution within the corneal layers. This approach provides insights into whether the drug primarily penetrates through the epithelium, stroma, or endothelium.

10.6.2 IN VIVO EVALUATION

In vivo evaluation of ocular drug delivery systems is a critical phase of development, providing essential data on the performance, safety, and therapeutic efficacy of formulations in biological systems. While in vitro studies offer initial insights, in vivo studies validate the findings by assessing drug behavior under physiological conditions. Key aspects evaluated include pharmacokinetics, efficacy, and safety, ensuring that the drug delivery system meets clinical standards.

Pharmacokinetics

Pharmacokinetic studies focus on determining the concentration of the drug in ocular tissues over time. These studies help assess the absorption, distribution, metabolism, and elimination of the drug when delivered through the ocular formulation.

Drug levels in the **aqueous humor** and **vitreous humor** are measured to evaluate the formulation's ability to target specific ocular compartments. For anterior segment diseases, such as glaucoma or dry eye syndrome, the drug concentration in the aqueous humor is critical. For posterior segment conditions, such as diabetic retinopathy or age-related macular degeneration, drug levels in the vitreous humor are of primary importance.

In a typical study, the formulation is administered to animal models, such as rabbits, due to the similarity of their eye anatomy to humans. Aqueous and vitreous humor samples are collected at specific time intervals post-administration. Advanced analytical techniques, such as liquid chromatography-mass spectrometry (LC-MS) or high-performance liquid chromatography (HPLC), are used to quantify drug concentrations.

Pharmacokinetic parameters, such as maximum concentration (C_{max}), time to reach maximum concentration (T_{max}), and area under the curve (AUC), provide insights into the formulation's release and retention characteristics. For example, a sustained-release hydrogel might demonstrate prolonged drug levels in the vitreous humor, ensuring consistent therapeutic effects with reduced dosing frequency.

Efficacy Studies

Efficacy studies are conducted to evaluate the therapeutic outcomes of the drug delivery system against specific disease targets. These studies assess whether the formulation achieves the intended clinical benefits, such as lowering intraocular pressure in glaucoma, reducing inflammation in uveitis, or inhibiting abnormal blood vessel growth in age-related macular degeneration.

Clinical outcomes are measured using both objective and subjective parameters. For example, in glaucoma studies, intraocular pressure is measured using tonometry to determine the effectiveness of the drug in lowering pressure levels. For retinal disorders, imaging techniques such as optical coherence tomography (OCT) or fluorescein angiography are used to monitor structural improvements in the retina and reductions in fluid accumulation.

Efficacy studies also involve comparisons with conventional formulations, such as eye drops or intravitreal injections, to demonstrate the superiority of advanced delivery systems like implants or microneedles. For instance, a biodegradable implant releasing anti-VEGF drugs may show longer-lasting effects and fewer administration requirements compared to intravitreal injections.

Irritation and Safety

The safety of ocular formulations is paramount, as the eye is a highly sensitive organ. In vivo safety studies evaluate potential irritation, inflammation, or toxicity caused by the formulation.

Rabbit eye models are commonly used for irritation assessment due to their anatomical and physiological similarities to the human eye. After administering the formulation, the eyes are examined for signs of irritation, such as redness, swelling, or excessive tearing. The Draize test is a standard method for assessing ocular irritation, involving a scoring system based on observable reactions.

Histological studies are also conducted to evaluate the impact of the formulation on ocular tissues. Tissue samples from the cornea, conjunctiva, and retina are examined under a microscope for any structural changes or inflammatory responses.

Safety studies also assess the long-term effects of the formulation, particularly for sustained-release systems or implants. Biodegradable materials are preferred to minimize the risk of accumulation or foreign body reactions.

CHAPTER XI

Intrauterine Drug Delivery Systems

11.1 INTRODUCTION TO INTRAUTERINE DRUG DELIVERY SYSTEMS (IUDS)

11.1.1 Definition and Overview

Intrauterine drug delivery systems, commonly known as IUDs, are long-term, reversible devices designed to deliver therapeutic agents directly into the uterus. These systems are widely recognized for their effectiveness, convenience, and minimal maintenance requirements, making them a preferred choice for contraception and other therapeutic applications. IUDs are small, T-shaped devices typically inserted into the uterine cavity by a trained healthcare professional. Once in place, they provide localized drug delivery, ensuring consistent and prolonged therapeutic action while minimizing systemic exposure.

Unlike systemic drug delivery methods, where medications are administered orally or intravenously and circulated throughout the body, IUDs focus on local drug delivery within the uterus. This localized action is particularly advantageous because it allows the drug to act directly on the target tissues, such as the endometrium, while reducing the risk of systemic side effects. For example, in hormonal IUDs like the levonorgestrel-releasing system (Mirena), the hormone is released in low doses over an extended period, directly affecting the uterine lining and cervical mucus. This minimizes the risk of systemic hormonal side effects such as mood changes or weight gain, which are more common with oral contraceptives.

Systemic drug delivery methods, while effective for many conditions, often involve higher doses of medication to ensure adequate drug levels at the target site. This approach can lead to unwanted side effects in non-target tissues. In contrast, the localized delivery achieved by IUDs ensures that therapeutic concentrations are maintained precisely where needed, allowing for lower overall drug doses. For instance, copper-based IUDs release copper ions that create an inhospitable environment for sperm, thereby preventing fertilization. The direct release of these ions within the uterus ensures effective contraception without affecting the rest of the body.

Local drug delivery methods other than IUDs, such as vaginal rings or topical gels, also aim to concentrate the therapeutic effect at the target site. However, IUDs offer a significant advantage in terms of longevity and ease of use. While vaginal rings typically need to be replaced monthly and gels require daily application, IUDs provide effective treatment for several years, with hormonal IUDs like Mirena lasting up to five years and non-hormonal copper IUDs lasting up to ten years.

The development and use of IUDs represent a significant advancement in modern medicine, offering solutions to longstanding challenges in contraception and localized therapy. By combining the benefits of long-term efficacy, reversibility, and minimal systemic exposure, IUDs provide a unique and effective approach to managing reproductive health. Their role in reducing unintended pregnancies and improving quality of life for individuals requiring localized hormonal or therapeutic interventions underscores their importance in contemporary healthcare. With ongoing advancements in materials and design, IUDs continue to evolve, further enhancing their effectiveness and patient acceptability.

11.1.2 HISTORICAL DEVELOPMENT OF IUDS

The development of intrauterine drug delivery systems (IUDs) has undergone significant evolution, transitioning from simple inert devices to sophisticated hormone-releasing systems. This progression reflects advancements in materials science, medical understanding, and patient-centered design, making IUDs one of the most effective and widely used contraceptive methods worldwide.

The origins of IUDs date back to ancient times, with early references suggesting the use of objects placed in the uterus to prevent pregnancy in animals. However, the modern era of IUD development began in the early 20th century. In the 1920s, Dr. Ernst Grafenberg introduced one of the first intrauterine devices, which combined silk sutures and silver wire. Although relatively primitive, it laid the groundwork for future innovations.

The introduction of plastic-based IUDs in the mid-20th century marked a significant milestone. These devices, such as the Lippes Loop, utilized inert materials like polyethylene, which were biocompatible and less likely to cause infections or tissue damage. Despite their effectiveness, these early IUDs had limitations, including high expulsion rates and a lack of long-term efficacy.

The 1960s and 1970s witnessed a transformative leap with the development of copper-based IUDs, such as the Copper T. These devices incorporated copper as an active component, which exerted spermicidal effects and enhanced contraceptive efficacy. The Copper T device demonstrated remarkable longevity, with some models providing effective contraception for up to ten years. Copper-based IUDs became a cornerstone of modern contraceptive options, widely used across diverse populations due to their non-hormonal nature.

The next significant advancement came with the introduction of hormone-releasing IUDs in the 1980s and 1990s. The levonorgestrel-releasing intrauterine system (LNG-IUS), marketed as Mirena, combined the mechanical contraceptive action of IUDs with the therapeutic effects of localized hormone release. This innovation not only provided effective contraception but also offered additional benefits, such as reducing menstrual bleeding and managing conditions like endometriosis. Mirena paved the way for smaller, shorter-duration devices like Skyla, catering to a broader range of patient needs.

In recent years, research has focused on biodegradable IUDs, which eliminate the need for device removal. These systems use biodegradable polymers to deliver drugs and naturally dissolve over time. This innovation addresses challenges associated with device removal, particularly in regions with limited healthcare access.

11.1.3 RELEVANCE IN MODERN MEDICINE

Intrauterine drug delivery systems have emerged as a critical tool in addressing unmet needs in contraception and hormone replacement therapy. Their ability to provide long-term, reversible, and effective solutions makes them highly relevant in modern healthcare, particularly in improving reproductive health and managing gynecological conditions.

Contraception remains a key application of IUDs, helping individuals and couples achieve family planning goals while reducing unintended pregnancies. With failure rates of less than 1%, IUDs are among the most effective contraceptive methods available. Hormonal IUDs, such as Mirena, offer additional benefits by addressing menstrual disorders, including heavy menstrual bleeding and dysmenorrhea. For individuals with contraindications to estrogen-containing methods, hormonal IUDs provide a safe and effective alternative.

In hormone replacement therapy, IUDs play a pivotal role in protecting the endometrium from hyperplasia in postmenopausal women receiving systemic estrogen. The localized release of progestins ensures endometrial protection without causing systemic side effects. This dual action makes IUDs a valuable option in managing menopausal symptoms and reducing the risk of endometrial cancer.

Beyond individual health, IUDs contribute significantly to global healthcare initiatives, particularly in population control and resource-limited settings. Non-hormonal IUDs like Copper T are widely used in family planning programs due to their affordability, ease of distribution, and long-term effectiveness. By empowering individuals to make informed reproductive choices, IUDs help reduce maternal mortality, improve economic stability, and enhance quality of life in communities worldwide.

The ability of IUDs to enhance local drug delivery is a major advantage in modern medicine. By releasing drugs directly at the target site, IUDs minimize systemic exposure and associated side effects. For example, in managing endometriosis, hormonal IUDs deliver progestins directly to the endometrium, alleviating symptoms while avoiding the systemic effects of oral or injectable therapies. This precision in drug delivery exemplifies the growing trend toward personalized medicine.

11.2 MECHANISM OF ACTION AND TYPES OF IUDS

11.2.1 MECHANISM OF ACTION

The mechanism of action of intrauterine drug delivery systems (IUDs) is multifaceted, aiming to prevent conception through various physiological and biochemical pathways. The contraceptive effects of IUDs are achieved by interfering with key stages of reproduction, including fertilization and implantation, and in some cases, ovulation. These mechanisms vary based on whether the device is hormonal or non-hormonal, but they collectively ensure high efficacy in preventing pregnancy.

Prevention of Fertilization Through Effects on Sperm Motility and Viability

One of the primary mechanisms by which IUDs prevent pregnancy is by inhibiting the motility and viability of sperm. Copper-based IUDs, for example, release copper ions into the uterine cavity. These ions create an inhospitable environment for sperm by altering the ionic composition of cervical mucus and the uterine lining. Copper ions are toxic to sperm, disrupting their motility and viability. This ensures that sperm are unable to reach and fertilize the ovum. Additionally, the physical presence of the IUD in the uterine cavity creates a mild inflammatory response, further enhancing its spermicidal effects by attracting immune cells such as macrophages and neutrophils, which phagocytize sperm.

Alteration of the Endometrial Lining to Inhibit Implantation

Both hormonal and non-hormonal IUDs modify the endometrial lining of the uterus, making it unsuitable for the implantation of a fertilized ovum. In the case of hormonal IUDs, such as those releasing levonorgestrel, the hormone causes the endometrial lining to become thinner and less vascularized. This inhibits the formation of a supportive environment required for implantation. Non-hormonal IUDs, like copper-based devices, achieve a similar effect through the inflammatory response they induce. The altered endometrial environment effectively prevents the establishment of pregnancy even if fertilization occurs, adding an additional layer of contraceptive efficacy.

Localized Hormone Release to Suppress Ovulation

Hormonal IUDs exert their contraceptive effects primarily through the localized release of progestins, such as levonorgestrel. These hormones act on multiple levels to prevent pregnancy. Firstly, they thicken cervical mucus, creating a physical barrier that impedes sperm entry into the uterus. Secondly, they suppress ovulation in some users by inhibiting the secretion of gonadotropins from the pituitary gland, which reduces the release of luteinizing hormone (LH) necessary for ovulation. While suppression of ovulation is not the primary mechanism for hormonal IUDs, it contributes to their overall efficacy in preventing pregnancy.

Hormonal and Non-Hormonal Mechanisms

Intrauterine drug delivery systems (IUDs) achieve their contraceptive effects through hormonal and non-hormonal mechanisms, each targeting specific physiological pathways to prevent pregnancy. These mechanisms are designed to optimize efficacy, reduce systemic side effects, and ensure long-term contraception.

Copper-Induced Spermicidal Effects

Non-hormonal IUDs, such as copper-based devices, rely on the spermicidal properties of copper to inhibit fertilization. Copper ions are continuously released into the uterine cavity from the device's surface. These ions create a toxic environment for sperm by disrupting their motility, viability, and ability to fertilize an ovum.

The mechanism of copper's spermicidal action involves multiple pathways. Copper ions interact with the enzymes and proteins on the sperm's surface, impairing their motility and reducing their ability to navigate through cervical mucus. Additionally, copper induces the production of reactive oxygen species (ROS) within the uterine cavity. These ROS not only disrupt sperm function but also damage their DNA, further reducing their fertilization potential.

Copper-based IUDs also stimulate a mild inflammatory response in the uterine lining. This response involves the recruitment of immune cells such as macrophages and neutrophils, which engulf and destroy sperm. The inflammatory environment creates a physical and chemical barrier that enhances the contraceptive effect of copper, ensuring that sperm are unable to survive or reach the ovum.

Examples of copper-based IUDs include the Copper T (Cu-T) and Cu-380A devices, which provide long-term contraception for up to 10 years, making them a cost-effective and low-maintenance option for individuals seeking non-hormonal birth control.

Local vs. Systemic Hormonal Actions

Hormonal IUDs, such as those releasing levonorgestrel (e.g., Mirena, Skyla), utilize localized hormone delivery to achieve their contraceptive effects. These systems provide a consistent, low-dose release of progestins directly into the uterine cavity, minimizing systemic exposure and reducing the risk of side effects associated with oral or injectable hormonal contraceptives.

The primary local action of hormonal IUDs is the thickening of cervical mucus. This hormone-induced change creates a dense barrier that prevents sperm from entering the uterus, effectively blocking fertilization. Additionally, progestins act on the endometrial lining, causing it to thin and become less receptive to implantation. This dual action ensures high contraceptive efficacy.

In some users, hormonal IUDs also exert systemic effects, although these are less pronounced compared to other hormonal contraceptive methods. By suppressing gonadotropin-releasing hormone (GnRH) secretion from the hypothalamus, hormonal IUDs can reduce the levels of follicle-stimulating hormone (FSH) and luteinizing hormone (LH). This suppression can inhibit ovulation in a subset of users, adding an extra layer of contraceptive protection.

The localized nature of hormonal IUDs allows for a lower overall dose of hormones, reducing the likelihood of systemic side effects such as mood swings, weight gain, or nausea, which are commonly associated with systemic hormonal methods like oral contraceptives or hormone injections.

11.2.2 TYPES OF IUDS

Non-Hormonal IUDs

Non-hormonal intrauterine devices (IUDs) are widely recognized for their effectiveness, longevity, and suitability for individuals seeking a hormone-free contraceptive option. These devices primarily utilize copper as the active agent to achieve their contraceptive effects, making them an ideal choice for individuals who prefer or require non-hormonal methods.

Copper-based IUDs, such as the Copper T and Cu-380A, are among the most commonly used non-hormonal devices. These IUDs are T-shaped, with copper wire or bands wound around their plastic frame. Copper, a biologically active metal, plays a central role in the contraceptive mechanism by creating a hostile environment for sperm within the uterine cavity.

The mechanism of action for copper-based IUDs involves several pathways. Firstly, the release of copper ions into the uterus impairs sperm motility, reducing their ability to swim effectively. This inhibition prevents sperm from reaching the ovum for fertilization. Additionally, copper ions compromise the viability of sperm by interacting with their enzymes and disrupting their cellular structure. Copper-induced production of reactive oxygen species (ROS) further damages sperm DNA and proteins, rendering them incapable of successful fertilization.

Another key aspect of the contraceptive effect of copper-based IUDs is their impact on the endometrium. The presence of copper generates a mild inflammatory response in the uterine lining, attracting immune cells such as macrophages and neutrophils. These cells engulf and destroy sperm that enter the uterine cavity, enhancing the device's contraceptive efficacy.

Non-hormonal IUDs offer remarkable longevity, making them an excellent option for individuals seeking long-term contraception. Devices like the Copper T and Cu-380A provide protection for up to 10 years, significantly reducing the need for frequent replacements or re-administration. This extended duration of action also makes them cost-effective, as a single device can provide years of reliable contraception.

The longevity of copper-based IUDs is due to the durability of the materials used and the slow, consistent release of copper ions. For example, the Cu-380A, one of the most widely used copper IUDs, has been shown to maintain its efficacy for up to a decade. Studies have demonstrated that the failure rate of copper-based IUDs is less than 1%, placing them among the most effective reversible contraceptive methods available.

Non-hormonal IUDs are particularly beneficial for individuals who experience side effects from hormonal contraceptives, such as mood swings, weight changes, or headaches. Additionally, they do not interfere with the menstrual cycle, allowing for natural hormonal fluctuations.

While non-hormonal IUDs are highly effective, they are not without challenges. Users may experience increased menstrual bleeding or cramping during the first few months after insertion. However, these symptoms often subside with continued use. For individuals seeking a hormone-free, long-term contraceptive solution, the benefits of copper-based IUDs far outweigh these temporary side effects.

Hormonal IUDs

Hormonal intrauterine devices (IUDs) represent a significant advancement in contraceptive technology, combining the mechanical benefits of IUDs with the therapeutic effects of localized hormone delivery. These devices are designed to release small, controlled amounts of the hormone levonorgestrel directly into the uterine cavity, providing highly effective and long-lasting contraception while minimizing systemic side effects.

Examples of hormonal IUDs include widely used devices such as Mirena and Skyla. These devices are T-shaped, made from biocompatible plastic, and incorporate a reservoir containing levonorgestrel. Once inserted into the uterus, the IUD releases the hormone at a consistent rate, typically between 10–20 micrograms per day, depending on the device.

The mechanism of hormonal IUDs involves multiple pathways that prevent pregnancy effectively. One primary mechanism is the **thinning of the endometrium**. Levonorgestrel acts on the uterine lining, causing it to become thin and less vascularized. This alteration makes the endometrium inhospitable for the implantation of a fertilized ovum.

Another critical mechanism is the **thickening of cervical mucus**. Levonorgestrel increases the viscosity of the mucus produced by the cervix, creating a physical barrier that hinders sperm movement. This prevents sperm from entering the uterus and reaching the ovum for fertilization.

In some cases, hormonal IUDs may also suppress ovulation by inhibiting the secretion of luteinizing hormone (LH) from the pituitary gland. While ovulation suppression is not the primary mode of action, it adds an additional layer of contraceptive efficacy for certain users.

Hormonal IUDs offer significant longevity, with devices like Mirena providing contraception for up to five years and smaller devices like Skyla lasting three years. This long-term efficacy makes them a convenient and cost-effective option for individuals seeking sustained birth control without the need for frequent maintenance.

The localized release of levonorgestrel from hormonal IUDs minimizes systemic hormone exposure, reducing the risk of side effects commonly associated with oral contraceptives, such as nausea, weight gain, or mood changes. Hormonal IUDs also provide additional health benefits, including the reduction of heavy menstrual bleeding and the management of gynecological conditions like endometriosis. For individuals with conditions such as anemia or dysmenorrhea, hormonal IUDs can offer significant relief by lightening or eliminating menstrual periods.

While hormonal IUDs are highly effective, they may cause certain side effects, particularly during the initial months of use. Users may experience irregular spotting or light bleeding, which typically resolves over time as the body adjusts to the device. The insertion procedure can also cause discomfort for some individuals, but this is a temporary concern and can be managed with appropriate care and guidance.

Biodegradable IUDs

Biodegradable intrauterine devices (IUDs) represent a promising innovation in contraceptive technology, leveraging advanced materials science to address some of the limitations of traditional IUDs. These devices are designed using biodegradable polymers that gradually break down within the uterine environment, eliminating the need for removal procedures. This feature makes biodegradable IUDs particularly appealing in resource-limited settings and for individuals seeking a more convenient and minimally invasive contraceptive option.

Biodegradable IUDs function similarly to conventional IUDs but offer the added benefit of natural degradation after their effective lifespan. These devices are typically made from biocompatible polymers such as polylactic acid (PLA), polyglycolic acid (PGA), or polycaprolactone (PCL), which degrade into harmless byproducts like carbon dioxide and water. These byproducts are safely absorbed or excreted by the body, ensuring no long-term residue remains.

The primary contraceptive mechanism of biodegradable IUDs depends on their design. Devices may incorporate active agents such as copper or levonorgestrel to prevent fertilization and implantation. For example, a biodegradable IUD with copper components releases copper ions into the uterine cavity, impairing sperm motility and viability. Similarly, a hormone-releasing biodegradable IUD delivers levonorgestrel locally, thickening cervical mucus and thinning the endometrium to prevent pregnancy.

One of the most significant advantages of biodegradable IUDs is the elimination of the removal procedure. Traditional IUDs, while effective, require a healthcare professional to remove them once their lifespan ends, which can be inconvenient or inaccessible for some users. Biodegradable IUDs naturally dissolve after completing their contraceptive duration, simplifying the process and reducing the risk of complications associated with removal, such as uterine perforation or infection.

Biodegradable IUDs are particularly beneficial in regions with limited access to healthcare facilities. For individuals who may not be able to return for device removal, these IUDs offer a safe and effective alternative, ensuring continued contraceptive protection without the need for follow-up visits. Additionally, the self-limiting nature of biodegradable IUDs enhances their appeal for first-time users or those hesitant about long-term contraceptive devices.

Despite their advantages, biodegradable IUDs are still in the developmental and early implementation stages. Challenges such as ensuring controlled degradation rates, maintaining mechanical strength during use, and achieving consistent drug release must be addressed. Researchers are exploring novel polymer blends and manufacturing techniques to overcome these hurdles and enhance the reliability of biodegradable IUDs.

Innovative Smart IUDs

Innovative smart intrauterine devices (IUDs) represent the next generation of contraceptive technology, incorporating advanced digital and sensor technologies to enhance their functionality. These devices not only provide reliable contraception but also offer real-time monitoring and feedback, allowing for personalized and precise reproductive health management. By integrating sensors for monitoring hormone levels and drug release, smart IUDs bridge the gap between conventional contraception and cutting-edge digital healthcare solutions.

Smart IUDs are designed to address limitations in traditional IUDs by enabling continuous monitoring of the device's performance and the user's physiological responses. Sensors embedded in the IUD can measure parameters such as hormone release rates, endometrial response, and uterine environment changes. These sensors communicate with external devices, such as smartphones or wearable health monitors, via wireless technology, providing users and healthcare providers with valuable insights into the device's effectiveness and the user's health status.

One key feature of smart IUDs is their ability to monitor **hormone levels** in real time. Hormonal IUDs, which release progestins like levonorgestrel, rely on precise dosing to achieve their contraceptive effects. Smart IUDs ensure that the hormone is released at consistent rates, preventing potential issues like under-dosing or over-dosing. If irregularities in hormone release are detected, the device can alert the user or healthcare provider, enabling timely intervention.

Another critical function of smart IUDs is the monitoring of **drug release dynamics**. Advanced sensors can track the degradation of the drug reservoir and predict when the device will require replacement. This feature eliminates uncertainty regarding the effective lifespan of the IUD, ensuring uninterrupted contraceptive protection. For example, if the device detects that hormone levels are declining earlier than expected, it can recommend follow-up with a healthcare provider.

Smart IUDs also have the potential to integrate additional functionalities, such as tracking menstrual cycles, detecting inflammation, or monitoring uterine pH levels. These capabilities expand the utility of IUDs beyond contraception, offering valuable health insights for conditions like polycystic ovary syndrome (PCOS) or endometriosis.

The development of **digital interfaces** for smart IUDs allows users to access data through dedicated mobile applications. These apps can display real-time information on the device's status, track reproductive health metrics, and provide reminders for follow-up appointments or device replacements. This level of engagement empowers users to take control of their reproductive health and fosters improved compliance with contraceptive regimens.

Despite their potential, smart IUDs face certain challenges, including the complexity of integrating electronic components into biocompatible and flexible materials. Ensuring the durability and safety of these components in the sensitive uterine environment is paramount. Additionally, addressing concerns about data security and privacy is critical to gaining user trust, as smart IUDs involve the collection and transmission of sensitive health information.

11.3 ADVANTAGES AND DISADVANTAGES

11.3.1 ADVANTAGES

Intrauterine drug delivery systems (IUDs) are among the most reliable and widely used contraceptive methods, offering numerous advantages that contribute to their popularity. Their effectiveness, convenience, and safety make them an excellent choice for individuals seeking long-term and reversible contraception.

Effectiveness and Longevity

IUDs are renowned for their exceptional contraceptive efficacy, with failure rates of less than 1% for both hormonal and non-hormonal types. This high level of reliability surpasses many other contraceptive methods, including oral pills and barrier devices, making IUDs one of the most dependable choices for preventing unintended pregnancies.

A key feature of IUDs is their longevity. Depending on the type of IUD, users can benefit from effective contraception for several years without the need for replacement or frequent follow-ups. Hormonal IUDs, such as Mirena, provide contraception for up to five years, while non-hormonal copper-based devices like the Copper T can last up to ten years. This long-term efficacy eliminates the need for daily or monthly administration, reducing the likelihood of missed doses and ensuring consistent contraceptive protection.

Reduced Systemic Side Effects

One of the most significant benefits of IUDs, particularly hormonal types, is the localized delivery of drugs. Unlike systemic contraceptives, such as oral pills or injections, which circulate hormones throughout the body, IUDs release hormones directly into the uterine cavity. This localized action minimizes systemic absorption, reducing the risk of hormone-related side effects such as weight gain, mood swings, and nausea.

Copper-based IUDs, which are non-hormonal, offer an additional advantage by providing effective contraception without introducing synthetic hormones into the body. This makes them an ideal choice for individuals who are sensitive to or prefer to avoid hormonal methods.

Reversibility

IUDs are highly reversible, allowing users to quickly regain their fertility after removal. This feature is particularly important for individuals who may wish to conceive in the future. Studies have shown that fertility rates return to baseline levels within a few months after IUD removal, demonstrating the minimal impact of these devices on long-term reproductive health. This rapid return to fertility makes IUDs an excellent option for individuals seeking temporary but reliable contraception.

Convenience and Cost-Effectiveness

The convenience of IUDs is one of their most appealing features. Once inserted, these devices require little to no maintenance, allowing users to focus on their daily lives without worrying about regular administration. This ease of use is especially beneficial for individuals with busy lifestyles or those who have difficulty adhering to daily contraceptive routines, such as taking oral pills.

IUDs are also highly cost-effective in the long run. While the initial cost of insertion may be higher compared to other methods, the extended duration of use—ranging from three to ten years—results in significant savings over time. For example, the cost of a single hormonal IUD like Mirena is offset by the elimination of monthly expenses for oral contraceptives or other short-term methods. This affordability makes IUDs a financially practical choice for many users, particularly in low-resource settings or healthcare systems with limited access to ongoing contraceptive supplies.

11.3.2 DISADVANTAGES

While intrauterine drug delivery systems (IUDs) offer numerous advantages, they are not without potential drawbacks. Understanding these disadvantages is essential for users and healthcare providers to make informed decisions regarding their use. Most issues associated with IUDs are rare or manageable with proper care and monitoring, but they must be considered in the context of individual health needs and circumstances.

Insertion-Related Complications

The insertion procedure for IUDs, although generally safe, can cause discomfort or pain for some individuals. Pain levels vary based on individual pain tolerance, uterine anatomy, and the skill of the healthcare provider performing the procedure. While most users experience only mild cramping during or shortly after insertion, others may report more significant discomfort that can last for a few days.

In rare cases, IUD insertion can lead to more severe complications, such as uterine perforation. Uterine perforation occurs when the IUD pierces the wall of the uterus, potentially causing pain, bleeding, and other complications. This condition is estimated to occur in approximately 1 in 1,000 insertions. Factors such as improper technique, postpartum insertion, or uterine abnormalities can increase this risk. Prompt diagnosis and removal of the IUD are necessary to prevent further complications, but these cases are uncommon with experienced practitioners.

Potential Side Effects

IUDs can cause side effects that vary depending on the type of device used. Non-hormonal IUDs, such as copper-based devices, may lead to irregular bleeding patterns, particularly in the first few months after insertion. Users often report heavier or longer menstrual periods and increased cramping, although these symptoms typically diminish over time.

Hormonal IUDs, while associated with fewer menstrual disturbances, may cause side effects related to the localized release of progestins. These side effects can include mood changes, acne, and breast tenderness. Although the localized action of hormonal IUDs minimizes systemic effects, some users may still experience these symptoms, especially during the initial adjustment period.

For most individuals, these side effects are temporary and improve within a few months. However, persistent or severe symptoms may require consultation with a healthcare provider to evaluate whether the IUD is the most suitable contraceptive option.

Risk of Infections

IUDs are associated with a small but notable risk of pelvic inflammatory disease (PID), particularly during the first 20 days after insertion. This risk is primarily linked to the introduction of bacteria into the uterine cavity during the insertion procedure. Individuals with pre-existing sexually transmitted infections (STIs) are at a higher risk of developing PID after IUD placement.

To minimize this risk, healthcare providers typically screen for STIs before inserting an IUD. Proper insertion techniques and sterile equipment further reduce the likelihood of infection. For most users, the risk of PID is low, but individuals with multiple sexual partners or those in high-risk groups should discuss their medical history with their provider before choosing an IUD.

Device Expulsion

Spontaneous expulsion of the IUD is another potential drawback, occurring in about 2–10% of users, depending on factors such as age, parity, and uterine anatomy. Expulsion is more likely to happen during the first year after insertion and is often accompanied by symptoms such as unusual cramping or bleeding.

When an IUD is expelled, it no longer provides contraceptive protection, necessitating replacement or consideration of alternative methods. Partial expulsion, where the IUD remains partially within the uterine cavity, can cause discomfort and requires prompt medical attention. Regular follow-ups with a healthcare provider can help detect expulsion early, and patients are often advised to check for the presence of IUD strings periodically to ensure the device remains in place.

11.4 DEVELOPMENT AND DESIGN OF IUDS

11.4.1 DESIGN CONSIDERATIONS

The development and design of intrauterine drug delivery systems (IUDs) involve meticulous considerations to ensure safety, efficacy, and user comfort. Modern IUDs are the result of advancements in materials science, biomedical engineering, and an understanding of uterine anatomy. These devices are carefully crafted to balance contraceptive effectiveness with minimal side effects, ensuring a positive experience for users.

Material Selection

The choice of materials used in IUDs is a critical factor influencing their safety and functionality. IUDs are made from biocompatible and inert materials to minimize the risk of irritation, allergic reactions, or adverse immune responses. For example, the plastic frame of many IUDs is constructed from medical-grade polyethylene, which is both durable and non-reactive.

In addition to the frame, materials used for drug delivery components, such as reservoirs or coatings, must enable controlled and sustained drug release. Hormonal IUDs, such as Mirena, incorporate polymers like polydimethylsiloxane (PDMS) or ethylene vinyl acetate (EVA), which allow for the steady release of levonorgestrel over several years. These polymers are chosen for their stability, biocompatibility, and ability to release drugs at precise rates, ensuring consistent therapeutic effects.

For non-hormonal IUDs, such as copper-based devices, the copper components are carefully integrated into the design. Copper wire or sleeves are used to ensure a consistent release of copper ions, which act as a contraceptive agent by impairing sperm motility and viability. The copper used is highly purified and coated to prevent corrosion, ensuring the longevity of the device.

Shape and Size

The shape and size of an IUD are critical design considerations that influence its effectiveness, comfort, and retention within the uterus. Most modern IUDs are T-shaped, a design that closely matches the natural anatomy of the uterine cavity. The horizontal arms of the T-shape help anchor the device within the uterus, preventing displacement or expulsion.

Tailored designs, such as frameless IUDs, have been developed to accommodate variations in uterine size and shape among users. Frameless devices consist of a flexible wire with copper or hormone-loaded beads, anchored directly into the uterine wall. This design is particularly beneficial for individuals with smaller or irregularly shaped uteri, as it minimizes discomfort while maintaining contraceptive efficacy.

The size of an IUD also plays a significant role in user comfort and acceptability. Devices designed for nulliparous women (those who have not given birth) are typically smaller and more flexible to reduce the risk of pain or complications during insertion. For example, smaller hormonal IUDs like Skyla are specifically designed for younger users or those with a smaller uterine cavity, offering effective contraception with reduced side effects.

In addition to comfort, the design of IUDs must ensure retention within the uterus to maintain contraceptive effectiveness. Features like flexible arms, anchor points, or frameless configurations help secure the device in place, even during physical activities or uterine contractions.

11.4.2 DRUG LOADING AND RELEASE MECHANISMS

The drug loading and release mechanisms of intrauterine drug delivery systems (IUDs) play a pivotal role in ensuring their therapeutic efficacy and user safety. These mechanisms are carefully engineered to provide controlled and consistent drug release, addressing both contraceptive and therapeutic needs. Two primary approaches are commonly used in modern IUDs: reservoir-based designs and surface-modified devices. Each approach offers distinct advantages, tailored to meet specific clinical and user requirements.

Reservoir-Based Designs

Reservoir-based designs are widely utilized in hormonal IUDs, where drugs such as levonorgestrel are encapsulated within a specialized polymeric reservoir. This design allows for the controlled and sustained release of the drug over an extended period, ensuring consistent therapeutic effects with minimal user intervention. The polymer reservoir is typically constructed from biocompatible materials like polydimethylsiloxane (PDMS) or ethylene vinyl acetate (EVA), which are selected for their ability to regulate drug diffusion.

The mechanism of drug release in reservoir-based IUDs relies on the gradual diffusion of the hormone through the polymer matrix. The rate of release is determined by factors such as the drug's concentration within the reservoir, the polymer's permeability, and the surface area of the device. For example, the levonorgestrel-releasing IUD, Mirena, is designed to release approximately 20 micrograms of the hormone per day during the initial phase, with a gradual reduction over time. This consistent release ensures effective contraception for up to five years while minimizing systemic hormone exposure.

One of the significant advantages of reservoir-based designs is their ability to provide long-term drug delivery without the need for frequent replacements or dosing. This makes them highly convenient for users seeking sustained therapeutic effects, whether for contraception or the management of gynecological conditions like heavy menstrual bleeding or endometriosis. The encapsulation process also protects the drug from environmental degradation, ensuring its stability and efficacy throughout the device's lifespan.

Surface-Modified Devices

Surface-modified devices are another innovative approach to drug delivery in IUDs. In these systems, the active drug is coated directly onto the surface of the device, allowing for localized drug action at the site of implantation. This design is particularly beneficial for non-hormonal IUDs, where drugs like copper or anti-inflammatory agents are applied to enhance contraceptive efficacy or address specific therapeutic goals.

The coating process involves the deposition of drug molecules onto the IUD's surface using techniques like spray coating, dip coating, or vapor deposition. These methods ensure uniform drug distribution and precise control over the coating thickness, which directly influences the release rate. For example, in copper-based IUDs, a thin layer of copper is applied to the device, allowing for the gradual release of copper ions into the uterine cavity. These ions create an inhospitable environment for sperm, reducing their motility and viability.

Surface-modified devices also enable the incorporation of additional functionalities, such as antimicrobial coatings to reduce the risk of infections or bioadhesive layers to improve retention within the uterine cavity. The localized nature of drug release minimizes systemic absorption, reducing the likelihood of side effects and ensuring targeted therapeutic action.

While surface-modified devices are highly effective for certain applications, their drug release profiles may be shorter compared to reservoir-based designs. This limitation makes them more suitable for short-term therapies or when immediate drug action is required. However, ongoing advancements in coating technologies and material science are addressing these challenges, expanding the potential applications of surface-modified IUDs.

11.4.3 MANUFACTURING TECHNIQUES

The manufacturing of intrauterine drug delivery systems (IUDs) requires precise engineering processes and stringent quality control measures to ensure their safety, efficacy, and reliability. The production methods employed are designed to meet exacting standards, with a focus on biocompatibility, durability, and controlled drug delivery. Modern manufacturing techniques, such as injection molding, extrusion, and coating, have significantly advanced the development of IUDs, allowing for innovative designs and enhanced functionality.

Precision Engineering

Precision engineering is at the core of IUD manufacturing, ensuring that the devices meet the specific structural and functional requirements necessary for their safe use. Techniques such as injection molding, extrusion, and coating are employed to achieve the desired shape, size, and drug delivery properties of IUDs.

Injection Molding

Injection molding is a widely used technique for fabricating the plastic components of IUDs, such as the T-shaped frame. This method involves injecting molten medical-grade plastic, typically polyethylene, into a mold that defines the shape of the device. The material is then cooled and solidified, resulting in a precise and consistent structure. Injection molding ensures that the IUD's dimensions are uniform, which is critical for its proper fit within the uterine cavity.

Extrusion

Extrusion is another essential technique used in the production of drug-releasing components of IUDs. In this process, polymers are melted and forced through a die to create long, continuous strands or tubes. These polymeric structures are used to form the reservoirs or coatings that encapsulate the drug. For example, the levonorgestrel reservoir in hormonal IUDs is typically fabricated using this method. The extrusion process allows for precise control over the thickness and composition of the polymer, which directly affects the drug release rate.

Coating

Coating is a critical step in the manufacturing of surface-modified IUDs. This technique involves applying a thin layer of the active drug or other functional materials onto the surface of the device. Methods such as dip coating, spray coating, or vapor deposition are used to achieve uniform coverage. For copper-based IUDs, a layer of copper is coated onto the device to provide sustained release of copper ions. Coating processes must ensure that the drug is evenly distributed and securely adhered to the surface to maintain consistent performance and minimize degradation.

Quality Control

Quality control is integral to the manufacturing process of IUDs, ensuring that every device meets regulatory standards for safety, efficacy, and biocompatibility. Rigorous testing and inspection are conducted at each stage of production to identify and eliminate defects.

Regulatory Standards

IUDs are classified as medical devices, and their manufacturing must comply with stringent regulations set by authorities such as the US Food and Drug Administration (FDA), European Medicines Agency (EMA), and International Organization for Standardization (ISO). These standards require manufacturers to demonstrate that their products are safe, effective, and free from contamination.

Testing and Validation

Quality control procedures include testing the mechanical properties of the IUD, such as its flexibility, tensile strength, and dimensional accuracy. Biocompatibility testing is also conducted to ensure that the materials used do not cause irritation, allergic reactions, or other adverse effects. For drug-releasing IUDs, extensive testing is performed to validate the drug release profile, ensuring that it meets the specified rate and duration. Analytical techniques, such as high-performance liquid chromatography (HPLC), are used to quantify drug levels and verify consistency across batches.

Sterilization and Packaging

Sterilization is a critical step in the final stages of manufacturing. IUDs are sterilized using methods such as ethylene oxide gas, gamma irradiation, or autoclaving, depending on the material's compatibility. After sterilization, the devices are packaged in sterile, tamper-proof packaging to maintain their integrity until use.

11.5 APPLICATIONS IN CONTRACEPTION AND HORMONE REPLACEMENT THERAPY

11.5.1 Contraception

Intrauterine devices (IUDs) play a vital role in preventing unintended pregnancies, offering one of the most reliable forms of contraception available today. These devices have transformed reproductive health by providing highly effective, long-term, and reversible birth control options for individuals worldwide. Their success is rooted in their ability to address a wide range of contraceptive needs while minimizing the burden of daily or frequent administration.

The primary mechanism of IUDs in contraception is their ability to interfere with the process of fertilization and implantation. Copper-based IUDs, such as the Copper T, release copper ions that disrupt sperm motility and viability, preventing sperm from reaching and fertilizing the egg. Hormonal IUDs, like Mirena, achieve contraception through the localized release of levonorgestrel, which thickens cervical mucus to block sperm entry and thins the endometrial lining, making it unsuitable for implantation. These mechanisms provide a dual layer of protection, ensuring a failure rate of less than 1%, which is comparable to sterilization procedures.

IUDs are particularly valuable for special populations, such as postpartum women, where their unique benefits address specific reproductive needs. Postpartum women often seek effective contraception to allow adequate spacing between pregnancies. Both hormonal and non-hormonal IUDs can be safely inserted immediately after childbirth, offering convenient and long-term protection. Hormonal IUDs like Mirena are also advantageous for postpartum women who experience heavy menstrual bleeding, as they reduce menstrual flow and improve iron levels. The long duration of action, ranging from 3 to 10 years depending on the type of IUD, makes them an ideal choice for women who want reliable contraception without frequent maintenance.

Case studies illustrate the widespread success of IUDs in diverse populations. The Copper T IUD has been extensively used in family planning programs worldwide, particularly in low-resource settings. Its affordability, longevity, and non-hormonal nature make it accessible and acceptable to a wide range of users. In India, family planning initiatives have incorporated Copper T IUDs as a cornerstone of their reproductive health strategy, reducing unintended pregnancies and improving maternal health outcomes. Similarly, hormonal IUDs like Mirena have gained popularity in high-resource settings, where users value their additional benefits, such as reducing menstrual discomfort and managing gynecological conditions. Clinical studies have shown that Mirena reduces menstrual bleeding by up to 90%, significantly improving the quality of life for individuals with conditions like menorrhagia.

In addition to their effectiveness and convenience, IUDs offer significant economic benefits. The upfront cost of an IUD, though higher than other contraceptive methods, is offset by its long duration of action. Over time, users save on the recurring expenses associated with pills, patches, or injections. For governments and healthcare systems, IUDs represent a cost-effective solution to reduce the economic burden of unintended pregnancies, including the associated healthcare and social costs.

11.5.2 HORMONE REPLACEMENT THERAPY

Intrauterine devices (IUDs) have emerged as a significant tool in hormone replacement therapy (HRT). Their localized hormone delivery offers targeted therapeutic effects while minimizing systemic side effects. This makes IUDs a preferred option for addressing specific gynecological conditions and protecting the endometrium in women undergoing estrogen therapy.

Endometrial Protection

Postmenopausal women on systemic estrogen therapy face an increased risk of endometrial hyperplasia. This condition, characterized by the abnormal thickening of the uterine lining, can lead to endometrial cancer if left untreated. Hormonal IUDs, such as those releasing levonorgestrel, play a crucial role in mitigating this risk.

Levonorgestrel acts locally within the uterine cavity to thin the endometrial lining. This localized action prevents the proliferation of endometrial cells stimulated by estrogen therapy. Unlike systemic progestins, which can cause side effects such as mood swings or weight gain, the localized delivery of levonorgestrel minimizes systemic exposure. This enhances patient compliance and reduces discomfort associated with traditional HRT regimens. Studies have shown that the use of levonorgestrel-releasing IUDs significantly lowers the risk of endometrial hyperplasia and maintains the protective benefits of estrogen therapy.

Gynecological Conditions

IUDs are highly effective in managing gynecological conditions like heavy menstrual bleeding and endometriosis. Levonorgestrel-releasing IUDs reduce menstrual blood loss by up to 90% in individuals with menorrhagia. This is achieved through their direct effect on the endometrium, which becomes thinner and less vascularized under the influence of levonorgestrel. For individuals with anemia caused by heavy periods, the use of hormonal IUDs offers a simple and long-term solution.

Endometriosis, a condition where endometrial-like tissue grows outside the uterus, causes severe pain and inflammation. Hormonal IUDs alleviate these symptoms by suppressing the growth of endometrial tissue through localized progestin delivery. This reduces the severity of menstrual pain and improves the quality of life for individuals with this chronic condition.

Hormonal IUDs are particularly advantageous in HRT for their long duration of action. Devices like Mirena provide effective endometrial protection and symptom relief for up to five years. This reduces the need for frequent medication adjustments and simplifies the management of chronic gynecological conditions.